INDIA AND AFRICA

Deepening the Security Engagement

INDIA AND AFRICA

DEEPENING THE SECURITY ENGAGEMENT

Editors

Ruchita Beri
Rajeesh Kumar

MANOHAR PARRIKAR INSTITUTE FOR DEFENCE STUDIES AND ANALYSES
मनोहर पर्रिकर रक्षा अध्ययन एवं विश्लेषण संस्थान

PENTAGON PRESS LLP

First published in 2024 by
PENTAGON PRESS LLP
206, Peacock Lane, Shahpur Jat
New Delhi-110049, India
Contact: 011-26490600

Typeset in AGaramond, 11.5 Point
Printed by Aegean Offset Printers, Greater Noida, U.P.

ISBN 978-81-971986-8-7 (HB)

www.pentagonpress.in

Contents

Foreword

The partnership between India and Africa has undergone significant transformation in recent years. Security cooperation is one of the critical focus areas, and this growing partnership is manifested in various forms. India and Africa are working to enhance their engagement across a broad spectrum, from maritime security to energy security, food security, and cybersecurity. This collaboration holds immense potential to advance the interests of the African continent in myriad ways. In addition, India has played an active role in addressing the growing need for skill development in Africa.

The evolving security engagement between India and Africa offers great potential for future cooperation. Both regions can benefit from increased intelligence-sharing, joint military exercises, and capacity-building programs. Under Prime Minister Modi's leadership, India has significantly strengthened security ties with African nations through various initiatives, including the India-Africa Forum Summit, India-Africa Defence Ministers Conclave, and India-Africa Defence Dialogue. These initiatives have facilitated crucial discussions on security challenges and opportunities for collaboration, resulting in several security cooperation agreements and a strengthened and resilient partnership between the two. Furthermore, during India's G20 presidency, the African Union became a permanent member of the G20. This significant development ensures that the G20 becomes an even more representative body and that the voice of Africa is heard in earnest.

One key area of partnership between India and Africa is in the field of maritime security. India and Africa have a shared geography and interests under the rubric of the Indo-Pacific, and Africa's increasing interest in the blue economy is reflected in the African Union's Integrated Maritime Strategy. India and African countries face similar security challenges in the maritime domain. These include terrorism, piracy, proliferation and smuggling of small arms and drugs, climate change, and inter and intra-state conflicts. Moreover, India's long coastline and vast Exclusive Economic Zone make maritime security a vital consideration, and partnership with Africa in this area can help to enhance security across the region.

Energy security is another area where India has significantly supported African countries. Sub-Saharan Africa has over 600 million people without access to electricity. Many countries continue to rely almost entirely on costly and polluting fossil fuels. India has been supporting African countries in developing their renewable energy sectors, offering financial and technical assistance. In addition, India is a founding member of the International Solar Alliance, a grouping that is dedicated to promoting solar energy globally, including in African nations.

India has been providing significant support to African countries in terms of food security. This has included technical assistance, training, and financial aid to improve agricultural productivity, food processing, and storage capabilities. The partnership has also featured joint research and development projects to enhance food security in Africa. Furthermore, India has played a crucial role in establishing food processing facilities in Africa, which has helped reduce food waste and prolong the shelf life of perishable produce.

The partnership between India and Africa has also been instrumental in building a safer digital environment in the region. India and African countries have formed a strong cybersecurity partnership through technical assistance, training, and joint initiatives. India has partnered with African countries to develop technologies and collaborate on cybercrime and critical infrastructure protection issues. In addition, India has been sharing its expertise in cybersecurity with African countries to help them build their cybersecurity strategies and capabilities.

Finally, skill development is becoming increasingly important across Africa, and India has been playing an active role in addressing this need. Prime Minister Narendra Modi has launched several initiatives to enhance the growing workforce's skills, and India provides training for African youth in traditional and non-traditional security fields under the Indian Technical and Economic Cooperation (ITEC) program. Over the last decade, Prime

Minister Modi and other Indian leaders have paid several visits to African countries, giving unprecedented impetus to bilateral security engagement across the continent.

The Manohar Parrikar Institute for Defence Studies and Analyses (MP-IDSA) is delighted to present an edited volume, "India and Africa: Deepening the Security Engagement," that provides an analyses of various issues related to India-Africa security relations. The chapters in this volume offer insights into the partnership's evolution, challenges and opportunities and provide a roadmap for future collaboration. I hope this volume will augment the existing literature on the subject and inspire further research on this important topic.

New Delhi
March 2024

Sujan Chinoy
Director General, MP-IDSA

About the Editors/Contributors

Sujan Chinoy is the Director General of the Manohar Parrikar Institute for Defence Studies and Analyses (MP-IDSA), New Delhi since 2019. A career diplomat from 1981-2018, he held several important diplomatic assignments, including as Ambassador to Japan and Mexico. A specialist on China, East Asia and politico-security issues, he anchored negotiations and confidence-building measures (CBMs) with China on the boundary issue from 1996-2000. On deputation to the National Security Council Secretariat (NSCS) from 2008-2012, his expertise covered external and internal security issues in the extended neighbourhood of the Indo-Pacific. Among his diverse foreign postings, he also served as Counsellor (Political) in the Embassy in Riyadh, Kingdom of Saudi Arabia. He was the Chair of the Think20 engagement group for India's G20 Presidency and a Member of the high-powered DRDO Review Committee.

Ruchita Beri is a Consultant with the Manohar Parrikar Institute for Defence Studies and Analyses (MP-IDSA), New Delhi. Earlier, Ms Beri served as Senior Research Associate and Centre Coordinator, Africa, Latin America, Caribbean and United Nations Centre at the MP-IDSA. She has over three decades experience in research on international relations, political economy and security of Sub-Saharan Africa, India–Africa relations and Emerging Powers in Africa and the Indian Ocean Region. She is a member of the Africa Committee of the Confederation of Indian Industry (CII). She is also a member of the Africa Experts Group at the Vivekananda International Foundation, New Delhi. She is the former President of African Studies Association of India (ASA). She has authored several research articles and edited and co-edited numerous books including *India- Africa: Building Synergies in Peace, Security and Development* (Pentagon Press, 2024), *Food*

Governance in India: Rights, Security and Challenges in the Global Sphere (Routledge, 2023).

Rajeesh Kumar is Research Fellow and Acting Coordinator at the ALAC&UN Centre, MP-IDSA, New Delhi. Prior to joining MP-IDSA in 2016, he held teaching positions at Jamia Millia Islamia, New Delhi and University of Calicut, Kerala. He was one of the Co-Chairs of the Think-20 Task Force on 'Reformed Multilateralism: Transforming Global Institutions and Frameworks' during India's G20 presidency. Dr Kumar is the author of the monographs titled - *Indian and Chinese Approaches to United Nations Peacekeeping in Africa* (MP-IDSA, 2024), *Principled but Evolving: India's Approach to Multilateral Peace and Security* (MP-IDSA, 2021) and *The International Committee of the Red Cross in Internal Armed Conflicts: Is Neutrality Possible* (Palgrave Macmillan, 2019). He is also the co-editor of *Eurozone Crisis and the Future of Europe: Political Economy of Further Integration and Governance* (Palgrave Macmillan, 2014) and *Islam Islamist Movements and Democracy in the Middle East* (Global Vision, 2013). His articles, opinion pieces, and reviews have appeared in Journals and Newspapers, including Strategic Analysis, India Quarterly, Journal of Defence Studies, Journal of Common Market Studies, Central European University Political Science Journal, The Indian Journal of Politics and International Relations, E-International Relations, The Hindu, The Diplomat, Japan Times, Tehran Times and The Outlook.

Festus Kofi Aubyn is the Regional Coordinator for Research and Capacity Building at the West Africa Network for Peacebuilding (WANEP-Regional) in Ghana. Previously, he served as a Research Fellow at the Kofi Annan International Peacekeeping Training Institute in Accra and as an Adjunct Professor at Webster University in Ghana. He has also been a guest lecturer at various institutions, including the Ghana Armed Forces Staff and Command College, the Ghana Military Academy, the Ghana Institute of Management and Public Administration, and the Legon Centre for International Affairs and Diplomacy (LECAID) at the University of Ghana. In September 2016, he was a visiting lecturer at the Department of Political and International Studies at Rhodes University in South Africa. His publications include "Challenging conventional understanding of statehood: West African realities" edited by Charles T. Hunt, Kwesi Aning, M Anne Brown and Volker Boege in the book Exploring Peace Formation-Security and Justice in the Post-Colonial States, Routledge,2018 and "Comparative Is Key to Ending Togo's Political Crisis" International Peace Institute (IPI) Global Observatory, in 2017.

Harriet Njoki Mboce is a lawyer, consultant, and policy advisor based in Kenya. Njoki is a former Visiting Fellow at the Institute for Defence Studies and Analysis on India-Kenya Maritime Security Co-operation. She is also a nominated Visiting Scholar at the Leiden Centre for Legal and Comparative Studies of the East African Community, Netherlands. Njoki is a practising advocate of the High court of Kenya, and a founding partner at the firm of Njoki Mboce & Company advocates. She teaches at the University of Nairobi, where she is also pursuing a PhD, with a focus on maritime delimitation disputes, an aspect of maritime security. She is an expert consultant in the same field. She is also a member of the implementing committee of the FishFORCE Academy model in Kenya on combating maritime crime.

Abhay Kumar Singh is Research Fellow and Coordinator of South East Asia and Oceania Centre at the Manohar Parrikar Institute for Defence Studies and Analyses, New Delhi. He is an Indian Navy veteran with extensive command and staff experience spanning 27 years. A surface warfare officer with a specialisation in Missile and Gunnery Warfare, he has commanded various naval platforms which include frontline frigate, submarine rescue & deep diving vessel, and fleet auxiliary. He has also served as Director (Military Affairs) in the Disarmament and International Security Division of the Ministry of External Affairs. Cmde. Singh is an alumnus of the Naval Academy, Defence Services Staff Course and Naval War College. He has an MSc (Defence and Strategic Studies) from the University of Chennai and an MPhil from Mumbai University. His publications include: *India–China Rivalry: Asymmetric No Longer: An Assessment of China's Evolving Perceptions of India*, New Delhi, KW Publishers, 2021 and "India's Pathways for Regional Prominence in Asia-Pacific: Prospects and Challenges", *Journal of Defence Studies*, Vol.12, Issue 4, October-December 2018.

Abhishek Mishra is Associate Fellow at the Manohar Parrikar Institute for Defence Studies and Analyses, New Delhi. His research focuses on India and

China's engagement in Africa, aimed at developing partnerships under the framework of South-South cooperation, including a specific focus on maritime security cooperation in the Indian Ocean Region. Abhishek holds a PhD in African Studies from the Department of African Studies, University of Delhi. His PhD thesis is titled "India's Maritime Cooperation with African Countries in Western Indian Ocean Region." Abhishek has given a lecture at Naval War College, Goa for the Naval Higher Commander Course on the theme "West IOR Island Nations and East Africa: Politico-Economic Perspective." He has also participated in the International Visitor Leadership Program (IVLP), sponsored by the United States Department of State on the theme "Enhancing Regional Maritime Governance and Cooperation in the QUAD" in October 2022. He also participated in the Paris Defence Young Leaders programme from 12-16 June 2023, hosted by the Institute for Strategic Research (IRSEM), a research institute of the French Ministry of Armed Forces. Before joining MP-IDSA, Abhishek was working on African issues at the Observer Research Foundation, New Delhi.

Benard Mouk is the Director at Innovation and Partnerships, Jaramogi Oginga Odinga University of Science and Technology, Bondo, Kenya. He has worked for over 20 years in research, extension, management and academic focusing on natural resource management, renewable energy, biodiversity, and climate change and science technology innovation. He holds a post doc in Bioenergy and Climate Change from University of Edinburgh, UK, PhD from Kyoto Prefectural University, Japan, MSc and BSc from Moi University. He also holds a certificate in Environmental Impact Assessment and Environmental Audit from Jomo Kenyatta University of Agriculture and Technology, International Certificate in Conservation from Royal Botanical Garden, Kew, UK. He was the Director of Programmes at the African Centre for Technology Studies and Vice President World Bioenergy Association. He is a board member of World Intellectual Property Organisation and member of the East African Community of Bioenergy Advisory Group.

Nitya Nanda is Director of the Council for Social Development; a social science think tank based in New Delhi. He is an economist and a public policy analyst with more than two decades of experience in research, consulting and teaching. His work covered issues and challenges in India and South

Asia, but often South-east Asian and African nations as well. He has been involved with more than 40 research/consulting projects, and in about half of them as the principal investigator. Previously, he worked at the National Council of Applied Economic Research (NCAER), CUTS International, and The Energy and Resources Institute (TERI). He graduated from the University of Calcutta and completed his master's and Ph. D from Jawaharlal Nehru University, New Delhi. He has worked on consulting assignments from several UN organizations, including UNCTAD, UNESCAP, UNDP and UNEP and other agencies like the World Bank and the European Commission. He has also been a consultant for different government ministries and agencies in India and contributed to formulating policies including as a member of committee/working group/advisory group formed by the Ministry of Commerce and Industry, Prime Minister's Economic Advisory Council and the NITI Aayog. His major publications include "Expanding Frontiers of Global Trade Rules: The Political Economy Dynamics of the International Trading System", Routledge, London & New York (2009), "Hydro-Politics in GBM Basin: The Case of Bangladesh-India Water Relations", TERI Press, New Delhi (2015), "India's Resource Security: Trade, Geopolitics and Efficiency Dimensions", TERI Press, New Delhi (2018), and "India's Industrial Policy and Performance: Growth, Competition and Competitiveness", Routledge, London & New York.

Shebonti Ray Dadwal, former Senior Fellow at the Manohar Parrikar Institute for Defence Studies and Analyses, New Delhi. Prior to joining MP-IDSA, she served as Deputy Secretary at the National Security Council Secretariat and was also Senior Editor with The Financial Express. Her research focus is on Energy Security. She has several peer-reviewed articles and papers focusing on Energy Security, including a monograph on The Geopolitics of America's Energy Independence: Implications for China, India and the Global Energy Market, and a book Rethinking Energy Security in India (2002). Her second book The Geopolitics of Gas: Common problems, Disparate Strategies is ready for publication. She has also co-edited a book Non-Traditional Security Challenges in Asia: Approaches and Responses, published by Routledge in 2015, and co-authored the IDSA Report on Security Implications of Climate Change for India (2009). She is a member of the CSCAP Study Group on Energy Security as well as member of the Core Group on Myanmar of the

MEA's Indian Council of World Affairs (ICWA). In April 2009, she was awarded a Chevening Fellowship by the Foreign and Commonwealth Office of the UK on completion of a course in Economics of Energy at the Institute for Energy Research and Policy, University of Birmingham, UK.

Essien D. Essien is an Associate Professor in University of Uyo, Nigeria. He teaches social ethics, human values, comparative religious and Christian ethics in the department of religious and cultural studies of the university. He is the editor of International Journal of Human Values and Public Life. He is a reviewer for many journals, nationally and internationally. He has published three books and has contributed journal articles and book chapters to over 40 publications. He received his PhD in social and religious ethics from the University of Ibadan, Ibadan, Nigeria. He has two Master's degrees in international relations and social ethics from the University of Uyo and Ibadan, Nigeria respectively. He is a laureate of The Council for the Development of Social Science Research in Africa and a recipient of Association of the Commonwealth University Centenary Award 2015. He is a Secretary, Faculty of Arts Research Committee and member, Departmental Research Committee of the University of Uyo, Uyo, Nigeria. He is a member of many professional bodies including the American Academy of Religion (AAR) and Association for Christian Ethics.

Cherian Samuel is Research Fellow in the Strategic Technologies Centre at the Manohar Parrikar Institute for Defence Studies and Analyses. He has written on various cyber security issues, including critical infrastructure protection, cyber resilience, cybercrime, and internet governance. His recent publications include a monograph on *Leveraging Cyber Power: A Study of the Approaches and Responses of the Major Powers* (2021), a co-authored book on *India's Strategic Options in a Changing Cyberspace* (2018), and a co-edited book on *Securing Cyberspace: International and Asian Perspectives* (2016). He was a nominated member of the Joint Working Group on Public-Private Partnership in the National Security Council and Principal Investigator in a project commissioned by the Ministry of Electronics and Information Technology on Global, Regional and Domestic Dynamics of Cybersecurity in 2017. His current research interests include the role of the military in cybersecurity.

Donald P. Chimanikire is a Lecturer, Faculty of Social Sciences, Midlands State University, Zimbabwe. He is also a Senior Lecturer in International Economic Relations. He is former Director of the Institute of Development Studies, University of Zimbabwe and former Chairperson of the Department of International relations and Social Development Studies of the same University. He was member of the Executive Committee of the Organization for Social Science Research in Easters and Southern Africa (OSSERA), based in Addis Ababa, Ethiopia, for several years. He has travelled extensively for research in a number of countries, China, India, Japan, Europe and the USA. He has contributed journal articles and book chapters to over 10 publications. He holds a Ph.D. degree in International Studies from Jawaharlal Nehru University, New Delhi and MA degree in International Relations from Kiev University, Ukraine.

Pranav Kumar is Vice-President, International Trade Policy and Compliance, Reliance Industries Ltd. He holds an M. Phil degree in Economics from IIT Bombay. He has over 28 years of professional experience in teaching, research, project management and policy advocacy with primary expertise on trade and development and regional economic integration. As a head of international trade policy division, he engages closely with the Government of India and industry members across all sectors on all aspects of Trade Negotiation and Policy Formulation and formulates the CII position on International and Trade Policy which feeds into the negotiation process for the Government of India. Previously he worked as a Senior Trade Policy Advisor with the joint international trade policy team (India Trade Policy Unit) of British High Commission and DFID India.

Kenneth King, Professor Emeritus at University of Edinburgh, Scotland, UK and former Visiting Fellow at the Manohar Parrikar Institute for Defence Studies and Analysis, New Delhi. Kenneth King was Director of the Centre of African Studies and Professor of International and Comparative Education at Edinburgh University for many years. He is now Emeritus Professor in its Schools of Education and of Social and Political Studies. His research has focused on the politics and history of international education, aid policy, and skills development, especially in the informal sector. He edited NORRAG News for 30 years until 2017. Since 2006, amongst other research, he has analysed China's educational aid to Africa, and published China's Aid and Soft Power in Africa (2013). From 2016 he has begun to research India's development cooperation with Africa, with a focus on skills and human resource development.

Introduction

Ruchita Beri and Rajeesh Kumar

In a rapidly evolving global landscape, characterized by dynamic geopolitical shifts and complex security challenges, the relationship between India and Africa has emerged as a pivotal axis of cooperation. India's engagement with Africa is rooted in historical ties, shaped by shared experiences of colonialism and a commitment to mutual development. Over the years, this relationship has evolved into a robust partnership, characterized by growing economic, political, and security cooperation. The Indian efforts to obtain full membership for the African Union in the G20 group during its presidency highlight the priority given to enhancing relations with the region. As both strive for peace, stability, and prosperity, their collaboration in the security domain has become increasingly relevant and consequential.

In recent decades, India's relationship with African countries has significantly progressed through structured engagements. This began with the first Indian Africa Forum Summit in 2008, followed by the second summit in 2011. The third summit in New Delhi in 2015 marked a renewed focus on strengthening the partnership between India and Africa. During this summit, the Delhi Declaration and the India-Africa Framework for Strategic Cooperation were signed, aiming to establish a long-term, stable partnership of equality and mutual benefit between the two regions. These documents offer a blueprint for cooperation in various fields, including political, economic, social, science and technology, cultural, security, and others.

India has played an active role in conflict resolution in Africa through its contributions to UN peacekeeping operations. This commitment underscores India's dedication to fostering peace and stability on the continent. In addition to peacekeeping efforts, India offers training for African military officers in its academies, enhancing the capabilities of African nations to manage their security challenges effectively. Indian navy also plays a crucial role in the Indian Ocean region, addressing natural disasters, piracy, and other security challenges. This engagement demonstrates India's commitment to ensuring maritime security and stability in the region, which is vital for the prosperity of both India and African nations. Furthermore, India's interests align with those of African nations on various global issues. Both regions face challenges such as climate change, cyber warfare, and the scarcity of energy, food, and water resources.

India's emergence as a leader of the Global South and Africa's economic progress have led both regions to play more prominent roles in addressing security challenges. Both India and Africa are part of the vast Indo-Pacific region, which is rich in resources. African countries have shown increasing interest in the blue economy, focusing on sustainable use of marine resources. The African Union's Integrated Maritime Strategy (AIM Strategy) emphasizes the importance of maritime resource development and security on the continent. India, with its extensive coastline and Exclusive Economic Zone, heavily relies on maritime trade, making maritime security a top priority. Enhancing security cooperation between India and African nations is crucial, given their shared interests in maritime security and resource management.

Similarly, the food, water, and energy nexus is critical for sustainable development, with increasing demand in both India and African countries. Despite abundant fossil fuel resources, Sub-Saharan Africa has the lowest energy access levels globally. Recent years have seen a global focus on low-carbon, clean energy, where Africa shows promising potential in renewable resources like solar, wind, and water. India, facing energy deficits, is keen on developing renewables. India, a major agricultural producer, owes its success to innovative farming solutions, including low-cost appliances, seeds, and water management techniques. African nations, facing similar agricultural challenges, are ripe for collaboration.

Africa's economic growth and digital transformation have spurred the adoption of new technologies, including mobile smart devices and social media, offering avenues for development. However, this progress also brings increased risks and vulnerabilities that could impede growth. It is crucial to implement effective policies to address the growing cyber threats, allowing

Africa to benefit from a digitized socio-economic space. Similarly, India faces escalating cyber threats and seeks to enhance its cybersecurity preparedness by establishing new security practices and procedures. India is keen to collaborate with African nations to address cyber threats and foster cooperation in cybersecurity technology.

Skill development is increasingly crucial in African countries, given the diverse needs across the continent. "Agenda 2063," the continent's development roadmap, emphasizes the urgent need for concerted action to tackle the challenges hindering the development of technical skills among African youth. Likewise, Indian government has initiated several programs to enhance the skills of the expanding workforce. India has a track record of training African youth in both traditional and non-traditional security fields through the Indian Technical and Economic Cooperation (ITEC) programme.

Against this backdrop, this volume examines the multifaceted dimensions of security cooperation between India and Africa, highlighting the shared interests, challenges, and opportunities that define their strategic partnership. It seeks to deepen existing partnerships between India and African countries while exploring new areas of convergence for mutual engagement. It examines the strategic imperatives driving their cooperation, the evolving security challenges they face, and the mechanisms through which they enhance mutual security interests. Delving into various issues and challenges, including conventional and non-conventional security threats, policies, and initiatives discussed during dialogues, this volume aims to provide a coherent exploration of the dynamic security relationship between India and Africa.

The first two chapters focus on the evolving security engagement between India and Africa. Festus Kofi Aubyn discusses how India's cooperation with Africa has expanded to include security, beyond economic and political realms. India has promoted African stability through peacekeeping, financial aid, and training at multilateral, regional, and national levels. He emphasizes the need for sustained strategic dialogue, robust support, and a holistic approach to address security challenges comprehensively.

Ruchita Beri's chapter examines the African security environment, current trends in defence cooperation and the drivers for India's security engagement with African countries. According to Beri, India's strategic interest in Africa stems from its shared philosophy of South-South cooperation and long-standing history. She highlights Africa's strategic importance due to its resources, security threats, and economic opportunities for India.

The next set of three chapters delves into India-Africa cooperation in maritime security. Njoki Mboce's chapter examines Kenya-India maritime cooperation. The chapter begins with a discussion about the drivers of cooperation. Mboce, goes on to draw out the common maritime security challenges. The chapter analyses the existing bilateral engagement and calls for greater maritime security collaboration between Kenya and India.

In his chapter, '2050 Africa Integrated Maritime Strategy and India's SAGAR Vision,' Abhay K. Singh explores maritime cooperation between India and Africa. Singh highlights alignment between India's SAGAR vision and Africa's AIMS, aiming for 'good order at sea.' He argues India's policy shows a willingness to shape the maritime environment for stability and sustainable development. Singh also notes India's shipbuilding industry could meet Africa's ship repair and building needs, fostering cooperative synergy in the maritime domain.

Abhishek Mishra's chapter delves into India's maritime cooperation with African countries, examining India's ascendancy as a maritime power in the Indian Ocean Region. Mishra argues that India's engagement with West Indian Ocean littorals varies in intensity and focus, mirroring the diverse needs of African nations. India has adeptly tailored its maritime security cooperation to address these varying priorities. The chapter also highlights the competition for influence in the West Indian Ocean between India and China, which presents both challenges and opportunities.

Moving on to energy security, Benard Muok's chapter explores the challenges and opportunities of achieving energy access in Africa, focusing on the Kenya case study. Despite having substantial energy resources, the continent is going through an energy crisis and lack of access to energy. The chapter also highlights the increasing interest of external actors in Africa's energy sector, with China being the most prominent. It also argues that the Global South should cooperate in capacity-building, policy formulation, technology transfer, upscaling innovation, and garnering funds for renewable energy cooperation.

In 'Energising the India-Africa Partnership,' Shebonti Ray Dadwal argues that there is immense potential for cooperation between India and Africa on the renewable energy front that has to be tapped. She discusses the similarities between India and Africa's energy landscape, thereby increasing the potential for cooperation. The author also argues that a substantial collaboration between India and Africa already exists in the hydrocarbon sector. There is increasing interest in developing cooperation in renewable energy. India and Africa can collaborate in the manufacture of high-tech equipment required for harnessing renewable energy.

Nitya Nanda's chapter focuses on food security and highlights its importance for India and Africa. According to the author, ensuring food sufficiency is crucial for food security in both regions. Nanda provides a historical overview of the food security scenario in India and Africa and argues that Africa can learn from India's experiences in dealing with food security challenges. Furthermore, the chapter calls for African support for India's struggles in the WTO, where India fights for fair practices in the international trade regime. This highlights the need for cooperation between India and Africa to address food security challenges. Nanda suggests that collaboration in agricultural research, trade, and investment could be a way forward for achieving food security in both regions.

Chapters 9 and 10 of the volume examine the intricacies of India-Africa cybersecurity cooperation. Essien D. Essien's chapter discusses cybersecurity challenges, including lack of end-user awareness, limited investment in information security, and a shortage of experts. The author suggests promoting education, training, and cybersecurity competitions. Collaboration among governments, private actors, and academics is essential, with consensual partnerships between Africa and India crucial for addressing cybersecurity challenges. These partnerships can facilitate joint research projects, knowledge sharing, and technology transfer, ultimately enhancing cybersecurity resilience to protect critical infrastructure in both regions. .

Samuel's chapter underscores the imperative for India and Africa to collaborate in cyberspace to address shared challenges. While digitization offers new economic prospects, it also brings vulnerabilities and threats. The chapter explores potential areas for cooperation, including capacity building, research, development, and innovation, and the creation of a legal and policy framework for managing cyberspace. Samuel stresses the importance of joint efforts by India and Africa to ensure a secure and stable cyberspace. This entails building trust and confidence among stakeholders, promoting information-sharing and collaboration among governments, businesses, and civil society, and enhancing the cybersecurity capabilities of both regions.

The last three chapters cover cooperation between India and Africa in the sphere of capacity building, knowledge transfer and skill development. Pranav Kumar's chapter underscores the critical role of skills in boosting trade and productivity in Africa. He highlights the shared challenge of skilling millions of youth entering the workforce annually in Africa and India. Kumar advocates for cooperation between the two regions to address skill development challenges, emphasizing the importance of a skilled workforce for sustainable economic growth, reduced unemployment, and poverty alleviation. He suggests that India's experience in skill development could benefit Africa, particularly in sectors like healthcare, IT, agriculture, and renewable energy.

Donald P. Chimanikire's chapter explores India's role in Africa's development, emphasizing capacity building and skill transfer. He highlights the need for processing raw materials in Africa to boost local industrial capacity and export earnings. Chimanikire argues that India's support for human resources development is vital for Africa's transformation, promoting South-South cooperation.

Kenneth King's chapter, "Skills Development in India and Africa: Interactive Agendas," explores potential synergies in skill development between the two regions. He notes their shared ambition to enhance skill capacity, addressing challenges in this sector. King delves into the historical context and current status of skill development in both India and Africa, emphasizing the need for a stronger partnership. He highlights areas of potential collaboration and suggests that India's expertise can offer valuable lessons for Africa's skill development initiatives.

In short, the multifaceted dimensions of security cooperation between India and Africa underscore the strategic partnership between the two regions. The evolving geopolitical landscape and complex security challenges necessitate deeper engagement and collaboration. Through structured engagements, both regions have made significant strides in enhancing their partnership, particularly in areas such as maritime security, energy security, food security, and cybersecurity. The chapters in this volume highlight the shared interests, challenges, and opportunities that define the security relationship between India and Africa, offering insights into the strategic imperatives driving their cooperation. As both regions continue to strive for peace, stability, and prosperity, their collaboration in the security domain will remain relevant and consequential in addressing global challenges. We hope this book will enable readers to understand India's security engagement with African countries.

1

India and Africa: Enhancing the Security Engagement

Festus Kofi Aubyn

Introduction

India-Africa relations have a long history that date back to the pre-colonial times. The relationship became stronger during the period of the anti-colonial struggles and during the formation of the Non-Aligned Movement (NAM) in 1961 in Belgrade under the leadership of Josip Broz Tito of Yugoslavia, Gamal Abdel Nasser of Egypt, Jawaharlal Nehru of India, Kwame Nkrumah of Ghana, and Sukarno of Indonesia. During the struggle for independence in Africa, India was among the most outspoken critics of apartheid and racial discrimination in South Africa and was also the first country to have raised the issue in the United Nations (UN) in 1946.[1] Over the past decades, India-Africa relations have evolved and grown steadily from a dominant focus on the political and economic spheres to issues of peace and security. The cooperation has occurred at the various multilateral forums, and at the regional and national levels. The relevance and the logic of the emerging security relations between India and Africa is a sound one that is based on common strategic interests.

Strategically, India has considerable geopolitical and economic interests at stake in Africa that requires a peaceful and stable domestic environment. Africa's security problems such as, localised conflicts, violent extremism, terrorism, piracy, cyber security threats and transnational crimes not only affect African countries, but also the national interests of India. For example, India's investment in the United Sudan's petroleum sector, which is estimated to be over $2 billion, will be at stake if the crisis in South Sudan continues to fester.[2] Ignoring Africa's internal problems therefore, can significantly endanger India's own future security and economic interests. Conversely, African countries and especially the African Union (AU) also look up to India as a significant partner for the continent's own future. India's attractiveness to Africa is based on the country's growing economy, role as a net security provider, competitive health, educational and agricultural sectors as well as business, infrastructure and training prowess.[3] Consequently, both India and Africa see the logic of enhancing their security cooperation due to the shared interest for stability in Africa. A stable and prosperous Africa will not only provide more investments and trade opportunities, but will also enhance the momentum of the strategic cooperation that will invariably dovetail India's growth story with that of Africa's Agenda 2063.[4] Given this mutual strategic understanding, India has partnered with Africa to promote security in the continent.

This chapter examines the nature and scope of this security cooperation and explores the possibilities for enhanced security engagement in the future. It begins with a contextual analysis of the foundation of the relationship, followed by a discussion on the India-Africa security cooperation at three levels: the multilateral, regional and national level. The limitations of the cooperation are also highlighted. The next section considers some practical ways in which India and Africa can enhance their security engagement at both the strategic and operational levels. The paper also explores ways in which India can coordinate its efforts with the multiple international actors in Africa such as the UN, EU, China, United Kingdom, France and the United States to minimise duplications and overlaps, maximise the resources and ensure synergy in international assistance to the AU and its Regional Economic Communities (RECs).

India in Africa: Contextualising the Relationship

The African continent has, in recent years, recorded significant achievements in economic growth and democratic governance. Most African economies, according to the African Development Bank, have sustained unprecedented growth rates, driven mainly by strong domestic demands, improved macroeconomic management, a growing middle class, and increased political stability.[5] The record of multi-party democracy and governance has also been encouraging despite the few cases of political upheavals in countries such as Togo Kenya and Burundi.[6] The extent of armed conflicts on the continent has also reduced by historical standards. For instance, statistics from the Armed Conflict Location and Event Data Project (ACLED) and the Uppsala Conflict Data Program (UCDP) shows a significant decline of conflict incidents in Africa since 2015.[7] Despite these encouraging transformations, the African continent continues to face multiple security threats that are not only national in scope but cross border and transnational.

Today, a number of African countries such as South Sudan, Democratic Republic of Congo (DRC), Central African Republic (CAR), Somalia, Mali and Libya still remain trapped in a vicious cycle of violent conflicts and its deadly consequences. The Sahel region especially, has witnessed an increasing spate of terrorist's attacks against innocent civilians, security forces and the United Nations peacekeepers, committed by the Al-Qaeda in the Islamic Maghreb (AQIM) and its affiliates such as the Movement for Oneness and Jihad in West Africa (MUJAO) and Al-Murabitoun.[8] The vast swathes of "ungoverned territory" coupled with inefficient security apparatus, bad governance, weak borders, arms proliferation, drug trafficking and socio-economic challenges (underdevelopment, poverty and unemployment) in the Sahel region has provided an ideal condition for violent extremism and terrorism to thrive.

Relatedly, Nigeria and its neighbouring countries like Cameroon, Chad, and Niger have also suffered constant attacks by Boko Haram despite the relentless efforts by the Multinational Joint Task Force (MNJTF) to restore peace in the Lake Chad Basin.[9] In Somalia, Al-Shabaab militants continue to launch deadly attacks against government officials, security personnel and personnel of the AU Transition Mission in Somalia (ATMIS) after more than a decade of offensive operations against the group.[10] Apart from the issues relating to terrorism and violent extremism, the incidence of political violence mainly caused by disputed elections and disagreements over presidential term limits have also triggered localised violence in a number of African countries such as Burundi, Kenya, Togo and the DRC. The consequences of these acts of violence have been enormous, ranging from the destruction of properties, injuries and loss of human life to arbitrary arrests and human right abuses of protestors. Furthermore, the threat of maritime piracy in the Gulf of Aden in East Africa and the Gulf of Guinea in West Africa, as well as, issues relating to irregular migration, cyber-crimes, health pandemics, climate change and transnational organised crimes such as the trafficking of narcotics, arms, and humans have further added to Africa's growing security conundrums.

In response to these complex security challenges, and in line with the provisions of its Constitutive Act and the Protocol Relating to the Establishment of the Peace and Security Council (PSC Protocol), the African Union (AU) and its member states have undertaken several conflict prevention, peacekeeping and peacebuilding interventions within the spirit of finding "African solutions to African problems." However, while African leaders have increasingly shown greater determination to solve their own problems, the magnitude and transnational nature of the threats, together with the huge financial commitments and capabilities needed has often stymied the efforts of the AU and its RECs. This has prompted the need to develop strategic partnerships with a number of multilateral agencies and bilateral partners to support the African efforts. India happens to be one of such important bilateral partners whose contribution to Africa's peace efforts over the years has been visible for all to see.

In the last two decades, India's economic engagement and commercial investments with the African countries has increased substantially. Trade with Africa has also seen an enormous increase from $11.9 billion in 2005-2006 to 98 billion in 2022-2023.[11] With the increasing number of investments and commercial interests, the stability of the African continent is important for India's own economic growth and development. From the African point of view, the security relations with India is meant to be a win-win cooperation, where Africa seeks assistance to maintain peace and stability on the continent, while India provides this support as a way of protecting its own strategic political, economic and commercial interests.

Nature and Scope of the Security Engagement

India's support to the African peace and security has mainly occurred at the multilateral level of the UN, at the regional level of the AU/RECs and at the national level with individual African states.

Multilateral Level (UN)

At the multilateral level of the UN, India has played a critical role in advancing African peace and security mainly at the decision-making level as well as through its financial and personnel contributions to UN peacekeeping operations in Africa. India's firm contribution to the UN is informed by its civilisational philosophy of non-violence and promoting peace across the globe.

At the decision-making level, India has played a very significant role regarding peacekeeping deployments to Africa during its non-permanent membership of the UN Security Council (UNSC) from 2011 to 2013.[12] India identified peacekeeping in Africa as a key agenda and suggested important ideas to enhance its effectiveness. The country used its position as a member of the UN Council to represent the interests, positions and concerns of the AU and its member states on various peacekeeping issues. A good illustration of this was India's call for a greater involvement of Troop Contributing Countries (TCCs) or Police Contributing Countries (PCCs) in the strategic decision-making process of new peacekeeping deployments, which is also a view shared by most African countries including Ghana, Egypt, Kenya, Nigeria, Rwanda, Uganda and Senegal.[13] During its latest UNSC tenure (2021-22), India proposed a four-point framework for UN peacekeepers to meet contemporary threats. This framework includes employing proven, cost-effective, and environmentally friendly technologies; establishing a strong information and intelligence foundation for early warning and response; ensuring the availability of technological advancements on the ground; and providing consistent training and capacity building for peacekeepers.[14]

This call has yielded some positive result because TCCs/PCCs are now often consulted at the initial stages before the UNSC determines the deployment of a new mission.[15] India has on various occasions also advocated for mission mandates to be rooted in ground realities and matched with the requisite resources as well as the need for greater financial and human resources for peacebuilding initiatives in post-conflict societies. These are important perspectives that are also shared by African countries. Additionally, India has consistently placed greater emphasis on the need for stronger partnership between the UN and the AU/RECs towards the maintenance of peace and security in Africa. On the issue of UN reforms, India and Africa have been working together to reform the Security Council. While India calls for the expansion of the UNSC to include permanent African representation, African countries have also supported India's aspirations for a UNSC permanent seat.[16] Both sides have supported each other's position at various forums and debates for a decisive action to be taken to correct what they call the historic injustice done to developing countries in the world.

On the peacekeeping front, Indian troops and police personnel have, since the 1950s, served in different capacities as Force Commanders, Deputy Force Commanders, Military Advisors, Staff Officers, Military Observers, formed Military and Police Units and as Police Advisors in different UN missions across Africa to help promote peace and stability in war-tone countries. Over the years, India has gained the track record as the largest troop contributor to the UN missions since its inception with a total contribution exceeding 1,95,000 troops and a significant number of police personnel.[17] Statistics from the UN Department of Peacekeeping Operations (DPKO) as of February 28, 2018 showed that India was the fourth largest contributor to UN missions with 6,712 personnel comprising military experts (44), police (589), staff officers (88) and troops (5991).[18] The country's participation in UN missions in Africa started in 1960 when two infantry Brigades were deployed to the UN Operations in the Congo (ONUC), out of which 39 lost their life. India subsequently provided two engineer companies, logistics company, staff officers and military observers to the UN mission in Mozambique from 1992-1994. Later in the 1990s, Indian Infantry battalions, signal companies, engineer companies, staff officers, quick reaction companies, attack helicopter units, medical units, logistic support units, staff officers and military observers were deployed to UN missions in Somalia (1993-94), Rwanda (1994-96), Sierra Leone (1999-2001) and Angola (1989-99).[19]

Since 2000, Indian military and police personnel have been deployed to the UN missions in Ethiopia-Eritrea (2006-08), DRC (2005), Sudan (2005),

Ivory Coast (2017) and Liberia (2007). In Liberia especially, for the very first time in the UN history India deployed an all-Female Formed Police Unit (FPU) in 2007 to the UN Operation in Liberia (UNMIL). With Indian support, most of these UN missions have either closed down or are on the path towards socio-economic recovery and development. The most recent missions to close down were the UN missions in Cote d'Ivoire and Liberia in 2017 where the security situation is now stabilised and rapid socio-economic transformation is taking place.[20] Currently, India is involved actively in peacekeeping missions in African countries such as the DRC, South Sudan and Western Sahara. Its largest contribution is in the DRC (MONUSCO), where 2,921 personnel made up of troops, military experts, staff officers and FPUs are serving in the mission.

To a large extent, Indian peacekeepers have contributed to the stabilisation of the most trouble spots in Africa where they have been deployed. The professionalism and commitment to service of the Indian peacekeepers in protecting civilians and building durable peace has always won the accolade and commendations of the UN and host countries in Africa. Below is for example an excerpt of a statement given by the Jonglei Acting Governor in South Sudan, Dr. Agot Alier, during the UN mission in South Sudan (UNMISS) medal day celebration in Bor for Indian peacekeepers in October 2017:

> The Indian battalion had played an important role in keeping the community safe as well as encouraging local peace efforts. They had also provided much-needed services to the community outside of their core mandate, such as medical care for local residents and support for local farmers with veterinary treatment for their animals.[21]

This is indeed a testament of the courage, dedication and professionalism exhibited by the Indian peacekeepers in executing their mandates in the UN missions in Africa. Nonetheless, cases of misconduct and alleged Sexual Abuse and Exploitation (SEA), brought against some Indian personnel in the UN missions in Africa, have been particularly worrying. The famous cash-for-sex scandal in the DRC involving Indian personnel in 2008 and recent allegations of SEA in the DRC and South Sudan are graphical cases in point.[22] SEA is an issue that does not confront India alone, but most TCCs/PCCs from Africa which requires joint sustainable remedies. Thanks to the Indian military for putting in place stringent measures to ensure that few of their peacekeepers do not trade the country's hard-won reputation for their own personal gratification.

Regional Level (AU/RECs)

India's security cooperation with Africa and its regional organisations has improved in the last decade. This evolving and dynamic relationship was placed under an institutionalised framework and structure in 2008 with the first India-Africa Forum Summit (IAFS-I) held in New Delhi in April that year and subsequently in Addis Ababa in May 2011 (IAFS-II) and New Delhi in October 2015 (IAFS-III).[23] At the IAFS-III in particular, India pledged to bolster its cooperation with Africa by enhancing capacity to contribute toward peacekeeping and peacebuilding efforts including support to the African Standby Force (ASF). Generally, the hosting of these forums undoubtedly demonstrates India's commitment and willingness to support the AU and its member states to maintain peace and stability in the African continent. Therefore, in line with the India-Africa Framework for Strategic Cooperation that emanated from the IAFS-I, the AU has received diverse support from India for the implementation of the African Peace and Security Architecture (APSA). This support has varied from the provision of financial support for the AU mission in Somalia (AMISOM), the African-led International Support Mission in Mali (AFISMA) and in the areas of capacity building and human resource development for conflict prevention, management and resolution. In the past, AFISMA benefited from a one mission dollar support and AMISOM's finances were also augmented with a two million dollars funding from India.[24] In 2016, Anurag Srivastava, the Ambassador of India to Ethiopia, Djibouti and AU, handed over a million USD cheque to AMISOM.[25] This cheque was received by Smail Chergui, the Commissioner for Peace and Security of the AU Commission, on behalf of AMISOM. These financial supports have been instrumental in overcoming some of the operational challenges and limited resources of the AU that has hindered the effectiveness of its operations. However, India does not have any specific programme of support for the AU/RECs such as the 'African Peace Facility' of the European Union (EU). Instead, the assistance from India has been given on an ad hoc basis in the form of grants to support specific peacekeeping efforts. It is important for India to have a holistic programme of support in order to have a more focused and engaged security interaction.

India's cooperation with the African RECs on peace and security is limited and yet to achieve its full potential. The focus of the relationship has mainly been on economic and commercial investments instead of security. Thus, economic issues have been prioritised over security issues. India's security engagement with the RECs is now expanding and gradually taking shape. It is vital, therefore, for India to develop mechanisms to further deepen its cooperation with the RECs to support their conflict prevention, management and resolution efforts. Nevertheless, some form of cooperation exists between India and the Southern African Development Community (SADC), the Economic Community of West African States and other RECs but mainly in the economic sphere.

National Level Engagements

At the national level, the cooperation has largely focused on defence cooperation through capacity building of African military personnel and infrastructures. To this end, a number of military personnel from African countries including Ghana, Nigeria, Tanzania, Zambia, Botswana, Lesotho and Seychelles have received different forms of training at various military establishments in India. Training teams from India have also been deployed to some African countries to build the capacity of military personnel for peacekeeping operations. There has been also the supply of military hardware to some African countries like Kenya and Seychelles.[26] India has also undertaken the building of operational and administrative facilities and infrastructures such as roads, airfields and communication networks in some of the African countries. Apart from the defence cooperation, India has also partnered with the Indian Ocean littoral states like Mozambique, Mauritius and Seychelles to combat maritime piracy around the Indian Ocean through joint patrols and initiatives.[27] The objective is to enhance the maritime security environment of the Indian Ocean region.

However, an area that is missing in India's security engagement with individual African nations is the cooperation between law enforcement agencies like the police institutions of both sides. The relationship appears to be more focused on the military. It is instructive to note that most of the non-traditional security challenges like violent extremism, terrorism, election violence, cybercrime and transnational organised crimes that confront Africa today falls within the constitutional mandate of the law enforcement agencies. The military is often called upon to play supporting roles or to assist when the law enforcement agencies are unable to effectively deal with a particular security situation. Moreover, in some African countries analysts have even questioned the relevance of the military, since inter-states conflicts are no longer popular. The nature of contemporary security threats has to do more with the "human security of the people" rather than the "national security of the state". In other words, with few notable exceptions, most African militaries are now playing more roles in international peacekeeping operations and in internal security operations rather than their traditional roles of protecting and defending the territorial integrity of states. In this regard, if India wants to make any significant lasting impact on African security, then it needs to rethink its bilateral security engagement to include cooperation in the area of law enforcement, especially with the post-conflict countries and fragile states to build the institutional and personnel capacities of national police and other law enforcement institutions.

Enhancing the India-Africa Security Engagement

Despite the achievements recorded so far, there remains potential for enhanced regional and bilateral security cooperation between India and Africa. Some of the issues that can be looked at to further enhance the security cooperation are discussed in the following paragraphs.

First, India and Africa can enhance their security engagement to deal with both the traditional and non-traditional security threats. So far, the cooperation framework on security does not effectively incorporate both traditional and non-traditional security issues. Most of the critical security challenges that confront Africa today are issues relating to terrorism, violent extremism, election violence, drug trafficking, arms proliferation, youth unemployment, energy insecurity, irregular migration, organised crime and environmental degradation.[28] The India-Africa security engagement, therefore, needs to go beyond the support for peacekeeping interventions and defence cooperation to address some of these non-traditional threats that underlie most of the conflicts in Africa.

Second, India and Africa can explore strengthening cooperation between the peace and security training and research centres/institutions of both sides. For example, there can be formal cooperation agreements in the areas of staff exchanges, joint research projects and publications, training programmes and conferences between Indian institutions like the Institute for Defence Studies and Analyses (IDSA) & the Centre for UN Peacekeeping (CUNPK) in New Delhi and African institutions such as the Kofi Annan International Peacekeeping Training Centre (KAIPTC) in Ghana, National Defence College in Nigeria, the Institute of Security Studies (ISS) in South Africa and the Kenyan Peace Support Training Centre (PSTC). In the KAIPTC, for instance, there are German, Austrian, French, Canadian, American, Nigerian and Swiss Military and Police Course Directors who are sent to the Centre for 2-4 years period to handle specific training courses funded by their governments. The Austrians, for instance, run the Humanitarian Assistance Course at the Centre which utilises both Austrian and African facilitators. Is it possible for India to explore some of these opportunities to share its experiences and help build the capacity of African security personnel? And can the African institutions also help train Indian security personnel who are selected for deployment to Africa for peacekeeping? Very often Africa tends to be on the receiving end but there is a lot India can learn from Africa in terms of training. In 2017, over 60 American soldiers were schooled in jungle warfare[29] by Ghanaian instructors at the Jungle Warfare School at the Achiase military base in Akim Oda, Ghana. This was an "eye-opening" experience for the US Soldiers because they were exposed to some of the things that they do not normally train in. In sum, the point being made is that the partnership between Indian and African institutions should be win-win cooperation.

Third, while Africa is grateful for the Indian support to the AU and its member states, like "Oliver Twist, Africa wants some more." India needs to maintain and increase its training and logistical and technological support to the implementation of the APSA, particularly the African standby force (ASF). India can help build the capacity of the AU forces in the fields of logistic management, communication and information systems. Additionally, India can consider having specific holistic programme of support to the AU and its RECs in order to have a more focused security engagement in line with African initiatives such as Agenda 2063 which is a long strategic framework for the socio-economic transformation of the continent.[30] The relationship with the RECs especially, has to be further strengthened. At the national level, India should take advantage of its good relationship with Africa, and help promote dialogues for political settlement of African conflict issues like the situation in South Sudan and the DRC.

Fourth, India's bilateral support to African countries should move beyond defence cooperation and be extended to the law enforcement agencies as well. Most of the security challenges in Africa today fall within the constitutional mandate of the law enforcement agencies. Therefore, building the institutional and personnel capacities of national police and other law enforcement institutions will go a long way to promote peace and stability in Africa especially in the post-conflict countries and fragile states.

Fifth, the presence of multiple development partners in Africa that are also providing similar supports to the AU and its member states undoubtedly have implications for India. It presents opportunities, but at the same time it can also be a source of increased competition among development partners. India can tap into the opportunities it presents and cooperate with other actors like the EU, China, USA, France, UK, Turkey, Germany and Canada on several key areas of mutual interests in African peace and security, where greater collaborative efforts can yield positive results. India can ensure that in its relationship with the various actors, African security issues will take a higher priority. To this end, trilateral dialogues such as India-Africa-UK security forums, India-EU-Africa security forums or India-Africa-US security forums can be initiated to allow for frequent exchanges of views and perspectives on security issues concerning Africa. However, Africa needs to play a more proactive role in shaping and directing any cooperation between India and its allies as well as setting the priorities for such cooperative efforts and initiatives.

Conclusion

The prospect of the India-Africa cooperation on peace and security is incontestable. The cooperation has a huge potential that needs to be vigorously explored. Both sides should make a concerted effort to further enhance the security engagement at the multilateral, regional and national levels, respectively. Significantly, India should consider increasing its financial and technical support to the AU and its RECs to take the lead role in maintaining peace and security in Africa. Moreover, India should also continue to support African countries' capacity building in areas such as defence, law enforcement and counter-terrorism. Moving forward, the relationship has to be based on the right concept of morality and mutual benefits. There is an adage that "If people make friends by their power, the friendship will break up when the power is lost; If people make friends by money, they will separate when money is gone; Thus, only heart-to-heart exchanges can last long." Hence, to further develop the security engagement, India and Africa should translate the strength of their traditional friendship into the driving forces for solidarity and honest cooperation, to advance Africa's stability through a sustained security and strategic dialogue. Thus, India has to play a more proactive role in ensuring peace and stability in Africa, given its growing trade and investment linkages with the continent.

NOTES

1 "India and the UN", at https://www.pminewyork.org/pages?id (Accessed 18 March 2018).
2 Salman Khurshid, "India Keen on Investment despite South Sudan Unrest", at https://www.livemint.com/Politics/F5WVfn2mGTDFP4t3a87i6I/India-keen-on-investment-despite-South-Sudan-unrest-Salman.html (Accessed 17 March 2018).
3 "A Case for Strengthening India-Africa Partnership", at https://www.brookings.edu/wp-content/uploads/2015/10/india-africa-briefing-book-brookings-india.pdf, (Accessed 18 March 2018).
4 "What is Agenda 2063?", at https://au.int/en/agenda2063 (Accessed 20 March 2018).
5 "Tracking Africa's Progress in Figures", at https://www.afdb.org/en/knowledge/publications/tracking-africa%E2%80%99s-progress-in-figures/ (Accessed 17 March 2018).
6 Festus Aubyn, "Compromise Is Key to Ending Togo's Political Crisis", at https://theglobalobservatory.org/by/festus-kofi-aubyn/ (Accessed 23 March 2018).
7 Ciara Aucoin, "Less Armed Conflict but More Political Violence in Africa", at https://issafrica.org/iss-today/less-armed-conflict-but-more-political-violence-in-africa, (Accessed 15 March 2018).
8 K. Aning and F. Aubyn, "Managing Complex Political Dilemmas in West Africa: The Role of ECOWAS in Mali", *New Routes,* Vol. 18 (2), 2013.
9 Kwesi Aning, Mustapha Abdellah and Festus Aubyn, "Responding to Boko Haram: Interrogating the Effectiveness of State and Regional Intervention Approaches," in James J. Hentz, Hussein Solomon (ed), *Understanding Boko Haram: Terrorism and Insurgency in Africa,* Taylor and Francis, London, 2016.
10 "ATMIS", at https://atmis-au.org/ (Accessed 17 March 2023).
11 Government of India, Ministry of External Affairs, "Remarks made by External Affairs Minister, Dr. S. Jaishankar at the Business Community Interaction", 8 July 2023, at https://www.mea.gov.in/Speeches-Statements.htm?dtl/36766 (Accessed 30 July 2023).
Ruchita Beri, "India's New Initiative in Africa: The Asia-Africa Growth Corridor", at https:/

/idsa.in/idsacomments/indias-new-initiative-in-africa-asia-africa-growth-corridor_rberi_130617 (Accessed 10 March 2018).

12 Ruchita Beri, "India's Evolving Security Relations with Africa", at https://www.brookings.edu/wp-content/uploads/2015/10/india-africa-briefing-book-brookings-india.pdf (Accessed 18 March 2018).

13 Ibid.

14 "Remarks by External Affairs Minister at the UN Security Council Open Debate on Technology & Peacekeeping", Ministry of External Affairs, Government of India, 18 August 2021.

15 "Deploying Peacekeepers", at https://peacekeeping.un.org/en/deploying-peacekeepers (Accessed 14 March 2018).

16 Jakkie Cilliers, "Working Together to Reform the UN Security Council", at https://www.brookings.edu/wp-content/uploads/2015/10/india-africa-briefing-book-brookings-india.pdf, (Accessed 19 March 2018).

17 "India and United Nations Peacekeeping and Peacebuilding", at https://www.pminewyork.org/pdf/menu/49151pkeeping.pdf (Accessed 16 March 2018).

18 "Troop and Police Contributions", at https://peacekeeping.un.org/en/troop-and-police-contributors (Accessed 17 March 2018).

19 "India and United Nations Peacekeeping and Peacebuilding", at https://www.pminewyork.org/pdf/menu/49151pkeeping.pdf,(Accessed 16 March 2018).

20 "UNMIL Farewell Ceremony in Honour of Police and Military Personnel", at https://unmil.unmissions.org/unmil-farewell-ceremony-honour-police-and-military-personnel (Accessed October 16, 2018); Bavier Joe, "U.N. Closes Ivory Coast Mission, Security Remains Fragile", at https://www.reuters.com/article/us-ivorycoast-un-peacekeepers-idUSKBN19L1VK (Accessed 16 October 2018).

21 United Nations, "UNMISS Force Commander Awards UN medal to Indian Peacekeepers in Bor", at https://peacekeeping.un.org/en/unmiss-force-commander-awards-un-medal-to-indian-peacekeepers-bor (Accessed 24 March 2018).

22 Rahul Singh, "UN Report Says Indian Peacekeepers Face Sexual Abuse charges", at https://www.hindustantimes.com/india/un-report-says-indian-peacekeepers-face-sexual-abuse-charges/story-MBLmkKV57x1Klr7O3kEUZK.html (Accessed 24 March 2018).

23 "Report on Partners in Progress: Towards A Dynamic and Transformative Development Agenda" *Third India-Africa Forum Summit,* 29 October 2015.

24 Ruchita Beri, "India-Africa Security Engagement" in R. Beri, (ed) *India and Africa: Common Security Challenges for the Next Decade,* Pentagon Press, New Delhi.

25 See "India Support AMISOM", at http://indembassyeth.in/india-supports-amisom/ (Accessed 21 March 2018).

26 A. Dutta, "Indo-African Defence Cooperation: Need for Enhanced Thrust", *Journal of Defense Studies.* Vol. 2, Issue 2.

27 Ruchita Beri, "India-Africa Security Engagement" in Ruchita Beri (ed.), *India and Africa: Common Security Challenges for the Next Decade*, Pentagon Press, New Delhi.

28 Festus Kofi Aubyn, "Countering Terrorism and Extremism in Africa: Drawing Lessons from the Indian Experience", in Ruchita Beri (ed.), *India and Africa: Common Security Challenges for the Next Decade,* Pentagon Press, New Delhi.

29 Courses thought include jungle navigation, ambush offence and defence tactics, and survival tactics, GraphicOnline, (2017), "Ghana Armed Forces train US counterparts in jungle warfare", at https://www.graphic.com.gh/news/general-news/ghana-armed-forces-train-us-counterparts-in-jungle-warfare.html (Accessed 20 March 2018).

30 "What is Agenda 2063?" https://au.int/en/agenda2063 (Accessed 15 March 2018).

2

India-Africa Security Relations: Drivers and Trends

Ruchita Beri

India-Africa relations have been founded on shared philosophy of South-South cooperation and long standing historical ties. Prime Minister Narendra Modi has often reiterated that Africa is "top priority" for India.[1] The steps taken by India's towards inclusion of the African Union as full member of the G20 group during its presidency is indicative of Africa's growing importance. The several high-level visits to African countries also reflect efforts towards building closer ties between the two regions. Over the years, India-Africa engagement has focused more on economic diplomacy rather than defence diplomacy. India's security engagement involves training and capacity building, participation in UN peacekeeping operations and maritime cooperation. Of late, India has expanded the cooperation between India and Africa in defence and security realm. It has launched several new initiatives and mechanisms to boost its ties with this important region. This chapter examines the security landscape of the continent and analyses the drivers and trends of India's security engagement with Africa.

Africa: Current Security Environment

In recent years, the African Union and its member states have adopted several policy documents that portray the continent's vision on political, economic and security issues. The *Africa Agenda 2063* is an ambitious vision for inclusive and sustainable growth of the continent. Notably, aspiration number four of this plan calls for a peaceful and secure Africa.[2] One of the flagship initiatives under this plan is "Silencing of Guns". This initiative aspires for the end of all conflicts in Africa. Unfortunately, there is no end in sight to conflicts and insecurity in the region. African countries are dealing with numerous security challenges from multiple conflicts, terrorism to unconstitutional changes in government.

Rise in Conflicts

According to Stockholm Institute for Peace Research (SIPRI) 22 out of 54 States in Africa faced conflict in 2022.[3] In particular, the Democratic Republic of Congo (DRC) in Central Africa, Ethiopia and Sudan in the Horn of Africa have of late, witnessed high-intensity conflict. In DRC, the resurgence of the March 23 (M23) rebel group in March 2022 led to intensification of conflict in the country. The Congolese are frustrated with the inability of the United Nations Organisation Stabilization Mission in DR Congo (MUNOSCO) to protect them, leading to deadly protests against the mission.[4] The MONUSCO is set to withdraw completely from the country by the end of 2024. Similarly, the East African Community Regional Force (EACRF-DRC) deployed in the country at the behest of Congolese government has also been ineffective in reducing the conflict and is also set to withdraw from the country.[5] Meanwhile the fighting between M23 rebels and the Armed Forces of the Democratic Republic of the Congo (FARDC) continues unabated, enhancing humanitarian crisis in the country.

Ethiopia has been ravaged with internal conflict for a few years now. In November 2022, the signing of peace agreement between the Tigray forces and the federal government had brought to an end two-year long deadly conflict in the country. The agreement led to normalization of relations between the Tigray and Ethiopian government. However, peace in the country was not for long as there was a fallout between the Amhara – the second most populous region in the country and the federal government.[6] The Amhara that had fought along the Ethiopian government forces against the Tigray, were unhappy with the peace accord, as it failed to address their concerns. Despite attempts to negotiate a peaceful solution, the military conflict between Ethiopian federal government and Amhara continues.

Sudan is in the news due to a deadly ongoing armed conflict. On 15

April 2023, fighting broke out between the Sudanese Armed Forces (SAF) led by General Abdel Fattah Al Burhan and the paramilitary force Rapid Support Group (RSF) headed by Mohamed Hamdan Dagalo in a power struggle to control the country. The ongoing conflict has led to horrific violence, destruction and massive loss of human lives across the country. During this conflict the Sudanese Armed Forces have been accused of bombing the RSF camps and also residential areas and critical infrastructure. Similarly the SAF have been blamed for atrocities against civilians, women in particular.[7] Despite various attempts to find a peaceful solution, hostilities continue with dire consequences for the region at large.

Surge in Terrorism

The terrorist attacks continue in Africa. Despite the African Union's efforts, terror groups are active in various parts of Africa.[8] According to the African Centre for the Study and Research on Terrorism (ACSRT) there has been a 99 per cent increase in the number of terrorist attacks in 2023 compared to the previous year.[9] The Sahel region dominates in terms of terrorist activities and attacks. The main terror groups include the Jama'at Nusrat al-Islam wal-Muslimin (JNIM), Islamic State Sahel Province (ISSP) and Islamic State West Africa Province (ISWAP). This expansion of terror violence took place along with significant change in security architecture and foreign presence in the region. After military coups in 2020 and 2021, the military junta in Mali distanced itself from France. In 2022, France announced closure of its counter-terrorist campaign *Operation Barkhane,* and withdrawal of its troops from the country. Subsequently, Mali invited the Wagner Group, a Russian private military company to the country.[10] The withdrawal of French troops from Sahel was followed by withdrawal of Taskforce Takuba comprising Special Forces from several European countries and the UN Multidimensional integrated Stabilization Mission in Mali (MINUSMA) from Mali.[11] This geopolitical shift has led to a surge in terrorist activities in the region.

In the Horn of Africa, the Al Shabaab terror group has strengthened its terror activities within Somalia and its neighbours like Kenya. In August 2022, the new Somali government led by Hassan Sheikh Mohamud launched a military offensive against the Al Shabaab. However, the Somali government's offensive has not stopped the group's activities. In June 2023, the Al Shabaab launched an attack on the African Union Transitional Mission in Somalia (ATMIS), resulting in the death of 54 peacekeepers.[12] It has also continued its attacks on the neighbouring countries – Kenya and Ethiopia. Al Shabaab has launched several attacks across the Kenya-Somalia border in the last one year. It has attacked the Ethiopian bases in South Western Somalia and targeted Ethiopian troops that are part of the ATMIS. The African Union forces, present in the country since 2007 are scheduled to withdraw by December 2024.[13] As the national government of Somalia readies itself to take over the complete security apparatus in the country, the continuous onslaught of Al Shabaab is a worrisome.

Apart from Somalia, terrorist activities of Boko Haram and ISWAP continue in Northern Nigeria and neighbouring Cameroon, Chad and Niger. There were also reports of clashes between the two jihadist groups in the Lake Chad region.[14] The only bright spot in the success achieved by the African forces in bringing down the terror activity in Mozambique. The security forces from Rwanda and the Southern Africa Development Community Mission in Mozambique (SAMIM) have helped in confronting and containing the terror challenge in Cabo Delgado region in the northeast of the country.[15] The persistent threat of terrorism in some pockets of continent underscores the urgent need for African countries to focus on coordinated efforts to address the fundamental root causes of this menace.

Rising Unconstitutional Changes of Government

The recent years have also seen a rise in unconstitutional change of government through military coups in Africa. West Africa seems to be most affected by this scourge. Between 2021 and 2023 there were six coups in West African countries (Burkina Faso, Chad, Guinea, Mali, Niger and Gabon). Another country that went through an undemocratic political transition is Sudan. In most of these countries, the putschists were motivated by governance deficiencies, mismanagement, corruption within political elites, deterioration in security situation, particularly failure to contain terrorism.[16] The recent coups have also displayed a significant geopolitical shift in the region. Both in the case of Mali and Niger the military junta called for an expulsion of French troops from the respective countries. Along with the exit of French and other Western troops, there has been a simultaneous call to welcome the presence of Russian private military forces in these countries.[17] The African countries have a complex task ahead to deal with this anti-West and anti-democracy trend in the region.

Choppy Maritime Environment

Maritime insecurity is another important concern for Africans. Africa has a long coastline of 26,000 nautical miles and 13 million square kilometers of exclusive economic zone. In recent years, oceans are often perceived as a reservoir of resources. Africa boasts of a marine industry worth $1 trillion per annum.[18] However, there are several challenges for a secure maritime domain in Africa. They include piracy, illegal unreported and unregulated fishing, drugs, narcotics, small arms and human trafficking etc. The high incidence of piracy off the East African coast in Gulf of Aden (GoA) and in Gulf of Guinea in West Africa, has brought the African maritime security challenges into world focus. The surge of piracy off the coast of Somalia and the Gulf of Aden during 2008-14, spanned a vast area including the maritime boundaries of countries like Kenya, Tanzania, Seychelles, Madagascar, and further off across the Indian Ocean, dangerously close to India's shores. After a lull the piracy in the Horn of Africa has resurfaced again. Since November 2023, more than 20 incidents of piracy were reported in the Gulf of Aden.[19] At the same time, piracy is also a problem in the Gulf of Guinea, which borders more than 3,700 miles of the West African coast. In recent years, this region has emerged as one of the most pirate-infested waters in the world, posing an urgent security threat to the maritime environment. While the African countries have launched several initiatives such the Djibouti Code of Conduct and its 2017 Jeddah amendment for Eastern Africa, Yaounde Code of Conduct for West Africa, the problem continues as unfortunately, a large number of African countries lack the capacity to ensure the security of their declared maritime zones.

India-Africa Engagement: Key Drivers

India has close and historical ties with Africa. In recent years, India has given high priority to engagement with African countries. While efforts have been made to augment cooperation in political, economic, scientific and cultural spheres. It is equally important that India boosts defence and security cooperation in the region. Africa, a continent of over a billion people with growing political and economic power is strategically important for India. This significance has grown for access of natural resources, economic growth, countering common security challenges, shaping India's multilateral ambitions and for connecting with the Indian diaspora.

Natural Resources

Africa is a key producer of natural resources that are important both commercially and strategically. The continent holds 10 per cent of the world's oil reserves and 8 per cent of the world's reserves of natural gas. There are many oil producing countries in Africa. Nigeria, Angola, Algeria, Egypt, Congo-Brazzaville, Gabon, Equatorial Guinea, Cameroon, Chad, the Democratic Republic of Congo (DRC) and South Sudan are the main oil producers in Africa. Algeria, Angola, Egypt, Nigeria and Libya produce 90 per cent of the natural gas on the African continent. There have been a series of major discoveries in recent years, in Egypt, Mozambique, Tanzania, Senegal, Mauritania and South Africa. It is projected that Africa – led by Mozambique and Egypt – may emerge as a major supplier of Liquefied Natural Gas (LNG) to global markets.

India is the world's third-largest oil importer. In recent years, it has been diversifying the source of its oil imports. This move is mainly to reduce the dependence on West Asia. Currently India sources around 63 per cent of its crude imports from West Asia.[20] Africa plays an important role in this diversification. Africa's share in India's oil imports is about 15 per cent and will increase in future.[21] India's main suppliers of crude oil in Africa are Angola, Nigeria, Algeria, Egypt and Equatorial Guinea. However, there is another side of India's energy ties with Africa. As most African countries do not have sufficient refining capacity, they normally import refined fuels. Africa is the second largest destination of India's refined petroleum.[22]

At the same time, Africa is estimated to contain 90 per cent of the entire world supply of platinum and chromium, almost half of the world's gold supply, and large share of other minerals like diamonds and uranium.[23] Democratic Republic of Congo, a country in central Africa accounts nearly 70 per cent of the world's cobalt, an important mineral used in production of Lithium batteries used in cell phones and laptops.[24] As the world moves towards clean energy, the demand for minerals needed for production of solar panels, wind turbines and electric vehicles will rise phenomenally. Hence, Africa's natural resources wealth is critical for global green transition. As an energy deficient country, India is moving towards renewable energy in a big way. Along with France, India launched the International Solar Alliance in 2015. Solar energy is an important part of India's energy mix. A large number of African countries are also moving towards renewables and have joined this Alliance. Partnership with African countries is essential for India's energy security and its shift towards sustainable energy.

Economic Potential

Over the years, India's economic engagement with Africa has increased. India's trade with Africa jumped from about US$ 34 billion in 2009 to US$ 98 billion in 2022-23. India is now Africa's third-largest trading partner. Investment has followed suit, with India now ranked Africa's fifth-largest source of Foreign Direct Investment (FDI).

Africa has tremendous economic potential and offers rewarding opportunities for global, more importantly Indian businesses with favourable returns. In 2024, according to the African Development Bank, eleven of the world's 20 fastest-growing economies will be from Africa.[25] At the same time, in 2024, the Gross Domestic Product (GDP) growth rate for the continent is expected to be 3.8 per cent. This is higher than projected global average of 2.9 per cent. Africa is predicted to have a fast population growth in the next decade which implies growth of middle class, increased business spending and household consumption. By 2030, Africa will have 1.7 billion people and a combined consumer and business spending of $6.7 trillion creating more opportunities for Indian industry and businessmen.

In recent years, there has been an improvement in the business environment on the continent. Top four African countries in terms of ease of doing business are Mauritius, Rwanda, Kenya and South Africa.[26] African countries have also taken steps to reduce the infrastructure gap on the continent. The African Union's Programme for Infrastructure Development in Africa (PIDA), launched in 2012, has made some progress. There has been fast digitalization and increased technological innovation in Africa. In the financial sector, for example, M-PESA, developed by Kenya in 2007, is at present Africa's leading mobile money service, with over 50 million active customers across seven countries.[27] The move towards regional integration, ostensibly to enhance intra-regional trade and growth, through the African Continental Free Trade Area (AfCFTA) signed in 2018, is another positive development in the continent.

Common Security Challenges

Over the years, terrorism has become the most important challenge to peace, security and development in Africa. The terror activities have grown exponentially in the continent, not only in terms of the number of attacks but also the number of countries affected due to proliferation of terrorist groups. While global terror groups such as the Islamic State of Iraq and Syria (ISIS) and Al Qaeda (AQ) have made their presence felt in the region, other local groups too have gained prominence over the years. The African Union and its precursor the Organisation of African Unity (OAU) have taken several measures to deal with this scourge, nevertheless the threat persists. India has also grappled with violent terrorism for several decades. Both India and Africa can learn from each other's experience in countering terrorism.

A secure maritime environment in the Indian Ocean Region (IOR) is crucial for both India and African countries for achieving sustained national development. Such security means not only guarding the coastline or territories, but also safeguarding the countries' interests in their exclusive economic zones (EEZs), as well as protecting trade and shipping routes, and sea-lanes of communications (SLOCs). Among Africa's 54 countries, 34 are coastal or island States. At the same time, 90 per cent of the continent's trade is conducted through the oceans.[28] Likewise for India, a peninsular country, a safe and secure maritime domain is vital. The maritime sector plays an important part in India's economic growth. Around 95 per cent of the country's international trade volume and 65 per cent of trade value is through the maritime route.[29]

Shaping India's Multilateral Diplomacy

Africa is significant for India's approach towards global governance and multilateral institutions. Since its independence, in multilateral forums, India continues to see itself as a leader of post-colonial States and an advocate for the Global South. India finds support for this leadership role, particularly in Africa. India's leading role in United Nations decolonization and anti-apartheid efforts, its proactive support for UN peacekeeping missions in the African continent are cases in point. Similarly, African countries have a critical role to play in India's quest for reformed multilateralism.[30] For India, a permanent seat in the UN Security Council is one of its highest multilateral policy priorities. With 54 countries, the voting weight of Africa in the UN is significant for any possible reform of the Council. Also, Africa is the prime and leading voice in two major coalitions on the issue of Security Council reform; African Group and L.69. While 54 African countries are all together in the African Group, 11 of them are also part of the L.69. Moreover, at a time of multilateralism facing profound crises, by ratifying the African (AfCFTA) in 2019, Africa has shown the world what reformed multilateralism can mean.

Indian Diaspora: A Contributor to India's Global Status

Indian Diaspora based in Africa is also an important link with the continent. In recent years, the Indian government has taken several initiatives to connect with the diaspora. Prime Minister Narendra Modi has made a concerted effort to engage with the Indian community during his visits to Africa. He has acknowledged that 'Africa had shaped the identity of Indian diaspora' and that 'Indians in the continent contribute to India's status across the world'.[31]

The African continent is home to three million people of Indian origin.[32] They are spread out across the region. In some countries like Mauritius they form a dominant strength (around 70 per cent of population). In other countries like South Africa, Kenya, Uganda, Tanzania, Nigeria, Madagascar, Zimbabwe, Zambia, Botswana and Mozambique, they have a significant presence.

India-Africa Security Relations: Recent Trends

India and Africa have a longstanding bilateral relationship. These relations are anchored on a partnership that respects each other's aspirations and priorities. In recent years, India's focus on nurturing closer relations with African countries is also reflected in the defence and security sphere.[33]

Setting up of an Institutional Mechanism

The most important landmark has been the setting up an institutional mechanism for a government-to-government dialogue on defence issues at the Defence Ministers' level. In 2020, India hosted the first India-Africa Defence Ministers' Conclave (IADMC) on the side-lines of the DefExpo2020 held at Lucknow.[34] This was planned as the first ministerial event on the run-up to the fourth India-Africa Forum Summit scheduled towards the end of year. However, the outbreak of the COVID pandemic prevented India from hosting the next India-Africa Forum Summit in 2020. Nevertheless, the impetus towards expanding defence and security dialogue with African countries continued. In 2021, India institutionalised a periodic dialogue, called India Africa Defence Dialogue (IADD) with African defence ministers, to be held once in two years on the sidelines of the DefenceExpo.[35] Subsequently, the IADD hosted by Indian Defence Minister, Rajnath Singh at Gandhinagar in October 2022, had helped improve the security relations between India and African countries.

Enhancing Capacity Building

Traditionally, skills enhancement and capacity building through the Indian Technical and Economic Cooperation (ITEC) programme is an important pillar of India's longstanding partnership with African countries. This programme offers courses for civilian and defence training. Over the years, several defence officers from Africa have trained at India's premier defence training establishments like the Defence Services Staff College or the National Defence College. These courses cover defence management, strategic studies, marine and aeronautical engineering.[36] Some of the alumni of the National Defence College have risen to occupy high positions in their respective countries. They include General Fredrick William Kwasi Akuffo, former President of Ghana. India also sends military training teams to an African country as per its requirement. For example, an Indian Military Advisory and Training Team is deployed at the Senior Defence Staff College, Jinja, Uganda since 2016.[37] Recently, at the IADD hosted by India's Defence Minister Rajnath Singh, India has proposed enhancement of defence training with African countries in mutually agreed areas.[38]

Contributing in UNPKO in Africa

India has supported the African efforts towards fostering peace and security through deployment of Indian peacekeepers for the United Nations Peacekeeping Operations (UNPKO) in the continent. India has participated in a majority of the UN peacekeeping missions in Africa. Currently, Indian peacekeepers are active in the UNPK missions in Democratic Republic of Congo, Sudan, South Sudan, Abyei and Western Sahara. These deployments have taken place with great risk to the safety and security of the peacekeepers. These are really challenging times for UN peacekeeping operations in Africa. Apart from threat of attack of non-State actors, the peacekeepers have also faced violent protests by the locals. The local population in Mali and DRC are very unhappy with the inability of the UN missions to bring peace in the respective countries and have often launched protests calling for the exit of peacekeepers from the country. In 2022, two peacekeepers of India's Border Security Force who were part of the UN mission in DRC, lost their lives during a violent protest by the locals. This is not the first time; over 175 Indian peacekeepers have made the supreme sacrifice while being deployed in a UNPKO. India has the highest casualty rate among the troop contributing countries.

In a bid to augment African capacities for conducting peacekeeping operations, India trains officers from African countries at the Centre for UN Peacekeeping (CUNPK) in India. In 2019, the Indian Army launched the inaugural Africa-India field Training Exercise called AFINDEX-19. Army contingents from 17 African countries participated in this exercise. The main objective of the exercise was to provide training and share best practices for conducting and planning humanitarian mine action and peacekeeping operations under the UN mandate.[39] In 2023, the second edition of this exercise was held at Pune, where in comparison, there was a greater representation from Africa. Military personnel from 25 African countries participated in the exercise.[40]

Expanding Maritime Security Cooperation

Maritime Security is a significant area of cooperation for both India and African countries. Prime Minister Narendra Modi reiterated this while announcing the ten guiding principles of the India-Africa relationship during his visit to Uganda in 2018. It is also reflected in India's cooperative and inclusive vision of Security and Growth for All in the Region (SAGAR), unveiled during his visit to Mauritius in 2015. In recent years, African countries have also focused on the maritime domain. In 2014, the African Union adopted the Africa's Integrated Maritime (AIM) Strategy 2050 that emphasises the maritime security challenges, and calls for sustainable development of the region's blue economy. Over the years, India has assisted African countries in surveillance of their Exclusive Economic Zone (EEZ) and Humanitarian and Disaster Relief (HADR) operations. In 2022, at the IADD held in Gandhinagar, Gujarat India called for sharing best practices and experiences to combat disasters and other challenges.

India has taken a fresh initiative to increase trilateral maritime cooperation with African countries. In 2022, the first India-Mozambique-Tanzania Trilateral Exercise (IMT TRILAT) was held off Dar-es-Salaam. This Exercise addressed common threats and enhanced interoperability.[41] India has also boosted trilateral maritime cooperation with the US and France in East Africa. Both France and the United States have similar interests as India and the African countries in keeping the waters of Indian Ocean Region open and free of piracy and other maritime security challenges. This is indicated by the Indian Navy's participation in the Exercise *Cutlass Express* in the last few years.[42] This Exercise was sponsored by the US-Africa Command (AFRICOM) and led by the United States Naval Forces off the East African coast and the Western Indian Ocean Region. In November 2022, the Indian Navy participated with France in joint surveillance and ocean mapping of the waters along with Mauritius, Mozambique Channel in the Western Indian Ocean region.[43]

Sharing Counter Terrorism Experience

The rise of terrorism is another area of common concern for India and African countries. Therefore, counter-terrorism is emerging as an important area of bilateral cooperation with countries suffering from the menace. At Gandhinagar, India has offered to provide counter-terrorism training to African countries. In 2019, India and Nigeria held a strategic and counter-terrorism dialogue at National Security Advisor level. During the meeting, the two sides agreed to maintain contact and a dialogue of understanding challenges faced in the sphere of terrorism and maritime insecurity.

Subsequently, an Indian Army's training team was despatched to Nigeria for a counter-insurgency and counter-terrorism programme for Nigerian Special Forces. In 2019, during Defence Minister Rajnath Singh's visit to Mozambique, cooperation in countering the growing challenge of radicalisation and terrorism was discussed.[44] Kenya is another country on Africa's eastern coast that has faced the brunt of terrorism. In 2021, during Indian Foreign Minister S. Jaishankar's visit to Kenya, the two countries discussed deepening security cooperation to include regular exchanges on counter-terrorism.[45] Egypt is an important African partner in India's fight against global terrorism. In 2018, the two countries signed an agreement to expand counter terrorism cooperation.[46] Morocco is another country in North Africa that shares India's concern regarding rising global trend of terrorism. In 2018, the two countries signed a key pact to affirm their commitment towards the fight against terrorism unleashed by terror group such as ISIS.[47]

Push for Defence Exports to African Countries

The recently held meetings with African countries like the IADD or the Army Chief's conclave have underlined the opportunity for the African partners to consider augmenting import of Indian defence equipment. In the last few years, Mauritius, Seychelles and Mozambique have been the top three countries from Africa to import arms from India. The Ukraine crisis has highlighted the importance of diversifying sources of weapons imports. Currently, Russia is the largest exporter of weapons to Africa, followed by China and European countries. India's defence public sector company, Bharat Earth Movers Limited has registered its branch office in Kenya.[48] This will help in facilitating any cooperation in the field of transfer and maintenance of defence equipment in the continent. At present only 10 per cent of India's defence exports are directed towards Africa.[49] The interest displayed by African countries indicates that this may change in future.

Conclusion

In the last decade, Africa has witnessed a surge in various security challenges. They range from conflicts, radicalisation and violent terrorism, coups, piracy and humanitarian disaster. As a traditional partner, India has supported African plans towards improving the security environment in the continent. In recent years, India has opened multiple pathways for defence and security cooperation between India and Africa. It falls within the series of steps taken by Prime Minister Modi's government to accord high priority to India-Africa engagement. It has increased interaction with African partners on matters related to security at the government-to-government level. The fresh initiatives, such as a new institutional mechanism through hosting of the IADD, the AFINDEX training exercise in India, the IMT TRILAT off the Tanzanian coast, deployment of military training team to Uganda and other African countries, indicates India's efforts towards building African capacities. India's continuous deployment of peacekeepers in Africa under the aegis of the UN denotes India's determination to provide support to this arduous task. India's efforts are towards showcasing itself as a reliable defence and security partner for the African countries.

NOTES

1 Press Trust of India, "Africa is top priority: PM Modi on India's proposal for African Union's G20 membership" *Economic Times,* 3 September 2023, at https://economictimes.indiatimes.com/news/india/africa-is-top-priority-pm-modi-on-indias-proposal-for-african-unions-g20-membership/articleshow/103324471.cms?from=mdr (Accessed 21 January 2024).

2 "Goals & Priority Areas of Agenda 2063", the African Union, at https://au.int/en/agenda2063/goals (Accessed 21 January 2024).

3 Richard Gowan, "Global and regional trends and developments in armed conflicts" *SIPRI Year Book 2023: Armaments, Disarmament & International Security* (Oxford: Oxford University Press, 2023), p. 47.

4 (AP), "UN sets December deadline for its peacekeepers in Congo to completely withdraw" *APNEWS,* Associated Press, 13 January 2024, at https://apnews.com/article/congo-un-peacekeeping-force-monusco-withdrawal-deadline-0f78c80422429cc0f6c233dd75e48366 (Accessed 21 January 2024).

5 Ibid.

6 Tegbaru Yared, "Africa must stand together to end Ethiopia's conflict", *ISS Today,* 7 December 2023 at https://issafrica.org/iss-today/africa-must-stand-together-to-end-ethiopias-conflict (Accessed 21 January 2024).

7 Alex de Waal, "Sudan is collapsing – here's how to stop it" *The World Today,* 2 February 2024, at https://www.chathamhouse.org/publications/the-world-today/2024-02/sudan-collapsing-heres-how-stop-it (Accessed 22 February 2024).

8 "African leaders to scale up efforts against unconstitutional changes of government; terrorism and foreign mercenaries", the African Union, 28 May 2022, at https://au.int/en/pressreleases/20220528/african-leaders-scale-efforts-against-unconstitutional-changes-terrorism (Accessed 24 July 2022).

9 Amani Africa, "Fight against terrorism and violent extremism" *Insights on the Peace and Security Council (PSC)* 22 February 2024 at https://amaniafrica-et.org/fight-against-terrorism-and-violent-extremism/(Accessed 22 February 2024).

10 Jose Antonio Latorre, "A change in Mali, the French out, Wagner in," 7 May 2022, at https://www.unav.edu/web/global-affairs/a-change-in-mali-the-french-out-wagner-in (Accessed 22 February 2024).

11 Angela Charlton, " European force battling extremists withdraws from Mali," 1 July 2022, at https://apnews.com/article/africa-france-united-nations-mali-2cc75f283c8fb6064e0b046f434cd33c (Accessed 22 February 2024).

12 "Conflict with Al-Shabaab in Somalia", Center for Preventive Action, 14 February 2024, at https://www.cfr.org/global-conflict-tracker/conflict/al-shabab-somalia (Accessed 22 February 2024).

13 Paul D. Williams, "Armies are leaving Somalia: What needs to happen to keep peace", *The East African,* 13 September 2023, at https://www.theeastafrican.co.ke/tea/news/east-africa/what-needs-to-happen-for-somalia-peace-after-au-withdrawal-4367546 (Accessed 22 February 2024).

14 "Nigeria: clashes between jihadists, more than 60 deaths feared" *Africanews,* 21 November 2023, at https://www.africanews.com/2023/11/21/nigeria-clashes-between-jihadists-more-than-60-deaths-feared/ (Accessed 22 February 2024)

15 "Mozambique Takes Aim at Terrorists in Last Stronghold", *ADF Magazine,* 23 January 2023 at https://adf-magazine.com/2024/01/mozambique-takes-aim-at-terrorists-in-last-stronghold/ (Accessed 22 February 2024).

16 Andrews Atta-Asamoah, "Africa's three waves of coups", *ISS Today,* 20 October 2023, at https://issafrica.org/iss-today/africas-three-waves-of-coups (Accessed 22 February 2024).

17 Samuel Ramani, 'Why Russia is the winner in the recent coup in Mali', 16 September 2020, at https://www.fpri.org/article/2020/09/why-russia-is-a-geopolitical-winner-in-malis-coup/ (Accessed 2 July 2022).

18 Ifesinachi Marybenedette Okafur-Yarwooda and Freedom C. Onuoha,"Whose Security is it? Elitism and Global Approach to Maritime Security in Africa" *Third World Quarterly,* 43 (12) 2023, at https://www.tandfonline.com/doi/full/10.1080/01436597.2023.2167706 (Accessed 22 February 2024).

19 "Somali pirates resurface, raising concerns for global shipping", 21 March 2024, at https://www.africanews.com/2024/03/21/somali-pirates-resurface-raising-concerns-for-global-shipping// (Accessed 22 March 2024).

20 "Diversification of Import of Crude Oil "*Starred Question No. 194* Lok Sabha, Government of India, 2 August 2021, at https://sansad.in/getFile/loksabhaquestions/annex/176/AS194.pdf?source=pqals (Accessed 22 February 2024); Ariel Cohen, "India, the Rising Power, Is Seeking Oil from the Middle East and Russia", 19 August 2022 at https://www.forbes.com/sites/arielcohen/2022/08/19/india-the-rising-power-is-seeking-oil-from-the-middle-east-and-russia/?sh=7df7bddd7b1e (Accessed 22 February 2024).

21 "Africa can play central role in India's oil diversification: Dharmendra Pradhan", *Mint,* 25 March 2021 (Accessed 22 February 2023).

22 Ibid.

23 "Africa well positioned to benefit from global green mineral boom", at https://lexafrica.com/2023/03/africa-well-positioned-to-benefit-from-global-green-mineral-boom/#:~:text=Africa%20is%20home%20to%20some,and%20uranium%20in%20the%20world. (Accessed 22 February 2024).

24 Ibid.

25 "Africa dominates list of the world's 20 fastest-growing economies in 2024—African Development Bank says in macroeconomic report", African Development Bank, 16 February

2024, at https://www.afdb.org/en/news-and-events/press-releases/africa-dominates-list-worlds-20-fastest-growing-economies-2024-african-development-bank-says-macroeconomic-report-68751 (Accessed 22 February 2024).

26 *Doing Business 2020, Fact Sheet Sub Saharan Africa,* World Bank, at https://www.doingbusiness.org/content/dam/doingBusiness/pdf/db2020/DB20-FS-SSA.pdf (Accessed 22 February 2024).

27 David G.W. Birch, "Happy Birthday M-Pesa", 23 March 2022, at https://www.forbes.com/sites/davidbirch/2022/03/23/happy-birthday-m-pesa/?sh=1baa89786d89 (Accessed 22 February 2024).

28 Ifesinachi Marybenedette Okafur-Yarwooda and Freedom C Onuoha,"Whose Security is it? Elitism and Global Approach to Maritime Security in Africa", *Third World Quarterly,*43 (12), 2023, at https://www.tandfonline.com/doi/full/10.1080/01436597.2023.2167706 (Accessed 22 February 2024).

29 Ministry of Ports, Shipping and Waterways, Government of India, *Maritime India Vision 2030,* 21 February 2021, at http://sagarmala.gov.in/sites/default/files/MIV%202030%20Report.pdf (Accessed 22 February 2024).

30 Ruchita Beri, "UNSC Reform: Africa holds the key", in Ruchita Beri and Arpita Anant (Eds.), *United Nations Security Council Reform: Perspectives and Prospects,* MP-IDSA Monograph Series No. 38, June 2014, at https://idsa.in/system/files/monograph/monograph38.pdf (Accessed 21 February 2023).

31 Indo-Asian News Service, "Africa Shaped Indian Diaspora's Identity: PM Modi In Mozambique" *NDTV,* 8 July 2016, at https://www.ndtv.com/india-news/africa-shaped-indian-diasporas-identity-pm-modi-in-mozambique-1429160 (Accessed 22 February 2024).

32 Rajneesh Kumar Gupta, "Indian Diaspora in Africa: A Profile", *Africa Trends,* April-June 2014, at https://www.idsa.in/africatrends/indian-diaspora-in-africa-a-profile_rkgupta_0614 (Accessed 20 February 2022).

33 Ruchita Beri, "Unpacking India's Defence Cooperation with Africa", *Journal of Defence Studies* 17 (3), 2023, at https://www.idsa.in/system/files/jds/jds-17-3_Ruchita-Beri.pdf (Accessed 22 February 2024).

34 "Lucknow Declaration Adopted at the 1st India-Africa Defence Ministers Conclave, 2020" Press Information Bureau, Ministry Of Defence, Government of India 6 February 2020, at https://pib.gov.in/newsite/PrintRelease.aspx?relid=199072 (Accessed 22 February 2024)

35 "India–Africa Defence Dialogue to be held alongside every DefExpo", Press Information Bureau, Ministry of Defence, Government of India, 21 September 2021, at https://pib.gov.in/PressReleasePage.aspx?PRID=1754522 (Accessed 22 February 2024).

36 Indian Technical and Economic Cooperation (ITEC) Programme, at https://www.itecgoi.in/about (Accessed 16 February 2023).

37 Press Information Bureau, Government of India, Indian Military Advisory and Training Team, Uganda 5 October 2017, at https://pib.gov.in/newsite/PrintRelease.aspx?relid=171410 (Accessed 22 February 2024).

38 "India Africa Defence Dialogue held on the sidelines of Defence Expo22 in Gandhi Nagar Gujrat; paves way for strengthening India-Africa defence relations", Press Information Bureau, Government of India, at https://pib.gov.in/PressReleasePage.aspx?PRID=1868820 (Accessed 22 February 2024).

39 Opening ceremony: Africa-India Field Training Exercise-2019, Press Information Bureau, Ministry of Defence, Government of India, 18 March 2019, at https://pib.gov.in/newsite/PrintRelease.aspx?relid=189450 (Accessed 22 February 2024).

40 "India-Africa joint military exercise 'AFINDEX-23' concluded at foreign training node, Aundh, Pune" Press Information Bureau, Ministry of Defence, Government of India, 29 March 2023, at https://www.pib.gov.in/PressReleasePage.aspx?PRID=1911766 (Accessed 30 June 2023)

41 "Indian Navy Participates In Maiden Trilateral Exercise with Mozambique and Tanzania," Ministry of Defence, Government of India, 29 October 2022, at https://pib.gov.in/PressReleasePage.aspx?PRID=1871827 (Accessed 22 February 2024).

42 "First Training Squadron participates In Cutlass Express 24", Press Information Bureau, Ministry of Defence, Government of India, 10 March 2024, at https://pib.gov.in/PressReleaseIframePage.aspx?PRID=2013170 (Accessed 22 March 2024).

43 Shishir Gupta, "India and France to conduct joint surveillance of South-West Indian Ocean", *Hindustan Times,* 8 November 2022, at https://www.hindustantimes.com/india-news/india-and-france-to-conduct-joint-surveillance-of-south-west-indian-ocean-101667905908997.html (Accessed 22 March 2024).

44 Ruchita Beri, "Rising Terrorism in Mozambique", 3 November 2021, at https://idsa.in/issuebrief/rising-terrorism-in-mozambique-rberi-031121; (Accessed 30 June 2023) See also, "India and Mozambique Sign Two MoUs to Further Strengthen Defence Co-Operation", Press and Information Bureau, Ministry of Defence, Government of India, 29 July 2021, at https://pib.gov.in/PressReleasePage.aspx?PRID=1580691 (Accessed 22 March 2024).

45 Dipanjan Roy Chaoudhary, "India-Kenya decide to widen Indo-Pacific; counter-terror partnership", *Economic Times*, 14 June 2021, at https://economictimes.indiatimes.com/news/defence/india-kenya-decide-to-widen-indo-pacific-counter-terror-partnership/articleshow/83517180.cms?from=mdr (Accessed 22 February 2024).

46 Dipanjan Roy Chaudhury, "India, Egypt sign MoU to exchange terrorism information", *Economic Times,* 13 July 2018, at https://economictimes.indiatimes.com/news/defence/india-egypt-sign-mou-to-exchange-terrorism-information/articleshow/53988210.cms?from=mdr (Accessed 22 February 2024).

47 Dipanjan Roy Chaudhury, "India, Morocco sign pacts to combat global terror including ISIS", *Economic Times,* 16 November 2018, at https://economictimes.indiatimes.com/news/defence/india-morocco-sign-pacts-to-combat-global-terror-including-isis/articleshow/66655266.cms?from=mdr (Accessed 22 February 2024).

48 Shobha Roy, BEML expects 20% growth in business during current fiscal 16 November 2022, at https://www.thehindubusinessline.com/companies/beml-expects-20-growth-in-business-during-current-fiscal/article66144435.ece (Accessed 30 June 2023)

49 Manu Pubby, "India trying to export weapons to African Nations", *Economic Times,* 12 April 2023, at https://economictimes.indiatimes.com/news/defence/india-trying-to-export-weapons-to-african-nations/articleshow/99070935.cms?from=mdr (Accessed 22 February 2024).

3

An Appraisal of the Kenya-India Maritime Security Collaboration

Harriet Njoki Mboce

Introduction

Kenya has a coastline of 536 km on the western Indian Ocean, an Exclusive Economic Zone (EEZ) with a total area of 142,000 km^2, and an extended Continental Shelf (CS) of 103,320 km^2.[1] India has a reported coastline of between 7516.6 km and 8000 km, and an EEZ area of 2,305,143 km^2.[2] Both Kenya and India are Indian Ocean Rim States. The dynamic, evolving, multi-jurisdictional and overwhelming nature of maritime security threats, coupled with the current posture of nautical activism and shifts in global dynamics, have caused maritime security synergism to be one of the most current, and prominent discussions around the world.[3] Seven core issues have heightened the centrality of Kenya-India maritime collaboration.

First, is their geographical positioning. Like conjoined twins, Kenya and India are linked by the Indian Ocean.[4] Second, both countries' centres of political and economic gravity are shifting seaward. Third, while providing them with great benefits, their said posture and geographical location expose them to a plethora of common challenges regarding their maritime order.[5] Fourth, the devastating nature and effects of maritime security threats experienced over the Indian Ocean in the past three decades are unprecedented and have been significantly unpredictable. Fifth, these challenges hinder realisation of optimum gains and must therefore be addressed. Sixth, the effective management of these risks requires an efficient collaborative security architecture.[6] Consequently, without collaboration, the two countries are adversely exposed.[7]

Nevertheless, while these circumstances are arguably obvious, the cooperation framework on maritime security between the two countries is glaringly insufficient. There is therefore dire need for a heightened maritime security cooperation between the two states. Hopefully, their historical, cultural, and economic linkages as well as developing diplomatic ties shall offer enough yarn to spin an efficient and effective engagement.[8] A core objective of this paper is to therefore investigate how this critical synergy can be achieved through various steps.

The research presented here was sponsored within the Africa Visiting Fellowship Programme at the Institute for Defence Studies and Analyses (IDSA), New Delhi.[9] The paper draws significantly on interviews with maritime experts as well as intelligence and security analysts. Given the sensitivity of the subject matter, the respondents requested anonymity. Names and affiliated organizations of these individuals have therefore been omitted from the text.

To realise its objective, this paper is divided into eight sections. Section I, which is the present section, offers the background of the research and the topic, and sets out the structure of this paper. Section II anchors the discussions by examining the definition of maritime security. This examination helps to draw out common maritime security threats between Kenya and India. Section III examines the need for maritime security collaboration between two States. Section IV analyses the nature and scope of the existing bi-lateral engagements between the two States, in tackling the common maritime security challenges.

Section V examines the nature and scope of existing collaborations between India and other African Indian Ocean Rim States (AIORS). It also examines the multilateral maritime security collaborations involving Kenya, India and other AIORS. Section VI exposes limitations to Kenya-India maritime security cooperation. Section VII presents recommendations for enhanced maritime security cooperation between the two countries. Finally, section VIII concludes the discussions.

Definition of Maritime Security

The definition of 'maritime security' is still part of a continuing debate.[10] There is however a consensus that the definition is relative, based on two core factors. The first factor is relativity based on perspective, circumstance, prioritization, capacity and capability of the relevant stakeholder(s) and 'end user(s).[11] The second factor is the constantly evolving nature and effects of maritime security threats. Nonetheless, various suggestions have been made as to how a uniform approach can be established, and certain elements have gained universal acceptance as critical parameters for defining maritime security.[12] The elements include safety of seafarers and other maritime domain users, safety of cargo and vessels, maritime resource sustainability, and maritime environmental protection.[13]

Need for Enhanced Collaboration

Common Maritime Security Threats between Kenya and India

Notwithstanding the lack of a common definition of maritime security, both Kenya and India share a significant range of common maritime security challenges. The threats are often classified as being either 'traditional' or 'non-traditional'. The traditional threats include piracy, armed robberies at sea, seaborne terrorist attacks and hijackings. Responses to these conventional threats are presently mainly characterised by military action.[14]

The non-traditional threats include: (a) environmental challenges such as climate change, ocean acidification, marine pollution and rise in sea levels, (b) fishing infringements such as illegal, unregulated and unreported (IUU) and over-exploration and exploitation of maritime resources, (c) trafficking of arms, drugs, humans and illegal immigration, (d) security of offshore installations, (e) maritime boundary disputes, and (f) inadequate maritime domain and the Blue Economy awareness.[15] The responses to these threats are presently anchored on military action and capacity—similar to responses to traditional threats—which is evidently largely a mismatch.[16] This gap with respect to combating non-traditional security threats is a potential area of deliberate collaboration between the two countries.

Below are specific scenarios to illustrate the commonality of these threats between Kenya and India.

The first scenario relates to maritime boundary disputes. Both Kenya and India share maritime boundaries with other States. The two countries have also been the subjects of enduring maritime boundary disputes. A significant number of traditional and non-traditional threats to the maritime security of these countries have been attributed to protracted maritime disputes.[17] For instance, IUU, piracy, and smuggling in the Kenya – Somalia Indian Ocean have been linked to the Somalia *vs* Kenya maritime boundary dispute which was determined by the ICJ in 2021.[18] On the other hand, the dispute between India and Bangladesh over the Bay of Bengal, which was determined by the Permanent Court of Arbitration in 2014, has presented similar challenges.[19]

Further, following increased incidents of piracy attacks in the Indian Ocean, Kenya's maritime waters were included in the piracy red list for twelve years—from 2009 to 2021. This was after the waters were designated as a high-risk area.[20] This designation resulted in an increase of maritime insurance premium for cargo destined for the port of Mombasa, as well as increased labour cost for seafarers aboard such ships.[21] Additionally, cargo ships destined for Mombasa took longer routes to avoid encountering pirates, while other cargo ships heightened their on-board security.[22]

The second scenario concerns seaborne terrorist attacks, where perpetrators exploit sea routes to smuggle themselves, their firearms and explosives. In India, this includes the 1993 and the 2008 attacks on the city of Mumbai.[23] In Kenya, this includes the 2002 attack on the Paradise Hotel in the City of Mombasa.[24] Seaborne terrorism continues to evolve and manifest itself in various ways. In Malindi, Kenya, recent attacks have involved kidnappings of tourists.[25] Further, the ports of Malindi, Mombasa and Lamu have been marked as being vulnerable to seaborne terrorist attacks.[26] A third related challenge common to both countries is that of illegal immigration through their respective connected maritime boundaries.

The fourth scenario is that both countries have independently adopted harnessing of the blue economy as a core area of their respective national focus.[27] This has seen both countries often allocating the exploration and exploitation of maritime domain resources to non-State corporations. In Kenya, the corporations are mainly foreign. The State benefit in such undertakings and oversight is significantly low as compared to cases where the exploration and exploitation is mainly managed by the State.

Fifth is that both countries have faced challenges relating to marine pollution and have specifically committed themselves to combatting this. Marine pollution occurs through various ways including the aforementioned exploration and exploitation as well as oil spills. While both countries have had relatively minor oil spills in their coastal waters, the possibility of a major oil spill occurring within their jurisdictions is today considerably higher, because of the significant increases in oil tankers, bulk carriers and container ships passing through the Indian Ocean, as well as the increased number of oil spills.[28]

In Kenya for instance, in 2005, an Indian oil tanker *MV Ratna Shalini* discharged five million litres of crude oil into Port Reitz creek at the Kilindini Harbour, which caused grave damage to marine life, including the destruction of mangrove trees as well as causing damage to the marine eco-system.[29] India has also had her significant share of oil spills. Of significant note, from the Indian Coast Guard report is that a significant number of the perpetrators of these spills are unknown.

Sixth are threats related to environmental concerns such as climate change and arising out of natural causes, such as, tsunami. The Indian Ocean tsunami of 2004 that originated in an earthquake in the Indian Ocean, hit the shores of 11 littoral states, including Kenya and India and killing over 226,408 people.[30] The relevant interventions included major rescue, relief and reconstruction of infrastructure. While most of the Indian Ocean is likely to be relatively safe from future tsunamis nevertheless, a larger earthquake is theoretically possible.[31]

Evidently, even in the absence of a common definition of maritime security, both countries have each adopted an inclusive approach to their definition of maritime security incorporating the elements discussed above.[32] The identified commonality of challenges coupled with the inclusive approach to their definition lays a strong basis for Kenya-India maritime security collaboration.

Geo-strategic and Political Basis for Maritime Security Collaboration

In addition to common threats as a basis for Kenya-India collaboration, there are also strategic, political and social factors. One of them is the fact that

India is currently positioning herself as a global maritime leader.[33] In this regard, India is keen on maintaining as many allies as possible, including Kenya.[34] On the other hand, as the most stable democracy in East Africa and given her geo-strategic location, Kenya is the gateway to the East African market of almost 500 million consumers.[35] Both Kenya and India therefore bear geo-strategic relevance to each other, especially in the area of maritime security, a fact which both countries have acknowledged.

Politically, both States have active diplomatic presence in each other's territories. In Kenya, India has both a High Commission in Nairobi and an Assistant High Commission in Mombasa.[36] Kenya also has a High Commission in India.[37] In addition to a committed diplomatic presence, the two countries display a great sense of diplomatic cohesion and co-operation with each other.

On both political and strategic fronts, India's maritime security strategy is captured in the "Security and Growth for All" principle, popularly referred to as 'SAGAR'.[38] SAGAR prioritises multilateral collaborative action including towards combating piracy and harnessing of the blue economy.[39] On the other hand, and just like India, Kenya's maritime security strategy also prioritises collaborative action towards combating piracy and harnessing of the blue economy.[40] In this context, the Kenya–India maritime security cooperation agenda in these two priority areas has been clearly articulated by both governments.[41]

The Kenya-India collaboration is also underpinned by strong historical and cultural ties. The two countries have a mutual historical trade network pre-dating the colonial period, and both grappled with the struggle against British colonialism.[42] Socially, both countries host a significant number of each others' citizens in various capacities. For instance, approximately one per cent of Kenya's population is of Indian descent. In 2017 the then-President Uhuru Kenyatta declared that the Indian community in Kenya should be regarded as the 44th tribe of the country.[43]

Given the need for a prioritised maritime security collaboration between the two countries, it is therefore necessary to examine how the Kenya-India maritime security collaboration is implemented.

Kenya-India Collaboration

In 2016, India's Prime Minister Narendra Modi visited President Uhuru Kenyatta of Kenya.[44] This was the first visit of an Indian Prime Minister to Kenya in thirty-five years.[45] During the visit, discussions between the two leaders culminated in the signing of seven Memoranda of Understanding (MoUs)/Agreements in the fields of defence, trade, and developmental assistance.[46] As part of defence cooperation, Prime Minister Modi handed over 30 field ambulances for use by the Kenya Defence Forces. Highlights of the visit included engaging in business forums, signing of seven MoUs, interaction with the Indian diaspora community in Kenya, and a lecture at the University of Nairobi.

Three key observations from this visit and its output are that out of the seven MoUs/Agreements, only one—the one on defence—touches on security. However, this defence MoU does not specifically touch on maritime security. The only specific reference to the Indian Ocean and the importance of the Blue Economy during this engagement was in the Joint *Communique* where the two leaders agreed to pursue initiatives in the sustainable management and extraction of ocean-based resources, as well as to finalize the agreement on Cooperation in the Blue Economy.[47] To date, the agreement on Cooperation in the Blue Economy is yet to be actualised.

Similarly in 2017, President Uhuru Kenyatta paid a State Visit to India. Whereas during this visit the discussions were also mainly on agriculture, commerce, technology, manufacturing and health sectors, there was a slight increased focus on maritime security and counterterrorism.[48] Nonetheless, yet again, none of the MoUs and Agreements signed related to maritime security collaboration.[49]

In addition to the said MoU on Cooperation in the field of Defence, there is also an MoU on Sharing White Shipping Information between the Indian Navy and the Kenya Defence Forces.[50] In 2023, after a joint survey between the Kenya Navy and the Indian Navy, Kenya received the Nautical Maritime Charts of the Lamu Archipelago.[51] Annually, India offers training to Kenyan Naval personnel in India.[52] The Kenya Navy has on several occasions equally hosted the Indian Navy at the Mombasa Port during the Indian Navy overseas deployment.[53] Additionally, the two States often undertake joint naval trainings to enhance inter-operability and strengthen maritime cooperation. It was only in December 2023, during President William Ruto's visit to India released a joint vision statement on India-Kenya Maritime Cooperation.

Clearly, Kenya-India collaboration on maritime security is significantly pale compared to its potential. The collaboration is also over-shadowed by the two countries' partnerships in other sectors such as agriculture, health, technology, manufacturing and disaster management.[54]

Existing Collaboration Between India and Other African States

An analysis of India's bilateral collaborations with other African Indian Ocean Rim States (AIORS) reveals that as it presently stands, Kenya-India maritime security collaboration pales in comparison to collaboration between India and other AIORS.[55] India has three distinct levels of priority accorded to AIORS: high, medium and low priority. Kenya seems to rank as medium priority. Apparently, India has more maritime security MoUs and agreements with other AIOR States such as Egypt, Seychelles and Madagascar than with Kenya. While this disparity is justifiable based on a country's national interests, it fails to correlate with the high levels of bilateral meetings and declarations of commitment made by both countries as illustrated above.

Both Kenya and India are members of the Indian Ocean Rim Association (IORA).[56] They are both also member states of the Indian Ocean Naval Symposium (IONS).[57] Both countries are also working together under the Asia-Africa Growth Corridor (AAGC), where the port of Mombasa in Kenya is accorded great significance.[58]

Limitations to Kenya-India Maritime Security Cooperation

There are significant challenges to international maritime security collaborations, including between Kenya and India, some of which are set out below.

The first limitation relates to maritime domain awareness (MDA).[59] Many people, including those tasked with maritime security roles, often have a limited or otherwise biased perspective when dealing with the scope, challenges, potential and the need to secure economic, strategic and other leverages within the maritime domain.[60] Consequently, this influences and greatly interferes with the respective countries' approaches to maritime security and collaboration.[61]

Second is the under-prioritization of maritime security. The general attitude for both Kenya and India towards maritime security threats has been mainly reactive as opposed to pro-active. Both States constantly relegate deterrence in respect of maritime security to the backburner in favour of land based economic interests such as agriculture and manufacturing.[62] Though no-doubt, the recent Joint Statement on Maritime Vision by both sides indicates an interest in cooperation in this important area.[63]

Third is the 'inward looking approach'. This is characterised by protectionist national interests, suspicion, and mistrust between the two countries.[64] Fourth is the gap between political commitment and execution at the bureaucratic level. While the heads of States of the two countries have over the years re-emphasized their commitment to bilateral collaboration in maritime security, there is a glaring gap at the implementation level. It is hoped that the unveiling of the joint statement on maritime vision is followed by implementation of this cooperation at an early date.

Fifth is multiple commitments and partners. As already demonstrated, India has a wide range of maritime security collaborations with several other AIORS. So does Kenya. Both States also have partnerships with non AIORS. This therefore often presents practical conflicts. Sixth is the multiplicity of stakeholders and laws involved in the maritime security industry both at domestic and bilateral levels.[65] Too often, this conflicts and poses inherent disruption to any collaboration attempts.[66]

Seventh is the resource burden related to prosecution, imprisonment, and rehabilitation regarding maritime offences. For instance, Kenya is the leading prosecutor of maritime security offenses among the IORA. This has proven to be extremely strenuous on Kenya's financial, technical and personnel capacity. In 2011, Kenya called onto other states to intervene.[67] This strain, especially where other states end up taking a back seat, has contributed to Kenya's cautious approach to collaborations especially in relation to enforcement of maritime offences.

Eighth is relativity in prioritised areas of interest in collaboration. Different States have their own unique deep rooted cultural circumstances, perspectives, ideologies, aspirations and priorities that influence their approach as well as implementation to international partnership arrangements. Often, there is a mismatch in their prioritised areas of interest in collaboration.[68]

Ninth is attitude. States have various sensitivities informed by the underlying concerns, experiences, and status. Kenya and India too often find themselves engaging at arm's length, especially in matters of intelligence sharing. There is also a tenth concern relating to the lack of an operative architecture for productive engagement and co-operation.

Recommendations

Below are recommendations on how Kenya-India cooperation in maritime security can be enhanced.

First is the need for the two countries to invest in the identification of common priority areas. This can be done not only by the state security agencies but also by facilitating the collaboration of think-tanks within their respective jurisdictions. One such think tank is the Maritime Centre situated at the University of Nairobi School of Law.[69]

Second is enhanced and joint maritime domain awareness for all levels of active stakeholders as well as the public.

Third is pro-active and deliberate prioritization of maritime security and mutual engagements in respect of the maritime domain. This can be achieved through firm and mutually beneficial bilateral agreements with the specific agenda of enhancing maritime security cooperation.

Fourth is alignment on specific aspects of collaboration, including in relation to identification of areas of training and capacity building, joint explorations and exploitation of resources, and joint monitoring and evaluation of the maritime exploitation and exploration undertaken by private corporations in the maritime domain.

Fifth is enhanced personnel training assistance especially for Kenya's Coast Guard, which is relatively young. India has demonstrated capacity for this because it is currently undertaking similar initiatives with both Mauritius and Mozambique.[70] India has also demonstrated capacity in ship building which Kenya can benefit from.

Sixth is establishing a Kenya-India framework for maritime defence co-operation like the one India signed with Madagascar in March 2018.[71] Both countries could also work on an enhanced joint maritime patrol system and enhanced information sharing.[72] This would alleviate maritime security threats such as piracy and illegal immigration.

Conclusion

Despite the lack of a common definition of maritime security, India and Kenya face significantly similar maritime security threats.[73] These threats are multi-jurisdictional in nature. The commonality of maritime security threats between India and Kenya, coupled with their shared Indian Ocean, necessitates a collaborative approach at various levels between the two countries in combating maritime security threats.[74] While the global context of international security collaborations is influenced by two contradicting schools of thought—protectionism characterised by suspicion, and multi-faceted multilateralism characterised by promiscuous international partnerships—the utility of strategic co-operation in this regard far outweighs severe protectionist concerns.[75] It is however necessary to effectively manage the collaboration in a balanced and mutually beneficial manner.[76]

NOTES

1 Harriet Njoki Mboce and Robert McCabe, "'Kenya: From 'Sea-Blind' to "Sea-Vision"," in Christian Bueger, et al, Ed. *Capacity Building for Maritime Security: The Western Indian Ocean Experience*, Springer, 2021.

2 Sohini Dudhat et al, 'Spatio-Temporal Analysis Identifies Marine Mammal Stranding Hotspots along the Indian Coastline'*Scientific Reports,* 12, 4128, 2022; Shaheed Khan and Swarna M Freeda Maria, '*Worldwide Hospitality and Tourism Themes*, Vol. 14 No. 6, pp. 579-585, at https://doi.org/10.1108/WHATT-05-2022-0053 (Accessed 09 April 2024).

3 Vishva Nath Attri and Narnia Bohler-Muller, eds. *The Blue Economy Handbook of the Indian Ocean Region,* Africa Institute of South Africa, 2018; Saroj Kumar Mohanty, 'Towards Estimation of the Blue Economy' in Vishva Nath Attri and Narnia Bohler-Muller, eds. *The Blue Economy Handbook of the Indian Ocean Region,* Africa Institute of South Africa, 2018 p. 64.

4 David Arase and Scarlett Cornelissen, *Routledge Handbook of Africa–Asia Relations,* London, Routledge,2018; Satinder Bhatia, 'Faculty Development Initiatives in Africa on Asian Studies – Key to Integration' *OmniScience: A Multi-disciplinary Journal,* Vol. 7, No. 3, pp. 27-35.

5 Lee Cordner, 'Progressing Maritime Security Cooperation in the Indian Ocean', *Naval War College Review*, Vol. 64, No. 4, 2011.

6 Lee Cordner, *Maritime Security Risks, Vulnerabilities and Cooperation,* Singapore, Springer, 2018.

7 Shivshankar Menon 'Security in the Indian Ocean' in Jivanta Schöttli ed. *Maritime Governance and South Asia: Trade, Security and Sustainable Development in the Indian Ocean,* Singapore, World Scientific, 2018.

8 Arase and Cornelissen (n 4); Bhatia (n 4).

9 'Harriet Njoki Mboce, Institute for Defence Studies and Analyses', at https://idsa.in/profile/hnmboce (Accessed 20 October 2018).

10 Christian Bueger, 'What Is Maritime Security?' *Marine Policy*, Vol. 53, 2015, p. 159.

11 Ioannis Chapsos and Elizabeth Ann Norman, 'Is Maritime Security Gender-Blind?', *Marine Policy*, Vol. 147, 2023.; Peter Chalk, *The Maritime Dimension of International Security: Terrorism, Piracy, and Challenges for the United States*, Rand Corporation, 2008.

12 Francois Vreÿ, 'Maritime Security Governance off Africa: Where to Assist?', at https://www.sun.ac.za/english/faculty/milscience/sigla/Documents/UNODC%20SIGLA/UNODC-SIGLA_AB%20Final%208%20Nov.pdf (Accessed 09 April 2024).

13 Lee Cordner, *Maritime Security Risks, Vulnerabilities and Cooperation*, Singapore, Springer, 2018; JL Suárez-de Vivero and JC Rodríguez-Mateos, 'Food Security as a Security Issue. A Perspective from Maritime Policy and Maritime Security Initiatives',*Ocean & Coastal Management*, Vol. 153, p. 140; Christian Bueger, *'We Are All Islanders Now'–Michel's Blue Economy Kaleidoscope and the Missing Link to Maritime Security, Journal of the Indian Ocean Region*, Vol. 14, No. 1, 2018, pp. 117–119.

14 R S Aswani, 'Non-Traditional Maritime Security Threats in the Indian Ocean Region: Policy Alternatives', *Journal of Public Affairs*, Vol. 22, 2022.

15 Mohanty (n 3); Antonios D Mazaris and Basil Germond, 'Bridging the Gap between Climate Change and Maritime Security: Towards a Comprehensive Framework for Planning', *Science of the Total Environment*, Vol. 635, 2018, pp. 1076-1080; Vishva Nath Attri (n.3), The term Blue Economy is an emerging concept encompassing the productive and sustainable engagement of maritime domain resources.

16 Zeba Rayee, *'India's Maritime Security: Opportunities and Challenges'* in Shantesh Kumar Singh and Shri Prakash Singh, *Non-traditional Security Concerns in India: Issues and Challenges,* Singapore, Palgrave Macmillan, 2022, p. 193.

17 Timothy Walker, 'Why Africa Must Resolve its Maritime Boundary Disputes', at https://www.files.ethz.ch/isn/194507/PolBrief80.pdf (Accessed 09 March 2024).

18 Anup Phayal, Aaron Gold and Brandon Prins, 'Interstate Hostility and Maritime Crime: Evidence from South East Asia' *Marine Policy*, Vol. 143, 2022; Philip Onguny, 'Why the Kenya-Somalia Maritime Dispute is Far from Over, Regardless of the International Court of Justice Ruling', *Africa Policy Journal*, Vol. 41, 2020; 'Judgments | Maritime Delimitation in the Indian Ocean (Somalia v. Kenya) | International Court of Justice,' at https://www.icj-cij.org/en/case/161/judgments (Accessed 13 January 2022).

19 'Bay of Bengal Maritime Boundary Arbitration between Bangladesh and India (Bangladesh v. India) | PCA-CPA,' at https://pca-cpa.org/en/news/bay-of-bengal-maritime-boundary-arbitration-between-bangladesh-and-india-bangladesh-v-india/ (Accessed 21 April 2023).

20 'Kenya Maritime Waters Removed from High-Risk List is a Boost to Trade,' at https://www.kenyahighcom.org.uk/news/kenya-maritime-waters-removed-from-high-risk-list-is-a-boost-to-trade (Accessed 21 April 2023).

21 Ibid.

22 Ibid.

23 *Acropolis Against Terrorism by Eric Gand*, at https://nuriakenya.com/product/acropolis-against-terrorism-by-eric-gand/ (Accessed 21 April 2023); Leonard C Orji, Oluchi G Dike and Mary Etim Ibok, 'Contemporary Terrorism: A World System Perspective', *Ibom Journal of Social*

Issues, Vol. 11, 2022, p. 13; P C Dheeraj, 'Seaborne Terrorism and Counterintelligence in India: Challenges and Concerns', *Journal of the Indian Ocean Region*, Vol. 14, 2028, p. 277.

24 Jonathan Fighel, 'Al-Qaeda–Mombasa Attacks 28 November 2002', International Institute for Counter-Terrorism, Herzlya. Israel, 2011.

25 Oscar Gakuo Mwangi, 'Five Reasons Why Militants are Targeting Kenya's Lamu County' (*The Conversation*, 14 February 2022), at http://theconversation.com/five-reasons-why-militants-are-targeting-kenyas-lamu-county-176519 (Accessed 21 April 2023).

26 Hamad Hamad, 'Maritime Terrorism: Why the East African Community is the next Potential Target of Maritime Terrorism', *Research on Humanities and Social Sciences*, Vol. 6, Issue 6, 2016.

27 Kariuki Muigua, 'Harnessing the Blue Economy: Challenges and Opportunities for Kenya', at https://kmco.co.ke/wp-content/uploads/2018/12/Harnessing-the-Blue-Economy-Challenges-and-Opportunities-for-Kenya-24th-December-2018.pdf (Accessed 09 March 2024). The blue economy encompasses all economic activities with a direct dependence on the ocean or coastal and marine resources. It also includes marine education and research.

28 S Sivadas, A Gregory and B Ingole, 'How Vulnerable Is Indian Coast to Oil Spills? Impact of MV Ocean Seraya Oil Spill', *Current Science*, Vol. 95, No. 4, 2008, pp. 504-512; Ministry of Defence-India, 'Indian Coast Guard on Alert as Oil Spill Reported from Haldia-Bound Portuguese Flag Container Ship', at https://pib.gov.in/pib.gov.in/Pressreleaseshare.aspx? PRID =1728093 (Accessed 21 April 2023).

29 Mboce and McCabe (n 1); Stellamaris Ndeve Muthike, 'Assessment of Kenya's Capacity to Effectively Prepare for and Respond to Oil Spill Incidents', at https://commons.wmu.se/cgi/viewcontent.cgi?article=1679&context=all_dissertations (Accessed 09 March 2024).

30 David Obura, 'Impacts of the 26 December 2004 Tsunami in Eastern Africa', *Ocean & Coastal Management*, Vol. 49, 2006, p. 873; Vijay Sakhuja, 'Indian Naval Diplomacy: Post Tsunami', at https://www.ipcs.org/comm_select.php?articleNo=1640 (Accessed 09 March 2024).

31 Obura (n 30).

32 'Maritime Security of India: Future Challenges', at https://idsa.in/keyspeeches/MaritimeSecurityOfIndiaFutureChallenges (Accessed 30 September 2018).

33 Ivan Lidarev and Harsh V Pant, 'India and Maritime Governance in the Indian Ocean: The Impact of Geopolitics on India's Involvement in Maritime Governance', *Contemporary South Asia,* Vol. 30, 2022, p. 269.

34 Chris Ogden, 'India's Relations with Her Neighbors', in Sumit Ganguly, Frank O'Donnell eds. *Routledge Handbook of the International Relations of South Asia*, London, Routledge, 2022.

35 Ministry of Foreign Affairs-Kenya, 'Kenya_Foreign_Policy.Pdf' (2014), at https://www.kenyaembassy.org.tr/uploads/Kenya_Foreign_Policy.pdf (Accessed 30 March 2023); 'Kenya's Foreign Policy – Foreign & Diaspora AAffairs | Kenya', at https://mfa.go.ke/fpolicy/ accessed 29 March 2023; US Embassy-Kenya Kenya and Ambassador Meg Whitman, 'Why Africa, Why Kenya?' (*U.S. Embassy in Kenya*, 29 March 2023) https://ke.usembassy.gov/why-africa-why-kenya/ (Aaccessed 21 April 2023).

36 At the commencement of this paper, 2017-2018, the Indian High Commission in Kenya is headed by Ambassador Suchitra Durai. The Ambassador and Mr. R. Chandramouli the First Secretary and Head of Chancery at the High Commission, during this time were the author's first actual contacts in respect of India-Kenya relationship representatives, in Kenya.

37 At the time of this paper, 2017-2018, the Kenyan High Commission in India is headed by Ambassador Florence Imisa Weche. The Ambassador, Deputy High Commissioner Belinda Amino and Mr. Fred Koigu Ndegwa all at the High Commission, were during the authorship

of this paper, the author's first actual contacts in respect of India-Kenya relationship representatives in India.

38 Commander Subhasish Sarangi, 'Unpacking SAGAR (Security and Growth for All in the Region)', at https://www.usiofindia.org/wp-content/uploads/2020/02/USI-Occasional-Paper_2_19-Unpacking-SAGAR-Final-print-File-1.pdf (Accessed 09 March 2023).

39 Ibid.

40 'National Defence Policy – Ministry of Defence – Kenya', at https://mod.go.ke/download/national-defence-policy/ (Accessed 29 March 2023).

41 See briefing by the Government of Kenya Spokesperson Mr. Manoa Esipisu in respect of the meeting between H. E. Uhuru Kenyatta's and Prime Minister Modi's discussion in Kenya in 2016, at https://www.youtube.com/watch?v=5Hv8ME5xuRw (Accessed 25 September 2017).

42 John Njenga Karugia, 'Connective Afrasian Sea Memories: Transregional Imaginaries, Memory Politics, and Complexities of National "Belonging"', *Memory Studies*, Vol. 11, 2018, p. 328.

43 Lotte Hughes, Steve Ouma Akoth and Celia Nyamweru, 'The Politics of Culture in Kenya since 2010: Implications for Pluralism' in Yash Pal Ghai, and Jill C. Ghai, eds. *Pluralism in Kenya,* The Katiba Institute and the Global Institute for Pluralism. Nairobi & Ottawa: The Katiba Institute and the Global Centre for Pluralism, 2018.

44 High Commission of India Nairobi, Kenya, 'Welcome to High Commission of India Nairobi, Kenya', at https://www.hcinairobi.gov.in/eoinrb_listview/NTc2 (Accessed 21 April 2023).

45 Ibid.

46 Ibid., The MoUs / Agreements are: Revised Double Taxation Avoidance Agreement (DTAA) 2. Bilateral agreement on exemption of Visa for holders of Diplomatic passports 3. MoU on Defence Cooperation 4. MoU on Cooperation in the field of standardisation, expertise sharing and mutual trade between Bureau of Indian Standards and Bureau of Kenya Standards 5. MoU on Cooperation in the field of National Housing Policy Development and Management 6. Line of Credit Agreement for US $15 million (first tranche of US $30 million) to IDB Capital Limited, Kenya, for development of various small and medium enterprises [SMEs] in Kenya 7. Line of Credit Agreement for US $29.95 million to the Government of Kenya for upgrade of Rift Valley Textiles Factory [RIVATEX East Africa Limited], Kenya.

47 Ibid.

48 Ibid.

49 Ibid.

50 'Defence PS Receives Nautical Charts of the Lamu Archipelago – Ministry of Defence – Kenya', at https://mod.go.ke/news/defence-ps-receives-nautical-charts-of-the-lamu-archipelago/ (Accessed 22 April 2023).

51 Ibid., Due to the sensitive nature of such a process, this process took about eight years to complete.

52 High Commission of India Nairobi, Kenya (n 44).

53 'Kenya Navy Hosts Indian Navy Ship TABAR – Ministry of Defence – Kenya', at https://mod.go.ke/news/kenya-navy-hosts-indian-navy-ship-trikand/ (Accessed 22 April 2023); Ryan White, 'Indian Navy Ships on Overseas Operational Deployment - Naval Post - Naval News and Information' (2 August 2021), at https://navalpost.com/indian-navy-ships-overseas-deployment/ (Accessed 22 April 2023).

54 Ruchita Beri, 'Asia Africa Growth Corridor: India's new initiative in Africa', *IDSA Comment*, at https://idsa.in/idsacomments/indias-new-initiative-in-africa-asia-africa-growth-corridor_rberi_130617 (Accessed 30 January 2018).

55 H Njoki Mboce, 'India–Africa Co-Operation on Maritime Security: Need for Deeper Engagement', *Strategic Analysis*, Vol. 43, 2019, p. 261.

56 The Indian Ocean Rim Association (IORA) is an inter-governmental organisation formed in 1997 to foster regional economic cooperation. IORA currently has 21 (of) 36 members states whose shores are swept by the Indian Ocean. It also has 7 dialogue partners that are individual sovereign states and not members of IORA, but with a special interest and/or capacity to contribute to IORA, particularly in the areas of common interest. IORA is the only ministerial forum that covers the Indian Ocean and includes important dialogue partners. IORA is mainly relevant to India and IORAAs because of its capacity to support their bilateral and sub-regional relationships. http://www.iora.net/en/about/about-iora (Accessed 21 March 2018.

57 'Welcome to Indian Ocean Naval Symposium, Indian Ocean Naval Symposium (IONS)', at https://www.ions.global/ (Accessed 22 April 2023).

58 The AAGC is an economic cooperation agreement between the governments of India, Japan and all the governments of African countries. It seeks to be a sea corridor linking Africa with India and other countries of South-East Asia and Oceania. This is proposed to be achieved by re-discovering ancient sea-routes as well as establishing new sea corridors that will link ports in Jamnagar (Gujarat) with Djibouti in the Gulf of Eden and similarly the ports of Mombasa and Zanzibar will be connected to ports near Madurai; Kolkata will be linked to Sittwe port in Myanmar.

59 Captain Dr Nitin Agarwala, Ram Erez and Suriya Narayanan, 'Enhancing Maritime Domain Awareness in the Indo-Pacific and the Eastern Mediterranean Regions: Indian and Israeli Perspectives' maritime 16; Steven C Boraz, 'Maritime Domain Awareness: Myths and Realities' (2009) 62 Naval War College Review 137; ibid MDA is principally understanding all that can be associated with the maritime area that could impact the economy, the environment or the security and safety of a country.

60 Darshana M Barua, "Expanding India's Maritime Domain Awareness in the Indian Ocean" 25 July 2016, at https://carnegieindia.org/2016/07/25/expanding-india-s-maritime-domain-awareness-in-indian-ocean-pub-64188 (Accessed 2 April 2018).

61 Ibid.

62 Professor Ian Taylor, at an interview conducted at IDSA on 30th January 2018.

63 Some of the various maritime security cooperation engagements between India and some African states are mentioned in various parts of this paper.

64 Jamal Barnes and Daniel Baldino, 'A Network Maritime Security Approach to Intelligence Sharing in the IOR', *Journal of the Indian Ocean Region*, Vol. 1, 2018.

65 Andrew John and others, 'A Decision Support System for the Assessment of Seaports' Security Under Fuzzy Environment', in Charalampos Konstantopoulos and Grammati Pantziou eds. *Modeling, Computing and Data Handling Methodologies for Maritime Transportation*Springer, 2018.

66 Ibid.

67 By Lillian Leposo CNN for, 'Kenya Ends Agreement with EU to Prosecute Suspected Somali Pirates - CNN.Com', at http://www.cnn.com/2010/WORLD/africa/10/04/kenya.eu.pirates/index.html (Accessed 22 April 2023).

68 Barnes and Baldino (n 64).

69 India already has a similar arrangement with Jordan, albeit in the area of IT under the 01 March 2018 MoU. The India/Jordan MoU seeks to set up next generation Centre of Excellence (COE) in Jordan for training of minimum 3000 Jordanian IT professionals over a period of 5 years and setting up of resource centre in India for Training of Master trainers in IT field from Jordan, at http://www.mea.gov.in/bilateral-documents.htm?dtl/29527/List_of_MoUsAgreements_signed_during_the_Visit_of_the_King_of_Jordan_to_India_March_01_2018 (Accessed 21 March 2018).

70 Gurpreet S. Khurana, interview on 26 January 2018.
71 List of MoUs/Agreements signed during the State visit of President to Madagascar (March 14-15, 2018), Ministry of External Affairs, Government of India, at http://www.mea.gov.in/bilateral-documents.htm?dtl/29673/List_of_MoUsAgreements_ signed_during_the _State_visit_of_President_to_Madagascar_March_1415_2018 (Accessed March 21, 2018)
72 Barnes and Baldino (n 64).
73 John C Hawley, *India in Africa, Africa in India: Indian Ocean Cosmopolitanisms*, Bloomington, Indiana University Press, 2008.
74 Gurpreet S Khurana, 'Multilateral Structures in the Indian Ocean: Review and Way Ahead', *Maritime Affairs: Journal of the National Maritime Foundation of India*, 2018.
75 Ibid.
76 Peter B Marlow, 'Maritime Security: An Update of Key Issues' Maritime Policy & Management, Vol. 37, 2010, p. 667.

4

2050 Africa Integrated Maritime Strategy and India's SAGAR Vision: Charting Convergences and Cooperative Synergy

Abhay Kumar Singh

There has been a remarkable awakening of maritime consciousness in Africa due to two contrasting imperatives. On the one hand, Lack of Good Order at Sea in the maritime milieu has been recognised as a serious strategic challenge. The menace of piracy is one of its most malevolent manifestations. On the other, imperatives of potential economic dividends of ocean-related resources and industries have the ocean as a new frontline of Africa's renaissance. The maritime domain serves as the gateway to the global market. In addition, Africa's marine environment is globally significant too, as a great deal of international shipping passes through our seas.

The maritime sector in Africa is underdeveloped, but it has the potential to be a greater source of employment and economic development, especially by increasing industries such as fisheries, shipbuilding, and tourism. If Africa is to successfully benefit from the potential of its maritime economy, the African maritime domain must be the site of safe, secure, and sustainable development. The African Union (AU) plays the key role in bringing together efforts to achieve this at multiple levels. The AU is the coordinator and driving force behind the implementation of several strategic documents, including the comprehensive 2050 Africa Integrated Maritime Strategy (AIMS), as well as specific endeavours, such as the Revised African Maritime Transport Charter.

2050 AIMS is an explicit expression of collective intent in ensuring stability in Africa's maritime domain towards the realisation of its vast potential for wealth creation.[1] The increased awareness about Africa's growing geopolitical salience of the Africa's maritime milieu and the resultant need for the African littoral to exercise control over their maritime space are the key drivers in the evolution this collaborative maritime strategy.[2] The AU Member States have also realised common maritime challenges and opportunities, and indeed, significant responsibilities for generating the desirable political will for implementing the strategy. The overarching vision of the 2050 AIM Strategy is to foster increased wealth creation from Africa's oceans and seas by developing a sustainable thriving blue economy in a secure and environmentally sustainable manner.[3]

Linked by sea lanes of the Indian Ocean, India and Africa have trade and cultural connections which go back to ancient times. *Periplus of Erythrean Sea*, a merchants' sailor guide, written towards the end of the first century AD, describes the thriving trade between India and the Western Indian Ocean region, which covered an area extending from the Somali Horn along the African coast of the Red Sea route to Egypt, and other African littoral countries.[4] The maritime connection has been at the core of India's historical and civilisational link with Africa, which has widened and deepened into a multifaceted partnership with trade, developmental cooperation, and strong societal linkages in the contemporary period.

Good Order at Sea in the Indian Ocean basin is of particular importance for India, the world's fastest-growing economy, region's most populous country, and geopolitical keystone. The collective approach towards ensuring stability in the IOR has been a key feature of India's regional engagements in general and with Africa, in particular. Institutional initiatives e.g. IONS and IORA along with deepening engagements with the AU and impetus for strengthening bilateral relations with African nations exemplify this approach. Prime Minister Modi, during his visit to Mauritius in March 2015, had outlined India's policy framework towards a secure and prosperous Indian Ocean region through an aptly framed acronym SAGAR which means ocean in Hindi and stands for **S**ecurity **a**nd **G**rowth for **A**ll in the **R**egion.[5]

The chapter aims to chart convergences between India's maritime engagement policy framework SAGAR and 2050 Africa Integrated Maritime Strategy and outlines contours of India-Africa maritime cooperation.

Ensuring Good Order at Sea: Collaborative Approach to Africa

Based on its robust economic growth in the 21st century era of globalisation and political stability in post-Cold War world, the McKinsey Global Institute (MGI), in its report in 2010 described the progress and potential of African economies as "lions on the move".[6] Overall, the African continent achieved a robust GDP growth averaging 5.4 per cent between 2000 and 2010. However, Africa's growth rate declined to 3.3 per cent in 2010 and 2015.[7] Notwithstanding, deceleration due to systemic factors of collapse of commodity prices and political factors, Africa's economic lions have shown resilience and are still moving forward. Youthful profile of demography, rapid technological change, and enhancing productivity are three key pointer towards sustained economic growth in Africa in the long term. It has been argued that Africa's economic fundamentals remain strong, but governments and companies will need to work even harder to keep the region's economies moving forward.[8]

In achieving the continent's development goals, maritime economic activities are expected to play a pivotal role. Of the 53 African countries, 38 are either littoral states or islands. Africa relies heavily on ships and ports to service its intercontinental trade. As per UNCTAD, Africa's ports account for 4 per cent of global containerized trade volume in 2018, much of which comprises imports of manufactured goods. Diversification of African economies and their progressive integration into regional and global value chains is expected to improve containerized trade and port traffic volumes. Africa's shipping and ports do not always match global trends and standards.[9] Africa's container ports and hinterland transport networks need to support these efforts by upgrading infrastructure and services, and improving performance, to match international standards. Infrastructure limitations, (for example, inadequate facilities and equipment) together with security, political, economic and legal constraints, are excluding most African countries from the benefits of these types of activities.[10] In addition to West African oil-producing regions, recent oil and gas discoveries in new regions in the East African Rift and the Mozambique Channel have enhanced potential energy profile of Africa. Overall, Africa holds 7.5 per cent of oil and 7.1 per cent of proven reserves.[11] The undeveloped fishing sector in littorals has hindered optimum harvesting of fisheries resources within EEZ of African littorals which could play a vital role in economic development and food security. It is estimated that Illegal, Unregulated and Unreported (IUU) fishing cost sub-Saharan Africa approximately US$1 billion a year in lost revenue.[12]

Notwithstanding the potential maritime economy, Africa has not given adequate attention to the oceans and the sea. Dr. Dakuku Peterside, the Director General of the Nigerian Maritime Administration and Safety Agency (NIMASA) has highlighted that "It is a well-known fact that African seas and oceans are usually overlooked when it comes to issues of sustainable development in Africa, to the extent that Africa is considered to be sea blind; sea blind because there is low-level awareness of the potential for wealth creation which abounds in the seas and oceans."[13] However, Africa is progressively turning its gaze to the sea with growing realisation of the relevance of the ocean as its future economic frontier and also the need for ensuring 'Good Order at Sea' in the Africa's maritime milieu.

On January 31, 2014 at the 22nd Summit of the African Union (AU) in Addis Ababa, African Heads of States and Governments adopted the 2050 Africa's Integrated Maritime Strategy (2050 AIM Strategy) and along with a plan of action for its implementation.[14] These initiatives "flag a recent pattern of African responses to maritime vulnerabilities that says something about a declaratory shift away from a period of self-imposed sea blindness."[15] It can also be seen as first true African efforts to reclaim the continent's maritime security agenda and to move it beyond the international counter-piracy agenda.

2050 AIM Strategy contains some really innovative ideas for collaborative maritime governance which includes a Combined Exclusive Maritime Zone of Africa (CEMZA) and Inter-Agency/Transnational Cooperation and Coordination on Maritime Safety and Security. These two initiatives are expected to grant Africa enormous cross-cutting geo-strategic, economic, political, social and security benefits, as it will stimulate collective efforts and reduce the risks of all transnational threats, environmental mismanagement, smuggling and arms trafficking.

The AIM Strategy draws attention to a broad array of real and potential threats that could result in mass casualties and inflict catastrophic economic harm to the African States. In addition to the loss of revenue, they could fuel violence and insecurity. Some of them, such as drug trafficking, could feed corruption, finance the purchase of illegal weapons, corrupt the youth, pervert democracy/rule of law, distort economies, and destabilise communal life. As the actors threatening Africa's maritime domain continue to grow in number and capability, there must be a corresponding African endeavour to address these at the national, regional and continental levels. Threats and vulnerabilities in Africa's Maritime Domain have been identified as:[16]

- (i) Transnational Organised Crimes in the maritime domain (includes Money Laundering, Illegal Arms and Drug Traffic, Piracy and Armed Robbery at Sea, Illegal Oil bunkering / Crude Oil Theft along African coasts, Maritime Terrorism, Human Trafficking, Human Smuggling and Asylum Seekers Travelling by Sea;
- (ii) Illegal, Unreported and Unregulated Fishing – IUU Fishing – and overfishing, and Environmental Crimes (includes deliberate shipwrecking and oil spillage as well as dumping of toxic wastes);
- (iii) Natural Disasters, Marine Environmental Degradation, and climate change;
- (iv) Strategic Communications Systems;
- (v) Vulnerable legal framework; and
- (vi) Lack of and/or poorly maintained aids to navigation and modern hydrographic surveys, up-to-date nautical charts and maritime safety information in a number of AU member states.

The AIMS is a spring-board for identifying areas of cooperation with external actors. The strategy document highlights 21 areas related to capacity building in the maritime sector.[17] These could be broadly aggregated into three segments i.e. Good Order at Sea, Trade, and Maritime Economy.

AIMS is, in essence, an ideal cooperative manifesto of collaborative intergovernmental approach in addressing existing and emerging challenges of maritime security in Africa's maritime domain. However, implementation of such a complex policy document would be a challenging task. During the African Union Extraordinary Summit held in Lomé, Togo in October 2016, the African Union finalised the African Charter on Maritime Security, Safety

Segments	*Capacity Building Requirement*
Good Order at Sea	• Maritime governance; • Maritime defence and security (military and civilian, public and private protective services); • Maritime education and scientific research (hydrography, oceanography, fisheries, coastal and inland training, research and transfer of technology); • Maritime safety of navigation (navigational warnings, meteorological services, and warnings, search and rescue services, hydrographic services, aids to navigation, ships' manning, etc.); • Access to sea and freedom of transit of land locked States;
Trade	• Maritime commerce; • Ports and harbours management; • Promotion of African vessel ownership; • Promotion of African Classifications societies; • Promotion of an African unified and harmonised Maritime Code; • Promotion of a Pan-African fleet; • Promotion and protection of African shippers' interests; • Promoting welfare of seafarers;
Blue Economy	• Wealth Creation; • Maritime infrastructure development; • Development of inland waterways; • Offshore exploration and exploitation; • Maritime tourism (ashore and afloat); • Fisheries and aquaculture industry; • Shipbuilding and ship repair industries; • Maritime transport and auxiliary services;

and Development in Africa (the Lomé Charter) which aims to take the African blue economy and maritime security agendas forward.[18] The Lomé Charter points to three key pathways. First, the charter aims to convert existing non-legally binding instruments viz. 2009 Djibouti Code of Conduct and 2050 Africa's Integrated Maritime Strategy (AIM Strategy) into legally binding treaties. Second, it aims to strengthen complementarities between the maritime security and safety and resource development for blue economy. Third, it articulates blue economy aspirations in more concrete terms.[19] Unarguably, the accomplishment of 'overarching, concerted and coherent long-term multi-layered plans of actions' articulated in 2050 AIMS and empahised in Lomé Charter would require policy coherence among Africa Union members. It has been argued that coherence would only be achieved through an institutional mechanism for 'effective coordination, information flow, and the nexus approach'.[20]

India's Maritime Vision SAGAR

Individual African nations, as well as African Union, increasingly look to India as a key partner in supporting their developmental goals and maritime ambitions. Similarly, India's engagement with Africa has shown renewed vigor at bilateral and multilateral levels in recent years. It is pertinent to note that India's maritime vision SAGAR was enunciated by PM Modi during a visit to Mauritius, a key member of AU, in March 2015. Five key elements of the SAGAR are:[21]

- India will do everything to safeguard its mainland and defend its interest. At the same time, India will work to ensure a safe, secure and stable Indian Ocean Region.
- India will deepen its economic and security cooperation with its maritime neighbours and island states.
- India will support and strengthen the regional mechanism for maritime cooperation for collective action and cooperative approach towards advancing peace and security in the region.
- India will seek a more integrated and cooperative future in the region that enhances the prospects for sustainable development.
- Indian Ocean states hold the primary responsibility for peace, stability, and prosperity in these waters. At the same time, there is a need to recognise stake of other nations.

During the 2nd Indian Ocean Conference at Colombo in August 2017, India's Foreign Minister Mrs Sushma Swaraj underscored India's engagement in the Indian Ocean and highlighted distinct but inter-related elements of India's SAGAR initiative.[22] These include "enhancing capacities to safeguard land and maritime territories & interests; deepening economic and security cooperation in the littoral; promoting collective action to deal with natural disasters and maritime threats like piracy, terrorism and emergent non-state actors; working towards sustainable regional development through enhanced collaboration; and, engaging with countries beyond our shores with the aim of building greater trust and promoting respect for maritime rules, norms and peaceful resolution of disputes." She argued that "the principles enshrined in SAGAR provide India with a coherent framework to address some of the challenges relating to economic revival, connectivity, security, culture and identity, and India's own evolving approach to these issues."

Prime Minister Modi further emphasised the historical and cultural linkages between India and Africa during his four nations visit to Africa in 2016. In an interview to a South African newspaper, he highlighted his key focus areas of India and Africa cooperation which included energy, food, and maritime security. He argued that "the four countries (Mozambique, South Africa, Tanzania and Kenya) I am visiting also straddle important sea lanes of communication; they are gateways to a number of landlocked countries that are our partners. Maritime security thus becomes an important aspect of our cooperation."[23]

It would be pertinent to highlight that vision of SAGAR reflects India's commitment to deepening her maritime engagements in the region to ensure 'Good Order at Sea' through a collaborative partnership in which Africa remain a valuable partner.

Charting Convergences and Cooperative Synergy

India's vision of SAGAR and 2050 AIMS has significant synergy as both emphasise on a collaborative approach in ensuring harmony, stability and rule-based order in the maritime commons in the IOR. Both recognise that states in the region have primary responsibility for ensuring 'good order at sea' in these waters. At the same time, both recognise stake of other nations as well.

Following this vision of SAGAR, Delhi Declaration 2015 signed during third India Africa Forum Summit on October 29, 2015 reaffirmed India's commitment to being a partner in Africa's progress towards a dynamic and transformative development. The Delhi Declaration recognised the importance of the oceans and seas to the livelihoods of people and that maritime security was a pre-requisite for the development of the blue/ocean economy. India affirmed to support Africa, as appropriate, in the implementation of Africa's AIMS in accordance with the International Maritime Law.

Ensuring Good Order at Sea

The menace of piracy in the African waters and resultant economic consequences highlighted the critical importance of collaborative efforts in ensuring good order at sea. Although, the threat from piracy in the Horn of

Africa has been contained to a large extent, piracy and armed robbery in other African littoral continue to remain a significant challenge along with other transnational crimes viz. arms/human smuggling. Illegal, unregulated and unreported fishing deny African littoral states their legitimate rights over resources within their EEZ. Capacity building assistance in enhancing maritime governance in African waters remains a key focus area of 2050 AIMS. India's commitment to deepening its security cooperation with AU littorals and Island states aims to address this critical void.

India had published its first maritime military strategy in 2007 which had outlined India's maritime security imperatives and its obligation towards ensuring stable order. Indian Maritime Strategy has since been revised in 2015. The title of the publication has been changed from 'Freedom to use the Sea' to 'Ensuring Secure Seas' as an acknowledgment of the active role the Indian Navy would play in strengthening and enhancing maritime security in the region in addition to its role in the national security calculus.[24] The strategy has outlined India's approach to meeting its obligation in the maritime neighbourhood.

The envisaged strategy for net maritime security transcribes three principles – preservation of peace, promotion of stability and maintenance of security. The key actions for net maritime security have been described as:

- Presence and Rapid Response.
- Maritime Engagement.
- Capacity Building and Capability Enhancement.
- Develop Regional MDA.
- Maritime Security Operations.

These actions are being performed by the Indian Navy in close coordination with friendly foreign maritime forces both regional and extra-regional. Indian Navy has developed strong institutional linkages with the maritime forces in the region. In addition, Indian Coast Guard has been pursuing engagement with other maritime security forces in the region. Strategic engagements through Indian Ocean Naval Symposium (IONS), Indian Ocean Rim Association (IORA), MILAN and other regional fora aims to shape maritime policy in a cooperative, balanced and mutually beneficial manner. India has been contributing to capability enhancement of smaller navies in the region through training assistance and material support. Over the past four decades, the Indian Navy has trained more than 11,000 foreign naval, coast guard and marine police personnel from about 40 countries, a significant portion of which includes countries in Africa. Material assistance has included the transfer of hardware by means of gift, sale, lease or attachment along with technical assistance which includes assistance for maintenance and support in the operation of vessels.

As the countries in African region lack surveillance capabilities, India has been contributing in this regard through assistance for development of Coastal Surveillance Radar System (CSRS) Chains in the region and sharing of merchant shipping information through networked systems aims at reducing surveillance gaps.[25] India has signed White Shipping Information with African countries like Mauritius, Seychelles, Kenya, Mozambique, and Nigeria. India and Tanzania have also exchanged a draft agreement on the sharing of white shipping information and the upgrade of surveillance systems. The motive behind such engagement is to improve linkages that are central to improving security cooperation in the maritime domain. Towards this end, India has requested and invited African countries in the WIOR to post international liaison officers at the IFC-IOR in New Delhi. Mauritius and Seychelles have already expressed interest to deputise their naval liaison officers.[26]

India has emerged as a leading defence exporter in the region as per a report published by India Exim Bank, titled 'Reinvigorating India's Economic Engagements with Southern Africa'. The report highlighted the presence of Indian military vehicle manufacturers such as Tata Motors and Ashok Leyland in the region. The report noted that "going forward, indigenously developed new age technologies in the maritime segment, including unmanned underwater systems, unmanned aerial systems and drones could also be exported to Africa." It is estimated that increased cooperation in areas of aerospace, defence, maritime equipment and vessels can ensure security and enhance technological capacity of Africa.[27]

Maritime Trade and Blue Economy

India has emerged as Africa's third-largest trading partner, having overtaken Japan and the United States, and is surpassed only by China and the European Union. India is ranked as Africa's fifth-largest source of foreign direct investment (FDI).[28] India's bilateral trade with Africa has now reached $89.5 billion in 2021-22 compared with $56 billion the previous year.[29]

India's growing trade and investment ties was emphasised by External Affairs Minister S. Jaishankar in his address to the 17th CII-EXIM Bank Conclave on India-Africa Growth Partnership in July 2022. He highlighted that with cumulative investments at $73.9 billion from 1996-2021, India is among the top five investors in Africa. He said that India's bilateral trade with Africa has now reached $89.5 billion in 2021-22 "through the Duty Free Tariff Preference (DFTP) Scheme that extends duty free access to 98.2 per cent of India's total tariff lines, India has opened its market to African countries. So far 33 LDC African nations have been entitled to get benefits under this scheme."[30] The African Continental Free Trade Area Agreement (AfCFTA) commenced in 2021 is expected to help Indian companies in enhancing and intensifying their business footprint in Africa.

Maritime capacity building infrastructure is a potential area of future engagement for India. The region has a very low presence of shipbuilding or boatbuilding industries. Indian industry could harness the potential for ship repairs/shipbuilding in Africa. With the region's growing maritime profile, the potential for ship repair, fisheries, and marine technical business is vast. Indian shipyards—those in the public sector as well as private ones—are improving their capabilities steadily. It would be a good business proposition for Indian Shipbuilding Industry to explore opportunities for local partnership in Africa.[31]

One of the key segment in the Delhi declaration 2015 has been to promote cooperation with Africa in the Blue/Ocean economy, towards the sustainable development of marine resources; place special emphasis on closer collaboration in developing sustainable fisheries, combating illegal and unregulated fishing, managing the marine resources, exploring non-marine resources, conducting hydrographic surveys, promoting eco-tourism, developing renewable energy, disaster risk reduction through modern early warning tools, pollution control and other coastal and ocean studies.[32] In addition, there is a renewed focus to intensify ongoing cooperation in training, capacity building, consultancy, and project implementation through concessional credit in infrastructure areas which includes water supply management, maritime connectivity, and road and railway construction and upgrading.[33]

Notwithstanding India's willingness to support Africa in its development goals, India being a developing country faces resource constraints. In order to surmount this constraint, India has partnered with Japan in envisioning the Asia Africa Growth Corridor (AAGC) for linking economies, industries and institutions, ideas and people among, and between Africa and Asia. India and Japan bring a shared repertoire of development cooperation strengths for Africa. The AAGC aims to synergise the strengths of India and Japan development programmes align them with development needs of Africa, and also its development priorities.[34]

The AAGC seeks synergy between India's "Act East" Policy and Japan's "Expanded Partnership for Quality Infrastructure" in order to improve growth and interconnectedness between and within Asia and Africa for realising a free and open Indo-Pacific region. Japan's contribution to the project will be its state-of-the-art technology and ability to build quality infrastructure, while India will bring in its expertise of working in Africa. The private sector of both countries is expected to play a big role by coming together to form joint ventures and consortiums and take up infrastructure, power or agribusiness projects in Africa. The Vision document of the AAGC was launched during the annual general meeting of the African Development Bank (AfDB) at Gandhinagar in May 2017 and a detailed study of the project is in progress.

Conclusion

Indian engagement in Africa has a rich tradition and history. In recent years, India has strengthened and expanded relations across all sectors, with a particular focus on building economic and maritime linkages quantitatively and qualitatively different from those of the past. The emerging policy contours indicate India's greater willingness for a more active role in shaping the maritime environment for stability and sustained development in the region. India's approach to Africa is focused on three main components: increased economic integration, building strategic partnerships, and deepening maritime cooperation with a special emphasis on maritime security with the countries in the region. There exist significant convergences between India's SAGAR vision and 2050 Africa Integrated Maritime Strategy (AIMS). Even though the implementation of 2050 AIMS remains a work in progress, India has recognised its critical role in ensuring maritime stability in the IOR. A collaboration between India and Africa in this regard at bilateral and institutional level is evident which needs to be accelerated.

NOTES

1 United Nations Educational, Scientific and Cultural Organization (UNESCO), "African Maritime Action Plan Adopted", 25 April 2014, at http://www.unesco.org/new/en/natural-sciences/ioc-oceans/about-us/ioc-sub-commissions/iocafrica/single-view-iocafrica/news/african_maritime_action_plan_adopted/, (Accessed 4 April 2018).

2 Elizabeth Sidiropoulos, "India-Africa Relations under Modi: More Geo-Economic?" *Brookings* (blog), 30 January 2016, at https://www.brookings.edu/opinions/india-africa-relations-under-modi-more-geo-economic/ (Accessed 13 March 2018).

3 "2050 Africa's Integrated Maritime Strategy (2050 Aim Strategy)". Africa Union, 16 December 2011, at https://au.int/sites/default/files/documents/30928-doc-2050_aim_ strategy_eng.doc (Accessed 16 March 2018).

4 Ajay Kumar Dubey and Aparajita Biswas, eds., *India and Africa's Partnership*, India Studies in Business and Economics, New Delhi: Springer India, 2016, p 12.

5 "Text of the PM Modi's Remarks on the Commissioning of Coast Ship Barracuda", at https://www.narendramodi.in/text-of-the-pms-remarks-on-the-commissioning-of-coast-ship-barracuda-2954 (Accessed 14 March 2018).

6 Charles Roxburgh et al., "Lions on the Move: The Progress and Potential of African Economies | McKinsey", June 2010, at https://www.mckinsey.com/featured-insights/middle-east-and-africa/lions-on-the-move.

7 Acha Leke and Dominic Barton, "What's the Future of Economic Growth in Africa?", *World Economic Forum*, 5 May 2016, at https://www.weforum.org/agenda/2016/05/what-s-the-future-of-economic-growth-in-africa/ (Accessed 14 March 2018).

8 Jacques Bughin et al., "Lions on the Move II: Realizing the Potential of Africa's Economies | McKinsey", September 2016, at https://www.mckinsey.com/featured-insights/middle-east-and-africa/lions-on-the-move-realizing-the-potential-of-africas-economies (Accessed 14 March 2018).

9 "Maritime Trade and Africa", UNCTAD Press Release, October 3, 2018, at https://unctad.org/en/pages/PressRelease.aspx?OriginalVersionID=476, accessed November 5, 2018 (Accessed 14 March 2018).

10 Mthuli Ncube and Michael Lyon Baker, "Beyond Pirates and Drugs: Unlocking Africa's Maritime Potential and Economic Development", *African Security Review* 20, no. 1, 1 March 2011, pp. 60–69, at https://doi.org/10.1080/10246029.2011.561019 (Accessed 14 March 2018).

11 "BP Statistical Review of World Energy 2018", *British Petroleum*, June 2018, at https://www.bp.com/content/dam/bp/en/corporate/pdf/energy-economics/statistical-review/bp-stats-review-2018-full-report.pdf (Accessed 14 March 2018).

12 Timothy Walker, "How Can Africa Improve Maritime Security?" *World Economic Forum*, 21 October 2015, at https://www.weforum.org/agenda/2015/10/how-can-africa-improve-maritime-security/ (Accessed 14 March 2018).

13 "Africa's Seas and Oceans Possess Huge Economic Opportunities — NIMASA DG, Other

Experts", *News Express* Nigeria, 25 July 2017, at http://newsexpressngr.com/news/detail.php?news=41698&title=Africas-seas-and-oceans-possess-huge-economic-opportunities-NIMASA-DG-other-experts (accessed 24 August 2018).

14 "African Maritime Action Plan Adopted", 2 February 2014, at https://www.maritime-executive.com/article/African-Maritime-Action-Plan-Adopted-2014-02-02 (Accessed 14 March 2018).

15 F. Vreÿ, "Turning the Tide: Revisiting African Maritime Security", *Scientia Militaria: South African Journal of Military Studies* 41, no. 2 (2013): 1-23–23.

16 "2050 Africa's Integrated Maritime Strategy (2050 Aim Strategy)".

17 "2050 Africa's Integrated Maritime Strategy (2050 Aim Strategy)".

18 "The African Charter on Maritime Security, Safety and Development in Africa (the Lomé Charter)", *Africa Union*, October 15, 2016, at https://au.int/sites/default/files/treaties/33128-treaty-0060_-_lome_charter_e.pdf (Accessed 14 March 2018).

19 Edwin Egede, "Africa's Lomé Charter on Maritime Security: What are the next Steps?," Piracy Studies, July 16, 2017, at http://piracy-studies.org/africas-lome-charter-on-maritime-security-what-are-the-next-steps/ (Accessed 14 March 2018).

20 Edwin Egede, "Maritime Security: Horn of Africa and Implementation of the 2050 AIM Strategy", Life & Peace Institute, 14 May 2018, at http://life-peace.org/hab/maritime-security-horn-of-africa-and-implementation-of-the-2050-aim-strategy/ (Accessed 14 March 2018).

21 Text of the PM's Remarks on the Commissioning of Coast Ship Barracuda.

22 Shushma Swaraj, "SAGAR – India's Vision for the Indian Ocean Region", 31 August 2017, at http://www.indiafoundation.in/sagar-indias-vision-for-the-indian-ocean-region/

23 Shannon Ebrahim, "Modi's Vision for India-SA Partnership" *IOL News*, July 10, 2016, https://www.iol.co.za/news/politics/modis-vision-for-india-sa-partnership-2043720

24 Directorate of Concepts and Transformation Strategy Indian Navy, *Ensuring Secure Seas: Indian Maritime Security Strategy*, 2015, at http://indiannavy.nic.in/sites/default/files/Indian_Maritime_Security_Strategy_Document_25Jan16.pdf

25 Abhay K Singh, "India as a Net Security Provider in the Indian Ocean Region: The Strategic Approach of a Responsible Stakeholder", in Jivanta Schottli ed. *Maritime Governance and South Asia: Trade, Security and Sustainable Development in the Indian Ocean*, New Jersey: World Scientific, 2018, pp. 63–78.

26 Srikant B. Kesnur and Abhishek Mishra, 'India's Maritime Agenda Pivots to Western Indian Ocean' (New Delhi: Observer Research Foundation, 6 September 2022), https://www.orfonline.org/research/indias-maritime-agenda-pivots-to-western-indian-ocean/ (Accessed 1 April 2023).

27 'India Could Fulfill Africa's Maritime, Aerospace and Defence Requirements: Exim Bank Report', *The Economic Times*, 1 November 2022, at https://economictimes.indiatimes.com/news/defence/india-could-fulfill-africas-maritime-aerospace-and-defence-requirements-exim-bank-report/articleshow/95227618.cms?from=mdr (Accessed 1 April 2023).

28 Ritika Passi and Ihssane Guennoun, eds., *Securing the 21st Century: Mapping India-Africa Engagement*, GP-ORF Series, New Delhi: ORF-OCP Policy Center, 2017, at https://www.orfonline.org/wp-content/uploads/2018/09/GP-ORF-India-Africa.pdf (Accessed 1 April 2023).

29 IANS, 'India among Africa's Top Investors, Bilateral Trade at $89.5bn in FY22: EAM', *Business Standard India*, 20 July 2022, https://www.business-standard.com/article/current-affairs/india-among-africa-s-top-investors-bilateral-trade-at-89-5bn-in-fy22-eam-122072000023_1.html. (Accessed 1 April 2023).

30 'Address by External Affairs Minister, Dr. S. Jaishankar at the 17th CII-EXIM Bank Conclave on India-Africa Growth Partnership', Ministry of External Affairs, Government of India, 19 July 2022, at https://www.mea.gov.in/Speeches-Statements.htm?dtl/35499/Address_by_External_ Affairs_Minister_Dr_S_Jaishankar_at_the_17th_CIIEXIM_Bank_Conclave_on_IndiaAfrica_Growth_Partnership (Accessed 1 April 2023).

31 Yogesh V. Athawale, 'Maritime Developments in the South Western Indian Ocean and the Potential for India's Engagement with the Region', *Strategic Analysis*, Vol. 36, No. 3 (1 May 2012): 424–39, https://doi.org/10.1080/09700161.2012.670537.

32 'Delhi Declaration 2015: Third India-Africa Forum Summit 29 October 2015', New Delhi: Ministry of External Affairs, Government of India, 29 October 2015, http://www.mea.gov.in/Uploads/PublicationDocs/25980_declaration.pdf (Accessed 1 April 2023).

33 'India-Africa Framework for Strategic Cooperation: Third India-Africa Forum Summit', New Delhi: Ministry of External Affairs, Government of India, 29 October 2015, http://www.mea.gov.in/Uploads/PublicationDocs/25981_framework.pdf (Accessed 1 April 2023).

34 Ruchita Beri, "India's New Initiative in Africa: The Asia–Africa Growth Corridor", *Institute for Defence Studies and Analyses*, 13 June 2017, at https://idsa.in/idsacomments/indias-new-initiative-in-africa-asia-africa-growth-corridor_rberi_130617 (Accessed 1 April 2023).

5

Militarisation in the Western Indian Ocean Region: Implications for India-Africa Maritime Cooperation

Abhishek Mishra

Introduction

The Western Indian Ocean (WIO) is a unique maritime region in which a number of contemporary maritime security challenges, capacity building responses, and naval interactions between States are prevalent. The region connects Europe, Middle East, Africa, and Asia. The region hosts several of the world's most important maritime chokepoints contributing to a significant amount of maritime trade. The WIO region comprises ten African countries, both mainland and island nations. They include Kenya, Tanzania, Mozambique, South Africa, Somalia, Mauritius, Seychelles, Madagascar, Comoros, and Réunion (France). This WIO region is a part of India's strategic maritime frontier, extending from the Persian Gulf, to the East Coast of Africa, and across the Malacca Strait. The region is home to natural resources and some of the world's busiest shipping routes and vital maritime chokepoints such as Gulf of Aden, Bab el Mandeb, Mozambique Channel, Strait of Hormuz, and the Cape of Good Hope.

During the first decade of the 21st century, the incidents of piracy increased drastically in the WIO region.[1] This was the result of the continued instability in Somalia due to lack of State protection, the vicious cycle of armed conflicts, and recurring humanitarian crises. The Somali pirate action groups took advantage of this situation, increased their sophistication and number of armed attacks at sea. Pirate attacks off Somalia's coast in the 1990s, were mostly sporadic and opportunistic efforts. However, this began to change in the first few years of the decade of the 2000s, with pirates using a more complex, efficient, and profit-oriented business model. This was linked to Somalian cartels, Somalian diaspora, wealthy investors within Somalia, and international financial networks. The severity of the challenge, in which no ships or seafarers from State were safe, led to an alarming national crisis. Nations acknowledged this challenge to their maritime trade and commerce, which subsequently led to a host of declarations by the United Nations Security Council (UNSC), most notably the UNSC Resolutions 1816 and 1851, calling on States to divert their resources and tackle the scourge of maritime piracy emanating off Somalia's coast.[2] Since then, naval forces from many countries like the United States, India, France, China, began conducting counter-piracy operations and escorting ships and vessels in the WIO region. The comprehensive response of the international community to the rise of Somalian piracy underlined the importance of the WIO region and sea lanes of communications (SLOCs) to global commerce, regional stability and energy security. Due to the dedicated multinational efforts to combat piracy, international partners and African countries have been able to successfully work together and contain the menace of piracy in the WIO region, especially since 2012.[3]

After reasonable success against piracy, the focus has now shifted to newer non-traditional and transnational maritime crimes. These range from Illegal, Unregulated and Unreported (IUU) fishing, to maritime terrorism, to trafficking in narcotics, small arms and wildlife products, climate change, and blue economy, among others.[4] The rise in these blue crimes have also coincided with the discovery of vast amounts of natural resources off the East African coast in the WIO region. The discoveries of energy resources like oil and gas, and mineral resources, in addition to the large number of physical infrastructure projects that are being planned and executed in East Africa, points to the potential of the East African region to become a major energy producer.[5]

The international communities' efforts are now being directed towards developing and maintaining partnerships with the littorals of this vital geographical region.[6] Countries like the US, France, Japan, India and China are at the forefront of such engagements. More recently, countries like Germany, The Netherlands, and the United Kingdom have also developed policies to promote their reach in the entire Indo-Pacific region.[7] India, along with Japan, has been one of the foremost proponents of including the East African shoreline in the Indian Ocean as part of their respective Indo-Pacific strategies.[8] Even though the US and Australia initially did not include the African east coast within the ambit of the Indo-Pacific, they now acknowledge the centrality of Africa within the Indo-Pacific discourse.[9] Much attention is being specifically directed towards the WIO region and its littorals, which have become a vital part of many extra-regional countries' strategies. From an Indian standpoint, while some of these countries' engagement in the WIO region has been welcomed, others have been perceived as security threats with implications for India's own status as the 'preferred security partner' in the Indian Ocean Region (IOR).[10]

Drivers of External Engagement in the Western Indian Ocean

The waters of the WIO are not only critical for the broader security and stability of the IOR, but also significant to the larger geopolitical imperative of the 21st century, where we are witnessing the strategic and economic rise of regional powers such as India and China, leading to a multipolar world. Owing to such a strategic importance of the region, where a great portion of world's shipping routes are located, it is imperative that external actors, and most prominently great and emerging powers have a significant stake in the WIO region. India and China significantly depend on energy supply from the Gulf to meet their growing economic needs, and both the countries have a major trade and investment linkage with mineral-rich Africa.[11] Hence, both India and China as growing economic and strategic giants have competing interests in this region as rivals. The sea lanes of communication (SLOCs) that pass through this region are critical to these two rising powers.

With the fall of the Soviet Union, the bipolarity of the world changed into American unipolarity. However, the rise of regional powers, especially that of China, to global prominence is a threat to such unipolarity led by the United States. Even though India, due to its advantageous geography is considered as the most capable resident power in the Indian Ocean, the United States too continues to play an important role in the region. The United States' significance in the region can be further understood by the fact that it continues to maintain a military presence on the island of Diego Garcia situated at the centre of the Indian Ocean.[12] France, on the other hand, has been a prominent power in the South-West Indian Ocean (SWIO). It was a formidable colonial power until the last century and it maintains strategic assets in the Indian Ocean, and particularly in the SWIO region. Such assets include possession of island territories (Scattered Islands) and EEZ along the Mozambique Channel, and military presence on Mayotte and Reunion. Mayotte and Reunion are overseas departments of France which are located outside the continental Europe situated portion of France. France maintains 2.8 million square kilometres of EEZ in the Indian Ocean, roughly 20 per cent of its total EEZ possession.[13] Hence, France is a sovereign power in the greater Indian Ocean.

For African countries too, their maritime domain offers tremendous potential for increase of trade and to achieve sustainable development. WIO States have a crucial interest in the development of the maritime domain, as it would provide them with enormous growth opportunities. The African Maritime Domain (AMD) provides a lifeline and a means of livelihood for various communities including fishing, transportation, tourism, marine resources, wave energy, maritime industry, harbour, and transport infrastructure.[14] External engagement in the WIO has been driven by several other factors.

Resource and energy security has been one of the foremost pull-factors that has drawn extra-regional powers like China and United States and regional powers like India and France closer to the WIO region. Oil and gas are central to the economic growth and development of the contemporary world. Energy security is crucial to sustain industrial and economic progress, and to meet the growing energy demands of both developed and developing States. As recent history has shown, concern about attacks by States and asymmetrical attacks on energy resources and shipping is a very real issue,[15] particularly important in the case of WIO as critical oil and gas routes traverse this region. Many governments on the eastern coast of Africa have relied on oil rents in order to diversify their national economies. Oil rents are the difference between the value of crude oil production at regional prices and the total cost of production, measured as a percentage of GDP. Over the last decade, there has been a significant amount of discovery and development of large offshore gas deposits, especially in Mozambique, Tanzania, and South Africa, particularly during 2010-2014. It is estimated that the combined discoveries off the southern coast of Tanzania and northern coast of Mozambique "indicate the presence of at least 150 trillion cubic feet (tcf) of natural gas."[16]

This has raised some concerns about security but offshore operations are not necessarily limited by a lack of security at sea. In order to develop any offshore oil fields, large investments are required and it usually takes years before production can begin. Therefore, international companies, together with the respective countries, provide military personnel for the security and safe passage of vessels. Although there is no history of oil and gas production – neither onshore nor offshore – in the East African region, it is now considered a so-called frontier region.[17] The revenues that would be generated from oil and gas production in the region are expected to have a transformative effect on national economies. In addition, countries wanting to diversify their oil imports away from the Middle East, are looking at Africa with keen interest. Asian economies particularly that of India, China, and Southeast Asian nations have a huge demand. Therefore, it is no surprise that various international oil companies are investing huge sums of money in the oil and gas sector across the WIO region.

India is among the world's largest importers of oil, and Africa's share of India's oil imports is quite substantial. India is attempting to diversify its sourcing of crude oil and liquefied natural gas (LNG). As a result, due to the proximity and absence of any choke points in trans-shipments, African nations are in a good position to fuel this growing Indian demand, which is looking to reduce its energy reliance on the Middle East.[18] India's State-owned companies have also invested billions of dollars in the region. In 2017, Oil India Limited and ONGC Videsh Limited decided to invest US$20 billion to build a liquid natural gas terminal in Mozambique for the Rovuma Offshore Area 1 gas field.[19] This represented India's single-largest investment in Africa.

Like India, even China's quest for energy security has been a primary driver of growing Chinese footprints in the WIO region.[20] It is looking for new exploration opportunities in countries like Kenya, Madagascar, and

Uganda by establishing joint ventures with local State-owned companies. China is already an established player in securing oil reserves in offshore deep-water blocs in Nigeria, Angola and Sudan. Due to the surge in domestic energy demand, China is now looking to diversify its natural resource imports. Most of the Chinese investments in Africa's oil sector are being led by China National Petroleum Corporation (CNPC), China Petroleum & Chemical Corporation (SINOPEC) and China National Offshore Oil (CNOOC). In many ways, China's appetite for energy would continue to grow in the coming years, and the countries on the eastern seaboard of Africa in the WIO would have an important role to play in its delivery.

India's Role in the Western Indian Ocean Region

Over the last decade, India is getting increasingly invested in Africa, both for political reasons but no less as an extension of its economic stake in the continent. The previous focus on development cooperation, extension of lines of credit (LOC), and capacity building in human resources and technology continues to be nurtured. At the same time, the Indian private sector is poised to play an increasingly important role by participating in projects of national development, regional connectivity, and maritime port connectivity in Africa. There is a perceptible and quantum increase in Africa's centrality in Indian foreign policy initiatives. This increase in greater cooperation with African countries has manifested itself primarily in the maritime domain.[21]

Abhijit Singh maintains that India's approach to maritime security cooperation with African countries has essentially revolved around India's central security concerns in African waters.[22] India has reached out to African States with offers of military aid, training assistance, and capacity building initiatives. India's maritime engagement with countries in the WIO region has over the years expanded and diversified into a broad-based security approach.[23] This approach has been complemented by regular naval visits and allied activities including patrolling of EEZs, and development of listening stations and posts.[24] Listening stations and posts are essentially monitoring stations. They are fitted with radars and surveillance gear for monitoring maritime communications.

Broadly, India's maritime engagement with African countries has evolved in four ways:

Firstly, through training of African maritime officers and practitioners, including civilians, by Indian naval institutes. These include the Indian Naval Academy in Ezhimala, Kerala, the Naval Institute of Education and Training Technology, Kochi, the National Institute of Hydrography, Goa, National Defence College, New Delhi and the Defence Services Staff College, Wellington, among others. Various kinds of marine science training courses are offered by India, which include marine engineering, ocean engineering, nautical science, water resource management, in addition to conducting both harbour training and sea training. Capacity building is an important aspect of India's maritime engagement with African nations. These include capacity building in oceanography, ship designing and construction, dredging, welding, fisheries, blue economy and port management. Furthermore, various Indian Training Teams are posted in African countries like a Tri-Services Training Team in Tanzania; a Training Team in Seychelles; an Indian Air Force Training Team (IAFTT) in Mauritius and Namibia; an Indian Army Training Team (IATT) in Lesotho and Namibia; and an Indian Military Training Team (IMTT) in Uganda. The Head of the Mauritius Police Force (MPF) and the Mauritian National Security Advisor are Indian officers[25] whereas Seychelles' maritime security advisor is an Indian naval officer.[26]

Secondly, by conducting anti-piracy patrols and long-term and sustained deployment of Indian naval ships in African waters. One significant threat and challenge to effective maritime governance around the Indian Subcontinent and across Sub-Saharan Africa is maritime piracy and armed robbery against ships. Piracy is defined as:

> "(A)ny illegal acts of violence or detention, or any act of depredation, committed for private end by the crew or the passengers of a private ship or private aircraft, and directed against another ship or persons or property on board a ship outside the jurisdiction of the territorial waters of a state."[27]

Piracy takes place in international waters, including the high seas, EEZs, and the contiguous zones. It is an extension of the act of taking another's possession by force. On the other hand, armed robbery is committed for private ends within a State's internal and archipelagic waters and territorial seas according to Resolution A.1025 (26) of the International Maritime Organization. Such acts that are committed in a State's territorial waters, usually within 12 nautical miles (nm) measured from the coast, are legally defined as acts of armed robbery.

At the heart of the piracy narrative lies the Indian Ocean. For India, the IOR is central to its maritime interests and concerns, as its economic development is crucially dependent on the sea due to the criticality of sea-borne trade and because of the vast economic potential of oceans which can be explored and exploited for resources. Therefore, safeguarding India's vast 7,500 kilometres long coastline, EEZ of two million square kilometres, and maintaining open and secure sea lines of communications (SLOCs), is of paramount importance. India has actively engaged in anti-piracy operations since 2008 in the Gulf of Aden and the Eastern Arabian Sea.[28] The Indian Navy has been continuously deployed in that region in order to not only escort Indian-flagged vessels, but also provide protection to ships of other countries. Indian naval assets were also been regularly deployed in the Mozambique Channel where it had provided security during the African Union summit in 2003.[29] The Indian Navy was called in for maritime security support when Mozambique hosted the World Economic Forum meeting in 2004. Since then, the Indian Navy has been regularly escorting UN-affiliated ships carrying food supplies to Somalia. One advantage of conducting independent operations was quick decision-making and single rules-of-engagement. The deterrent value of a singular rule of engagement, and the kinetic means adopted by Indian naval ships helped New Delhi to conduct successful anti-piracy operations.

Incidents of piracy in Africa's eastern coast have declined in the last few years due to the dedicated efforts of the Indian and foreign navies. However, there is a need for continued vigilance and correct reporting of untoward incidents and suspicious approaches by ships. Now, piracy in the IOR and the WIO is contained, rather than eliminated or eradicated, as a latent threat continues to remain.[30]

Thirdly, through greater collaboration on maritime information sharing. Effective maritime enforcement capacity is dependent upon a nation's strong Maritime Domain Awareness (MDA).[31] This capacity is vital for promoting marine safety, stopping illegal activity, responding to vessels in distress, tracking at-sea transshipments, and protecting territorial waters from illegal incursions by foreign vessels. Given the complexity of India's maritime neighbourhood in which India is seeking to attain its strategic objectives, bolstering MDA capabilities, especially in the aftermath of the 2008 Mumbai terror attacks, is an imperative for India. India has been helping its maritime neighbours in setting up coastal surveillance networks. This facilitates sharing of MDA. In this context, India launched the Information Fusion Centre-Indian Ocean Region (IFC-IOR) in Gurugram in December 2018. The Centre has currently established links with 25 partner countries, 45 multi-national agencies, and hosts 12 International Liaison Officers.[32] The IFC-IOR can help ensure situational awareness of regional maritime activities. The Centre collects, analyses and disseminates information related to maritime safety and HADR requirements at sea. In furtherance of this goal, the Indian Navy has been engaging with various friendly foreign navies for concluding and signing of agreements for exchange of *White Shipping Information*, in order to enhance India's MDA in the IOR.[33]

Till date, India has signed the White Shipping Information with Mauritius, Seychelles, Kenya, Mozambique, Tanzania, and Nigeria. India became an observer to the Indian Ocean Commission in March 2020 and the Djibouti Code of Conduct (DCoC) in September 2020. India has expressed interest in deputing liaison officers at the Regional Maritime Information Fusion Centre (RMIFC) and the European Maritime Awareness in the Strait of Hormuz (EMASOH). India has also requested and invited African countries in the WIO to post international liaison officers at the IFC-IOR in New Delhi. Mauritius and Seychelles have already expressed interest to depute their naval liaison officers.

The Indian Navy has also conducted hydrographic surveys for many littorals in the WIO region. In contrast to many coastal countries having no or very limited hydrographic capability, India possesses enough knowledge and capacity in this sphere. It is estimated that 64 per cent of African waters have not yet been systematically surveyed.[34] India has MOUs for hydrographic surveys with Mauritius, Tanzania and Seychelles. In addition, Indian survey ships have also cooperated with Kenya and Mozambique.

Growing Militarisation in the WIO Region

Maritime security in the WIO region has been primarily associated with piracy off the coast of Somalia, which threatened international commerce and the safety of seafarers. This prompted various countries to deploy their naval warships in order to contain the menace of piracy. Due to the support from the international community, piracy and armed robbery in WIO has declined in recent years. Although pirate attacks have reduced, new threats and challenges have emerged like illicit fishing, grey-zone maritime attacks, weapons smuggling, and drug trafficking. These threats have emerged concurrently with growing external naval engagement and growing militarisation in the WIO, as part of which countries are setting up dual-use military bases, regularly deploying naval warships, and investing heavily in hard infrastructure.

Although African countries do have genuine infrastructural deficiencies which require investments, not all the big-ticket investments and hard infrastructure projects are aligned with the national development priorities of African countries. The WIO region has emerged as a theatre of geostrategic competition where multitude of regional and external actors are vying to carve out a space for themselves and protect their national interests. African governments and leaders have been cautious and vocal about the growing contestation in the WIO region.[35] They have voiced their concerns and want to promote their own interests by leveraging and balancing the external powers.

However, the extensive foreign presence and growing militarisation of the region is a source of tension for African countries and could have a destabilising impact on the region. This situation in the WIO region has been termed by Christian Bueger and Jan Stockbruegger as the emergence of a "militarisation dilemma".[36] Greater external naval operations will be needed to suppress maritime threats and address the new maritime insecurities in the region. However, increasingly countries like the US, China, France, the European Union, and India are viewing others as strategic rivals. This is particularly true of the US and India and their concern and opposition to China's growing presence in the WIO region. Therefore, greater naval presence and operations risk importing geopolitical tensions to the WIO region, which could undermine international cooperation efforts.

Christian Bueger argues, neither more nor fewer external naval presence present a favourable outcome for the region.[37] With the increase in naval presence, there is a risk of greater strategic competition. However, lesser naval engagement and operations could weaken efforts to secure shipping lanes, for which African littorals rely on high-end naval capabilities provided by external actors. Piracy and transnational blue crimes pose severe challenges to African countries in the region, given the volume of trade that goes on this increasingly significant maritime trade route. Afghanistan's opium production for example, fuels maritime crimes throughout the WIO and provides important funding for violent non-State actors. According to Stable Seas, 19 active violent non-State actors operate in the Western Indian Ocean region.[38] This is in addition to concerns over the rise in sea level due to climate change and ocean pollution like dumping of toxic waste, and emission of fumes by ships, along these important trade routes in the WIO. Therefore, African countries would continue to require support for improving their capabilities.

Implications for Indian Interests in WIO Region

The growing presence of a number of external actors and the ensuing geopolitical competition for power and influence in the WIO, presents India with significant challenges. Traditionally, India has considered the IOR as its 'backyard' and has maintained and developed friendly relations with all IOR littorals. This is especially true in the East African countries, where India had enjoyed a long history of maritime and trade links. Eastern and Southern Africa is also home to a substantial Indian diaspora. Therefore, it comes as no surprise that India views East Africa, encompassing the WIO region, as its gateway to continental Africa, and is interested in the peace, stability, and security of the region. However, with a multitude of actors now attempting to increase their footprint in this important maritime space, India is being challenged. The foremost challenge for India has been the rapid expansion of the People's Liberation Army Navy (PLAN) in the Indian Ocean.[39]

In 2020, the PLAN surpassed the US Navy to become the largest navy in the world in terms of the total number of warships commissioned. The Chinese Navy is investing heavily in shipbuilding, military capability, modernisation of forces and command structure. China usually sends to the Indian Ocean its Type 052C Destroyer, Type 054A Frigate, and supply ships as part of its anti-piracy deployments in the Gulf of Aden off the coast of Somalia.[40] However, what has been the cause of alarm for India is the sighting of Chinese intelligence and survey ships off the coast of Andaman and the Lakshadweep Islands.[41] This has become a regular feature and poses a challenge as it allows the Chinese to systematically map the seabed across the vast swath of the Indian Ocean. Rather than the quantum of China's deployments in the IOR, it is the nature of these deployments, which is raising alarm.[42] Under the cloak of its 'benign' deployments in the region, the Chinese Navy is in fact conducting surveillance operations in the IOR to learn about the strategic dynamics and hydrological conditions in the region. This is indicative of China's desire to have a long-term presence in the region. China's intent behind increasing their presence in the IOR is guided by its desire to develop an understanding and assessment of other countries' operational capacities by observing them in their respective waters. In the Indian Ocean, it is unlikely that China is pursuing any form of a full-spectrum domination strategy; rather, it is a strategy of incremental control.

Initially, China is looking to have an incremental presence by studying the operational environment. Chinese submarines in the Indian Ocean tend to spend a lot of time in South Asia, around the Andaman Islands or Sri Lankan waters, before eventually venturing into the Western Indian Ocean. The motive behind such operations lies in the Chinese desire to understand the bathymetry, i.e., the measurement of depth of waters in oceans and seas, and temperature profile in these waters, to utilise such knowledge and conduct operations that would give China the opportunity to maintain and sustain its long-term presence in the Indian Ocean. For India, this presents a direct challenge to its aspirations to become a 'net security provider' or 'preferred security partner' for the IOR littorals. As the PLAN's ability to maintain and sustain its presence in the Indian Ocean is enhanced, India's freedom of navigation may get restricted.[43] This could soon overcome the advantages of geography in the Indian Ocean that India currently enjoys. In many ways, China has been successful in combining a series of measures in terms of infrastructural developmental, through the Belt and Road Initiative (BRI) and the Maritime Silk Route (MSR), by funding and constructing ports like Lamu (Kenya) and Bagamoyo (Tanzania), aided by diplomacy, and increased naval deployments, to become a force that could dominate the WIO region.

India's official position regarding the presence of regional and extra-regional powers in the IOR was evident during Prime Minister Narendra Modi's speech in Mauritius and the Seychelles in 2015. Prime Minister Modi noted that,

> "...those who live in this region have the primary responsibility for peace, stability and prosperity in the Indian Ocean...we recognize that there are other nations around the world, with strong interests and stakes in the region."[44]

France's sustained presence in the WIO is welcomed by the Indian security establishment. Both countries enjoy a strategic partnership but lack a regional dimension for their ties. Securing cooperation in the WIO could fill this gap. Already, India and France have expressed interest to collaborate on third-country projects in WIO littorals in a host of areas like port connectivity, blue economy, tourism, skill development, connectivity, and healthcare, among others.[45] In May 2022, the Indian and French Navy jointly conducted patrols off Réunion Island in the WIO region.[46] The Indian Navy's P-8I maritime reconnaissance aircraft conducted the patrols, with French personnel on board. These joint patrols help to strengthen interoperability between the two partners and enhance their maritime domain awareness capabilities in the region, which is useful for surveillance and monitoring of foreign ships, illicit activities in the maritime domain, which is particularly widespread in the WIO region.

Additionally, in April 2021, India and France conducted the 21st edition of the bilateral exercise 'VARUNA-2023' in the western Arabian Sea, under which a wide array of naval operations at sea and anti-submarine exercises were conducted and best practices were shared.[47] India has also increased its collaboration with the US as was evident with the Indian Navy participating in 2023's edition of the US AFRICOM-directed multilateral naval exercise Cutlass Express, which works towards promoting maritime security, coordination, and information exchange, among the WIO countries.[48] The Indian Navy trained the contingents from various participating African navies in different fields, across the spectrum of maritime security operations.

The presence and role of regional powers like France in the WIO does not pose any direct security threat to India. On the contrary, India and France have expressed their desire to work together in order to play a greater role in collaborating with African countries and shaping the maritime security architecture in the WIO region. There are many opportunities for both India and the US to explore and collaborate. The signing of the Logistics Exchange Memorandum of Agreement (LEMOA) with the US in August 2016 has been beneficial for Indian warships operating in Gulf of Aden and Indian Ocean.[49] Through this, Indian Navy's warships have access to fuel from US Navy tankers deployed in the region. The US could also play a pivotal role in the Indian Ocean, since it has been an active dialogue partner of the IORA since 2012. Now that France too has become a full-fledged member of IORA, through its department of Réunion, there are many opportunities for India, France, and the US to work together for ensuring freedom of navigation and shared mutual prosperity in the WIO region. However, China's increasing foray in the WIO has become a source of concern and consternation for all these powers. China's tendency to prop up African elites and secure deals on low interest rates and the rapid pace of infrastructure construction, has made other powers question its motives. Moreover, although there is no direct evidence of asset seizure in Africa, the opaque nature of Chinese deals, confidentiality clauses, and increasing unilateralism and belligerence, have served to caution regional powers about China's exact motives and strategy in the WIO region.

Conclusion

Over the last two decades, India's maritime cooperation with African countries has evolved in conjunction with two developments. First, India, sitting astride critical sea-lanes of communication, in the IOR is emerging as a maritime power. The Indian Navy is increasingly positioning itself as a regional security provider with the principle objective of effectively patrolling the regional commons. The Indian Navy has assumed the role of a security stabiliser in the IOR, as a source of positive deterrence and provider of regional goods. Second, there has been a growing maritime consciousness amongst African States about the importance of securing their maritime domain and sustainable use of marine resources in order to foster wealth creation and development. India's maritime cooperation with these WIO littorals have taken place under different circumstances, and are at varying degrees of intensity, or have different priorities. India has recognised the varying priorities of African countries and has fine-tuned its own maritime security cooperation in order to respond effectively to the emerging challenges.

The growing contestation for influence in the WIO presents India with both challenges and opportunities. Both India and China are fully aware of their respective capabilities and understand the costs of provoking each other. Therefore, both countries have strived to increase their respective maritime surveillance and monitoring capabilities. They have also taken care not to engage in any form of direct conventional confrontation. India continues to rely on its shared historical, colonial linkages with African countries, and the proximity to East Africa and WIO, is an advantage.

Going forward, India's efforts and her goal to become a leading provider of public goods in the IOR and be recognised as a 'preferred security partner' of IOR littorals would be contingent on the cooperation and support of African countries in the WIO region. The manner in which India's maritime engagement with African countries have evolved, is likely to follow the same trajectory in the near future, albeit with a broader focus and ambit. India can take the lead in shaping the emerging maritime security architecture in the WIO region by working to improve the collective maritime competence of African nations and secure her vision of Security and Growth for All in the Region (SAGAR).

NOTES

1 Rulah Odeh Alsawalqa and Denis Venter, "Piracy and Maritime Security in North-Western Indian Ocean: From the Gulf of Oman to the Waters off the Somali Coast", *Insight on Africa* 14(1), 3 December 2021 at https://journals.sagepub.com/doi/full/10.1177/0975087821 1049224. (Accessed 13 December 2023).

2 United Nations Security Council, "Resolution 1816 (2008)/ adopted by the Security Council at its 5902nd meeting on 2 June 2008" at https://digitallibrary.un.org/record/627953?ln=en. (Accessed 13 December 2023).

3 Arun Prakash, "The Menace of Piracy: India, the International Community and a UN Response", Atlantic Council, 21 May 2009 at https://www.atlanticcouncil.org/blogs/new-atlanticist/the-menace-of-piracy-india-the-international-community-and-a-un-response/. (Accessed 16 December 2023).

4 Christian Bueger and Timothy Edmunds, "Blue crime: Conceptualising organised crime at sea", *Marine Policy*, 119, September 2022 at https://www.sciencedirect.com/science/article/pii/S0308597X20300270. (Accessed 16 December 2023)

5 "East Africa's Oil and Gas Boom: Promise and Peril", Brookings, 20 February 2014at https://www.brookings.edu/events/east-africas-oil-and-gas-boom-promise-and-peril/. (Accessed 15 December 2023).

6 Christian Bueger, Timothy Edmunds and Robert McCabe, *Capacity Building for Maritime Security: The Western Indian Ocean Experience,* Palgrave Macmillan, Cham, October 2020, p. 307.

7 Abhishek Mishra *Reflections on the Indo-Pacific: Perspectives from Africa*, December 2021, Observer Research Foundation at https://www.orfonline.org/wp-content/uploads/2021/12/ORF_Monograph_Reflections-on-the-Indo-Pacific-Perspectives-from-Afric.pdf. (Accessed 16 December 2023).

8 Elizabeth Roche, "India's view of Indo-Pacific stretches from east coast of Africa to west coast of US: Shringla", *Livemint*, 3 November 2020 at https://www.livemint.com/news/india/india-s-view-of-indo-pacific-stretches-from-east-coast-of-africa-to-west-coast-of-us-shringla-11604423464721.html. (Accessed 16 December 2023).

9 Rushali Saha, "Western Indian Ocean: Missing Piece in the U.S. Indo-Pacific Strategy", *South Asian Voices*, 26 September 2022 at https://southasianvoices.org/western-indian-ocean-the-missing-piece-in-the-u-s-indo-pacific-strategy/. (Accessed 19 December 2023).

10 "Indian Navy Over The Years Has Emerged as a Combat Ready, Credible and Cohesive Force, and is The 'Preferred Security Partner' in the Indian Ocean Region: President Kovind", *Press Information Bureau*, 25 March2022 at https://pib.gov.in/PressReleaseIframePage.aspx?PRID=1809533. (Accessed 13 December 2023).

11 S.N. Yadav, *India, China and Africa: New Partnership in Energy Security*, Jnanada Prakashan, February 2009, New Delhi: India.

12 Blake Herzinger, "The power of example: America's presence in Diego Garcia", *The Interpreter*, Lowy Institute, 15 February 2021 at https://www.lowyinstitute.org/the-interpreter/power-example-america-s-presence-diego-garcia. (Accessed 19 December 2023).

13 Armistead Maupin, "France in the Indian Ocean: A Geopolitical Perspective and its Implications for Africa", SAIIA Policy Insights No.42, South African Institute of International Affairs (SAIIA), March 2017 at https://hal.archives-ouvertes.fr/hal-02536811/document. (Accessed 19 December 2023).

14 "The Geostrategic Importance of Africa's Maritime Domain: Opportunities and Challenges", African Union, 14 October 2010 at https://au.int/sites/default/files/newsevents/workingdocuments/27459-wd-keynote_address_of_h.e._the_dcp-1_0.pdf. (Accessed 13 December 2023).

15 Thean Potgeiter, "Maritime security in the Indian Ocean: strategic setting and features", Paper No. 246, Institute for Security Studies, August 2012, pp.1-24 at https://media.africaportal.org/documents/Paper236.pdf. (Accessed 16 December 2023).

16 D.M. Richmond, "Oil, Gas and Renewable Energy," in *Regional State of the Coast Report: Western Indian Ocean*, United Nations Environment Programme/Nairobi Convention Secretariat, Nairobi: Kenya, 2015 at https://wedocs.unep.org/handle/20.500.11822/9668. (Accessed 13 December 2023).

17 B. Augé and R. Nakayi, "Eastern Africa: a New Oil and Gas Frontier?", *L'Observatoire des Grands Lacs enAfrique*, 24, 2014, pp.1-14.

18 Nidhi Verma, "Africa can play a central role in India's oil diversification, says minister," *Reuters*, 24 March 2021 at https://www.reuters.com/article/us-india-africa-oil-idUSKBN2BG2SZ/. (Accessed 15 December 2023).

19 "ONGC Videsh, partners to invest $20 b in Mozambique LNG project", *The Hindu Business Line*, 19 June 2019 at https://www.thehindubusinessline.com/companies/ongc-videsh-partners-to-invest-20-b-in-mozambique-lng-project/article28077931.ece. (Accessed 15 December 2023).

20 Kate O'Shaughnessy, "China's Western Indian Ocean Step Up", *Australian Institute of*

International Affairs, 16 October 2023 at https://www.internationalaffairs.org.au/australianoutlook/chinas-western-indian-ocean-step-up/. (Accessed 22 December 2023).

21 Abhishek Mishra, *India-Africa Maritime Cooperation: The Case of Western Indian Ocean*, ORF Occasional Paper 221, Observer Research Foundation, November 2019 at https://www.orfonline.org/wp-content/uploads/2019/11/ORF_OccasionalPaper_221_India-Africa-Maritime.pdf. (Accessed 13 December 2023).

22 Abhijit Singh, "Reenergizing India-Africa Maritime Relations", IDSA Comment, 28 October 2015, Institute for Defence Studies and Analyses, New Delhi: India, at https://idsa.in/idsacomments/reenergising-india-africa-maritime-relations_asingh_281015. (Accessed 13 December 2023).

23 Abhishek Mishra, no. 221.

24 Listening stations and posts are essentially monitoring stations. They are fitted with radars and surveillance gear for monitoring maritime communications.

25 "Why does Mauritius have an Indian security advisor?", *Firstpost*, 5 October 2023 at https://www.firstpost.com/opinion/vantage-why-does-mauritius-have-an-indian-security-advisor-13202682.html. (Accessed 16 December 2023).

26 David Brewster, "Modi builds India's sphere of influence in the Indian Ocean", *The Interpreter,* Lowy Institute, 17 March 2015 at https://www.lowyinstitute.org/the-interpreter/modi-builds-india-s-sphere-influence-indian-ocean. (Accessed 16 December 2023).

27 United Nations General Assembly, *Convention on the Law of the Sea*, 10 December 1982 athttps://www.un.org/depts/los/convention_agreements/texts/unclos/unclos_e.pdf. (Accessed 16 December 2023).

28 "Anti-Piracy Operations, Gulf of Aden Deployment" at https://www.indiannavy.nic.in/content/anti-piracy-operations-gulf-aden-deployment/page/0/1. (Accessed 13 December 2023).

29 "Indian warship to ensure security to African Summit", *Times of India*, 4 July 2003 at https://timesofindia.indiatimes.com/india/indian-warships-to-ensure-security-to-african-summit/articleshow/60159.cms. (Accessed 19 December 2023).

30 Timothy Walker and Denys Reva, "Is Somali piracy finally under control?", *Institute for Security Studies*, 21 April 2022 at https://issafrica.org/iss-today/is-somali-piracy-finally-under-control. (Accessed 22 December 2023).

31 Maritime Domain Awareness has been defined by the International Maritime Organization. Definition premised on "effective understanding" of anything associated with the maritime domain which may impact the security, safety, economy, or the environment. MDA is a nations' ability to gather, process, analyse, and share real time information about what is occurring at sea.

32 Information Fusion Centre-Indian Ocean Region (IFC-IOR) at https://www.indiannavy.nic.in/ifc-ior/. (Accessed 19 December 2023).

33 White shipping means sharing and exchange of advance information regarding identity and movement of non-military commercial vessels. There is a particular colour code for ships. White is the colour code for commercial vessels whereas grey is for military vessels, and illegal ships are coded as black. After a White Shipping information agreement is signed between two nations, they are then able to share data about commercial vessels.

34 "International Cooperation", National Hydrographic Office 2023, at https://hydrobharat.gov.in/international-co-operation/. (Accessed 19 December 2023).

35 Leaza Jernberg, *The Great Game is Afloat: Africa and Indian Ocean Geopolitics*, Africa Report No. 40, *Institute for Security Studies*, October 2022 at https://issafrica.s3.amazonaws.com/site/uploads/AR-40.pdf. (Accessed 22 December 2023).

36 Christian Bueger and Jan Stockbruegger, "Maritime security and the Western Indian Ocean's

Militarisation Dilemma", *African Security Review* 31(2), 2022 at https://www.tandfonline.com/doi/full/10.1080/10246029.2022.2053556. (Accessed 22 December 2023).

37 Ibid.

38 "Violence at Sea: How Terrorists, Insurgents, and other Extremists Exploit the Maritime Domain," *Stable Seas*, One Earth Foundation, August 2020 at https://www.stableseas.org/post/violence-at-sea-how-terrorists-insurgents-and-other-extremists-exploit-the-maritime-domain. (Accessed 28 December 2023).

39 Rahul Singh, "Closely tracking Chinese presence in Indian Ocean, says navy chief", *Hindustan Times*, 1 December 2023 at https://www.hindustantimes.com/india-news/closely-tracking-chinese-presence-in-indian-ocean-says-navy-chief-101701437600606.html. (Accessed 22 December 2023).

40 Joshua T. White, "China's Indian Ocean Ambitions: Investments, Influence and Military Advantage", *Brookings*, April 2020 at https://www.brookings.edu/wp-content/uploads/2020/06/FP_20200615_chinas_indian_ocean_ambitions_white-1.pdf. (Accessed 22 December 2023).

41 Ajay Banerjee, "Indian Navy tracked Chinese 'survey' ship in Bay of Bengal for 36 days", *Tribune India*, 27 October 2023 at (Accessed 22 December 2023).

42 Dinakar Peri, "Chinese research vessels operating close to India's area of national interest pose a challenge: Navy Chief", *The Hindu*, 29 April 2023 at https://www.thehindu.com/news/national/large-presence-of-chinese-vessels-in-indian-ocean-region-india-keeping-close-watch-navy-chief/article66793087.ece. (Accessed 22 December 2023).

43 Srikant B. Kesnur and Abhishek Mishra, "India's Maritime Agenda Pivots to Western Indian Ocean", ORF Issue Brief No. 576, *Observer Research Foundation*, September 2022, at https://www.orfonline.org/research/india-s-maritime-agenda-pivots-to-western-indian-ocean. (Accessed 28 December 2023).

44 "Text of PM's remarks on the Commissioning of Coast Ship Barracuda", *Press Information Bureau*, Government of India and Prime Minister's Office, 12 March 2015 at https://www.pib.gov.in/newsite/erelcontent.aspx?relid=116881. (Accessed 28 December 2023).

45 Dipanjan Roy Chaudhury, "India, France explore 3rd country projects in Western Indian Ocean region", *The Economic Times*, 24 October 2019 at https://economictimes.indiatimes.com/news/defence/india-france-explore-3rd-country-projects-in-western-indian-ocean-region/articleshow/71743985.cms. (Accessed 2 January 2023).

46 Dinakar Peri, "India, France carry out second joint patrol in Southern Indian Ocean", *The Hindu*, 16 May 2022 at https://www.thehindu.com/news/national/india-france-carry-out-second-joint-patrol-in-southern-indian-ocean/article65419890.ece. (Accessed 2 January 2023).

47 "21st Edition India France Bilateral Naval Exercise 'Varuna' – 2023", at https://indiannavy.nic.in/content/21st-edition-india-france-bilateral-naval-exercise-%E2%80%98varuna%E2%80%99-%E2%80%93-2023-0#:~:text=The%20first%20phase%20of%20'Varuna,India%2DFrance%20strategic%20bilateral%20relationship. (Accessed 2 January 2023).

48 "Participation of *INS Trikand* in International Maritime Exercise/Cutlass Express 23 (IMX/CE-23)", *Press Information Bureau*, 10 March 2023 at https://pib.gov.in/PressReleaseIframePage.aspx?PRID=1905563#:~:text=With%20long%20reach%20and%20a,wide%20spectrum%20of%20naval%20operations.&text=by%20PIB%20Delhi-,INS%20Trikand%20participated%2 0in%20Sea%20Phase%2DI%20of%20the%20International,05%20to%2009%20March%202023. (Accessed 2 January 2023).

49 Abhishek Mishra, "Exercise Cutlass 2021: Prospects of alignment of Indo-U.S. interests in the Western Indian Ocean", *Observer Research Foundation*, 9 August 2021 at http://20.244.136.131/expert-speak/exercise-cutlass-2021. (Accessed 2 January 2023).

6

Enhancing Energy Access in Africa through Renewable Energy Development: Successes, Challenges and Prospects

Benard Muok

Introduction

Energy gives life to economic and social development: it lies at the basis of household activities, food production, transportation, health, education and security. Yet, out of the world's estimated 1.5 billion people who live without electricity access and 2.4 billion who rely on traditional cooking fuels, more than 95 per cent are either in sub-Saharan African (SSA) or developing Asia and 84 per cent are in rural areas.[1] Sub-Saharan Africa remains the region with the highest energy poverty in the world making the region to miss modern energy services, which are crucial to human well-being and economic development. Although investment in modern energy supply (pre-dominantly electricity) is on the rise in the region, these gains are outpaced by the population growth. To date more than 620 million people in Africa still live without access to electricity and nearly 730 million people use hazardous, inefficient forms of cooking with severe impact on health as well as being a major contributor to environmental degradation.[2]

According to the New Climate Economy working paper that contributed to the Africa Progress Panel 2015 report, the reliance on traditional biomass for cooking in sub-Saharan Africa results in 600,000 lives lost annually due to exposure to biomass smoke. Reliance on biomass for cooking continues to increase with high population growth outstripping clean energy access options. The economic impacts of this are astounding with $36.9 billion per year or 2.8 per cent of GDP including $29.6 billion lost due to time spent in collecting firewood.[3] The situation not only makes Africa less competitive in the global market, but also has a negative impact on the Human Development Index (HDI) such as life expectancy, education, and per capita income. According to recent World Bank report, approximately 200 million Africans live between the international poverty benchmarks of USD 1.25 and USD 2.00 per day.[4]

Sub-Saharan Africa is rich in energy resources especially renewable energy resources such as solar, wind, geothermal, biomass. The solar radiation climatology of Africa is such that more than half of the continent has solar radiation intensities of more than 7000 kWh/m2/day. The hydropower resource of the continent is huge especially in the central and eastern parts of the continent with the Grand Inga of Democratic Republic of Congo alone having a potential of about 50,000 MW. There is a significant geothermal potential along the East African Rift Valley spanning Djibouti, Ethiopia, Kenya and Tanzania. High-wind potentials exist along the coastal and mountainous parts of the continent. Biomass in the form of fuelwood is the dominant fuel in the household sector in the whole continent and most especially in the tropical zones. There is vast land for biofuel production in most African countries. Despite this potential the region has very poor energy supply, making the region to have highest access deficit in electrification rate, only just managing to stay abreast of population growth.

Making reliable and affordable energy widely available is therefore, critical to the development of the region that accounts for 13 per cent of the world's population and only 4 per cent of its energy demand.[5] Renewable energy technologies have the potential to significantly enhance energy access thus, contributing to economic and social development of Africa where many communities live in isolated areas with no access to electricity or to clean water, primary health care, education and other basic services, all of which are largely dependent on access to electricity. Despite the advantages that increased use of renewable resources such as solar could potentially bring to the country in terms of energy access to spur rural development, the uptake continues to be low due to barriers such as technological, economic, financial, market, public acceptance, infrastructural as well as legal and administrative barriers.

As with other SSA countries, Kenya is endowed with vast renewable energy (RE) resources, which can be exploited to enhance energy access especially to the poor, most of who are not connected to the national grid. Most of renewable energy sources are based in rural areas therefore, their production and use could be is especially beneficial in rural areas where such projects can contribute to agricultural and infrastructure development, health and education services, communications and small business enterprise. Further, unlike grid electricity that can only be used where connection makes economic sense, renewable energy wind, solar, woody and non-woody biomass and small hydros can be used for both on-grid and off-grid systems. Despite the potential of renewable energy, Kenya's electricity generation is currently based on large-scale hydropower, fossil fuels, and geothermal, while other renewable energy sources play only a minor role.[6]

The Kenyan solar market is one of the most advanced in Eastern Africa, and indeed in Africa. Traced back through the 1980s, it is one of the classic examples of a market driven technology adoption led by the private sector. It is estimated that the overall solar market has increased by more than 100 per cent in Kenya with an estimated 300,000 solar home systems (SHS) installed and generating about 8-10MWp.[7] Lighting Africa sales results collated from manufacturers of quality tested products indicates that over 2.2 million units of solar lighting products have been sold in Kenya since 2009 and expected to grow to over 2.7 million by 2016.[8] While solar market continues to grow rapidly to the level that is now considered as playing a big role in enhancing energy access especially in the rural areas of Kenya, there is no doubt that a large segment of the population, especially the poor, have been left out or at best forced to rely on poor and counterfeit products due to the high cost of buying quality solar solutions.

On the other hand, most of the African improved cookstoves sector emerged in the 1980s. Kenya was a leading country in this, which led to the development of the Kenyan Ceramic Jiko (KCJ). Since then, countless stakeholders in various countries have developed numerous types of stoves to address both urban and rural communities. However, despite this concerted effort, penetration rates show that there is still much to be done. In East

Africa, Global Alliance Clean Cookstoves' East Africa Regional Analysis (2012) indicates that Uganda and Tanzania show particular room for improvement with estimated penetration rates of 8.4 per cent and 5 per cent respectively, compared to 36% for Kenya and 50% for Rwanda.[9] However, penetration is not the only consideration. The overall quality of stoves; fuels savings, emissions reduction and durability, are equally important. Many of these countries face similar challenges to scaling up the improved stove sector and increasing improved cook stoves (ICS) adoption. Affordability of quality stoves, low demand and consumer awareness in certain rural areas, expanding distribution networks, accessing finance for working capital and improving the overall quality of stoves in the market are common challenges present across East Africa. This situation has restricted the growth of both the sector and businesses with it, making it difficult for many producers to commercialize at scale. This chapter will attempt to explore the achievements and barriers to achieving energy access in Africa by using the Kenya case study and its recent development in solar market and improved cook stoves.

Low Capacity for Local Manufacturing

Manufacturing is widely believed as a basis of economic development of a country. Literally, no country has been able to achieve growth and accumulate wealth without developing a strong manufacturing industry. Though Africa has been slow to adopting manufacturing, the truth is that the continent must invest in manufacturing to spur industrialisation. While improved cookstove market has been led by a strong push for locally manufactured products, the same cannot be said about solar. In the solar sector, there are very small steps towards local manufacturing. For example, in Kenya, there are only two companies involved in some form of production. Solinc East Africa is known to locally assemble solar panels. Sunlight designs its products in Kenya, but, gets them manufactured in China due to technological setbacks.

On the cookstoves side, despite the gains in local manufacturing of cookstoves, major grey areas still exist. Discussion on the topic must focus on the quality of locally manufactured stoves compared to imported stoves. In general, imported cookstoves that are designed in engineering labs and are industrially manufactured offer better fuel efficiency and lower emissions than artisanal stoves. A recent technical assessment found that centrally produced stoves outranked artisanal stoves both in emissions and efficiency.[10] Imported stoves may also be perceived as holding higher prestige, leading to increased adoption rates despite their higher cost when compared with domestically produced stoves. Despite the said advantages of imported stoves, locally produced technologies offer other advantages, which merit consideration. Artisanal stoves are more likely to rely upon regionally available material and manufacturing capacities. Local manufacturing engenders community stove production networks (often trained by NGOs and aid organizations) which increases opportunities for skilled labour and faster rates of repair and maintenance services.[11] The big question is how to promote local manufacturing at the same time ensuring high quality? Can quality assurance and design standardization be sufficiently achieved when stoves are locally produced?

Among the challenges facing local manufacturing are high cost of money especially for startup companies and high cost of land. In addition, expensive and unreliable electricity supply adds to high cost of production not to mention the bureaucracy involved in setting up business and getting necessary documentation. Other issues that are worth considering include low capacity of both human capital and infrastructure as bottleneck in local manufacturing and low funding of science technology and innovation. These have further limited innovation and commercialization of research and development outputs.

Access to Renewable Energy Technology

Renewable energy projects are not just capital-intensive investments; they also require the transfer of technology and knowledge. While Africa has made strides in technological development, there still exists a big gap with the other continents. Most renewable energy technology still belongs to the developed world. With technology ownership still dominated by the developed countries and protected by intellectual property, local manufacturing in Africa cannot thrive. In Kenya, for example, pico solar products of two companies Sunlight Products and Mibawa are being designed in Kenya however, their manufacturing is being done in China due to patenting of moulds in China, which limits Kenya from manufacturing the products in the country. The situation is not unique to Kenya but is replicated in several other African counties. The disadvantage of this is not only that it is denying Africa job creation in the green energy sector, but also has a reflection in the pricing of the products often beyond the purchasing power of the poor and the population at the bottom of the pyramid. The big question is how can IP work for Africa and not against Africa?

Distribution Models

The growing interest in energy access generated by the United Nations Sustainable Energy for All initiative (SEforAll) and the Sustainable Development Goals (SDG) has seen many players enter the renewable market including the civil society, government and other development agents. Due to this increasing interest and expansion of the market, different distribution models are being employed with varying rate of success or lack of it. This paper discusses two models (1) Community based energy, and (2) ICT driven pay-as-you-go (PAYG).

The community energy centres has become popular in many areas of Africa especially areas not connected to the national grid. The system is mainly based on an off-grid system. The Centre consists of mounted solar panels often up to 250 KW generation capacities where portable solar lanterns are charged and rented to the surrounding communities. The centre could also have out computer services such as typing, printing and photocopying and a social hall with a connection to channel television network. The University of Oslo in collaboration with the Energy Resource Institute (TERI), African Centre for Technology Studies and other local partners established such a system in Ikisaya village in Kitui County, Eastern Kenya.

The use of informal market instrument, a system whereby end consumers of a product can pay for a product in several installments, would help to broaden access to renewable energy systems. Due to the low-income status of the African society, many people are unable to pay full amount for a solar water heater or photovoltaic or other renewable energy facilities in a single installment. Allowing them to spread the payment over a period of time (six months to one year or even longer) would be helpful. A number of NGOs, the private sector and financial institutions are employing this system to scale-up renewable energy markets, which would help to increase access to these facilities and consequently more modern energy services. For large scale electricity generation using renewable technology, a hire-purchase type of agreement, underwritten by development bank(s) or similar institutions, but with interest of no more than 3 per cent per annum have been tried. The advent of ICT driven innovation in marketing has further given more options especially for the poor who cannot afford the cost of technology by giving them options of instalment payment or pay-as-you-go (PAYG). M-KOPA products are one of the well-established systems employing PAYG. While this can be classified as a success case, the ongoing discourse is questioning if the products are really cheap in the long run.

Consumer Capacity and Awareness

While scholars have always argued that low penetration of clean energy is associated with high poverty levels in Africa, lessons learnt from development of mobile phone market in Africa gives a different picture. The rapid adoption of mobile phones in some of the poorest countries in the world has far exceeded expectations. Mobile phone subscriptions on the continent have risen from 16 million in 2000 to 376 million in 2008.[12] This suggests that the problem may not be poverty per se, considering that at least 50 per cent of the entire populations in 38 of the 49 sub-Saharan countries live without electricity, the question is why are the same poor Africa population able to acquire mobile phone sets but not solar lanterns? These are issues that need to be addressed by the industry players with a view to coming up with long-term strategies. One could argue that the packaging of the message to consumers needs to be thought through to identify the real issues that will appeal to consumers.

Awareness, perceptions and user expectations regarding use, benefits and impact of renewable energy is a prerequisite for adoption and sustained use. Solar solutions for example, offer several benefits to consumer including income and fuel savings. A question that need to be asked is does the consumer understand the 'triple benefits' (economic, social and environmental) including their role in household health, livelihoods, local environmental quality and regional climate benefits? The proposers of renewable energy solutions must bring out this message at a level that the customers can identify with. We have to look at the benefits from the consumers' perspectives and not ours. Consumers seldom adopt innovations without good reasons.

Related to this is the consumer capacity to understand and use the products. Most of the products such as solar and cookstoves come without instruction to users including maintenance and after sale services. This means that the consumers may not always be handling the products properly resulting in breakages, and in the absence of after sale services these products are often disposed of before their intended life span. The other issue to do with awareness is the ability to discern counterfeit and genuine products. The influx of solar products in the market for example, has led to growth of high number of counterfeit products. With the low capacity to differentiate between counterfeit and genuine products, the consumers are left exposed and this could hurt the market in the long run when they lose faith in the products.

Policy Framework and Political Good Will

There is need to develop a comprehensive strategy, policy and investment programme for a transition to the use of sustainable energy. Considering that this is an urgent need, the policies need to have clear targets and timeline for monitoring achievement. Such a system should be anchored on the use of renewable energy and energy efficiency. Such policies should be driven by the state in partnership with private sector and active civil society participation. In addition, there should be the formulation of comprehensive sustainable energy and trade policy for renewable energy technologies and strategies for the implementation of energy policies. Suffice to mention that there has been a strong move among the African countries to formulate energy polices in the past few years. However, more often these policies are not fully implemented. Many policies in the past have passed their implementation life in the shelves of senior government officials. New policies should address all issues such trade, production, distribution, consumption, investment in renewable energy and end-use and demand-side energy efficiency. There is need for a paradigm shift in energy development.

Policy consideration should involve: putting in place market and fiscal policies that promote renewable energy; promote open energy markets to remove legislative and commercial barriers to entry and promote transparent competition in supply and; Promote non-electricity producing renewables e.g. cooking is the main energy need of the poor and this will not change even when electricity becomes available. Promotion of improved cook stoves, small-scale biogas for cooking, solar thermal technologies

Policy plays a central role in driving deployment of renewable energy market. These policies must be long-term and predictable to create confidence in the market. Policies that change after a short period are most likely to compromise investors' confidence. For example most of the Feed-in Tariff (FiT) Policies in Africa are often blamed for low investment in renewable energy. For example, Kenyan was formulated to promote renewable energy solutions (incl. wind, biomass, small hydro, geothermal, biogas and solar and municipal waste energy) in 2008 and revised in 2010 and 2012. Under the FiT system, investment security and market stability for investors in electricity generation from renewable energy solutions is provided whilst encouraging private investors to operate their power plants prudently and efficiently to maximize returns.

Policy environment needs to include a strong regulatory framework and institutions including standards to ensure even playing field to the sector players. Influx of counterfeit products in the market is blamed on lack of standards and/or weak regulatory enforcement. Together with policies, there is need for strong political goodwill to mainstream renewable energy in the country's economy. This should be reflected from the National Budget Policy to the local government structures. Many a time, the budget for energy development focuses mainly on the large power production project and renewable energy receives only lip services from the leaders.

Waste Management

Scholars are in agreement that renewable energy such as solar power facilities reduces the environmental impacts of combustion used in fossil fuel power generation, such as impacts from greenhouse gases and other air pollution emissions. Unlike fossil fuel power generating facilities, solar facilities have very low air emissions of air pollutants such as sulphur dioxide, nitrogen oxides, carbon monoxide, volatile organic compounds, and the greenhouse gas carbon dioxide during operations. In addition to these benefits of solar development, construction and operation of solar facilities creates both direct and indirect employment and additional income in the regions where the development occurs.

Solar modules have an expected lifespan of at least 20 years so most of the systems in Africa have not yet reached the end of their useful lives. With ever increasing solar product entering the market, it is a matter of time before e-waste becomes an environmental threat. Recycling of solar panels may face issues, specifically, there are not enough locations to recycle old solar panels, and there are not enough non-operational solar panels to make recycling them economically attractive. Recycling of solar panels is particularly important because the materials used to make the panels are rare or precious metals, all of them being composed of silver, tellurium, or indium. Due to the limitability of recycling the panels, these recoverable metals are likely to go waste, which may result in resource scarcity issues in the future.

There is need to consider extended producer and stakeholder responsibility that will aid the take-back-schemes for solar products that are no longer in use. This should be considered hand-in-hand with design for disassembly so that it becomes easier to promote recovery, reuse, and recycling. The lack of awareness regarding the manufacturing process of solar panels and the issue of recycling these, as well as the absence of much external pressure, are the causes of the insufficiency in driving significant change in the recycling of the materials used in solar panel manufacturing, a business that, from a power-generation standpoint, already has great environmental credibility. Some legal and regulatory frameworks on management of E-waste already exist in some counties. These frameworks are, however, inadequate and poorly enforced therefore there is need for enforcement of the frameworks, as well as revising them to match with the current trends. E-waste management board should be established to implement guidelines on E-waste management

Role of International Cooperation

In recent years, many global summits have been working to raise awareness on the negative consequences of global warming, focusing on the reduction of CO_2 emissions. Indeed, it seems that the most rapid way to reduce the production of greenhouse gases is to adopt clean energy technologies, and alternatives to fossil fuels. The Kyoto Protocol (1997) represented the first attempt to divide the effort and monetary costs of this research among its adhering nations, specifying aims and rules for each of them. Later, the Paris Climate Change Conference (COP21 in 2015) marked a strong commitment of 196 countries to combat climate change; they acknowledged the risks climate change poses to the global environment and committed to adopting alternative energy sources. One of the important outcome of the Dubai Climate Change meeting (COP28 in 2023) was a first time acknowledgement of the need to move away from fossil fuels.[13]

Developing countries currently host 80 per cent of the global population. By 2035, their economic development is projected to drive them to account for 70 per cent of the world's energy demand. Renewable energy projects are not just capital-intensive investments; they also require the transfer of technology and knowledge. With high level of poverty and low gross domestic product (GDP), developing countries can hardly afford to invest significantly in renewable energy. Through political cooperation, nations with more experience at reducing emissions could assist other countries in creating strategies to do so as well, and may be able to provide technical and financial assistance to weaker economies.

South-South Cooperation

There have been significant changes in Africa recent years in terms of the development co-operation and partnerships. While in the past Africa looked to the North for all its development needs, in the recent years South-South Cooperation (SSC) is increasingly playing an important role in Africa trade and economic development. South-South investment has also shown unprecedented dynamism in the last decade. In summary, Africa's total trade with non-African developing countries increased from US$34 billion in 1995 to US$97 billion in 2004, and then jumped to US$283 billion in 2008 and US$595 billion in 2012.[14] This is an enormous increase taking place at a time when there is a decline in the African trade with the North.

This positive trend of South-South Cooperation has been recorded primarily in the increased inflows of resources, especially to the benefit of African countries. Despite this, many states also face major challenges because of increased dependence on raw materials and the greater pressure of competition from other countries in the South in the case of light manufactures. The challenges for Africa in SSC seem to revolve around Africa's haphazard approach to development. The effect has been the failure to develop relevant institutions in Africa, both technical and academic, to facilitate and deepen and benefit more substantially from these partnerships.

Strong policy and legal and institutional framework that could govern and promote their interests in partnerships beyond political dialogue and engagement is necessary if Africa has to achieve a level playing group. The current scenario shows Africa has to fully invest in South-South partnerships. Most of the efforts to date to improve these partnerships across the board appear to have been left to non-Africa partners. The stronger Southern partners from outside Africa seem to fully fund and finance the partnerships, rather than work through joint ventures. In the end, SSC partnerships seem to strengthen the visibility of the provider, rather than be based on mutual interest of the partnerships.

Technology Transfer

Technical knowledge developed in more experienced countries can be transferred to and used by new partner states. Developing countries could address the IP issues and consider how this could be of support to their acquisition of technology rather than being an impediment.

Level the Playing Field for the Renewable Energy Industry

In order to maximize the full potential of renewable energy, the markets need to be redesigned to support its development. Redirect trade policy toward supporting renewable energy technologies (such as reducing import duties on RE equipment).

Removal of Import Tariffs and other Trade Barriers

On short-term bases, the reduction or as appropriate elimination of tariffs and non-tariff barriers on renewable energy facilities may help to stimulate the nascent renewable energy industry in Africa. This should be done in a way to protect local industries. More importantly, emphasis should be laid on strengthening the production capacity of renewable energy facilities; putting in place measures to reduce the burden of high cost of energy and promoting investments on renewable energies.

Training of African Personnel

Training of African personnel on renewable energy technologies is an important factor that would help to scale-up renewable energy market in the continent. This would help to minimise the over-reliance on foreign experts in the installations and maintenance of renewable energy technologies, consequently helping to reduce the cost of renewable energy services.

Global Fund

There is a need to champion and support the development of international financial instruments that support renewable energy and energy efficiency. There is also a need for innovative financing mechanisms to fully transition from a carbon-based economy with suggestions including the Tobin Tax and Carbon Taxes going toward renewable energy programmes.

The South-South Cooperation Trust Fund (SSCTF) is one example of a financing mechanism. Largely funded by the government of Brazil, the SSCTF seeks to support African countries in mobilising and taking advantage of development solutions and technical expertise available in the South. The Fund also seeks to promote South-South partnerships and knowledge sharing among middle-income countries (MICs) and between MICs and least-developed countries (LDCs) in Africa. The Fund's focus areas include agriculture and agri-business, health, social development and clean energy. It supports: Provision of technical assistance in the preparation of policy and sector studies, research and analysis; Capacity-building and human resources development; Organisation of seminars, workshops, conferences and consultations and sharing of knowledge and experiences; and Implementation and piloting of innovative approaches to solve development challenges in African countries.

Conclusion

While there exist regional and international processes to support renewable energy development that Africa could take advantage of, the absence of African governments' policies on partnership development strategies, alongside the absence of mechanisms to coordinate the activities of different implementing agencies, make it difficult for African countries to pursue mutual partnerships in a comprehensive manner. Many countries appear to be guided by political statements and directives from those in position of power with no policy and institutional framework. In cases where such policies exist, there has been slow and non-implementation of the policies. Africa needs to focus its effort to benefit from the increasing trade relationship with the non-African developing countries to develop its renewable energy resources while embracing the international processes and support from the North.

NOTES

1 'International Atomic Energy Agency Energy poverty,' at http://www.iea.org/topics/energypoverty/ (Accessed 30 March 2017).
2 G.O. Young, "Synthetic Structure of Industrial Plastics" in *Plastics*, 2nd ed. Vol. 3, New York: McGraw-Hill, 1964, pp. 15–64.
3 'Power, People, Planet: Seizing Africa's Energy and Climate Opportunities,' Africa's Progress Report 2015, at https://www.seforall.org/sites/default/files/l/2015/06/APP_REPORT_2015_FINAL_low1.pdf (Accessed 09 March 2024).
4 'World Bank World Development Indicators (WDI) (database),' World Bank, Washington, DC., 2014.
5 'Africa Energy Outlook 2022', World Energy Outlook Special Report, at https://www.iea.org/reports/africa-energy-outlook-2022 (Accessed 09 March 2024).
6 'Draft Energy and Petroleum Policy 2015', at https://repository.kippra.or.ke/bitstream/handle/123456789/621/The%20National%20Energy%20and%20Petroleum%20%20%20Policy%202015.pdf?sequence=1&isAllowed=y (Accessed 09 March 2024).
7 Benard O. Muok and Willis Bernard Makokha, 'Accelerating Energy Access to the Rural Poor in Kenya through Pico-Solar Market Development', *International Journal of New Technology and Research (IJNTR),* Vol. 3, Issue 10, 2017, pp. 37-44.
8 Lighting Africa, Off-grid Solar Market Trends Report, 2016, at https://www.energynet.co.uk/webfm_send/1690, (Accessed 20 March 2017).
9 'East Africa Regional Intervention Options Executive Summary', at https://cleancooking.org/binary-data/RESOURCE/file/000/000/182-1.pdf (Accessed 09 March 2024)
10 J. Jetter, et. al., "Pollutant Emissions and Energy Efficiency under Controlled Conditions for Household Biomass Cookstoves and Implications for Metrics Useful in Setting International Test Standards", *Environmental Science And Technology*, Vol. 46, 2012, pp. 10827-10834
11 Gregory L. Simon, et al. 'Current debates and future research needs in the clean cookstove sector', *Energy for Sustainable Development,* Vol. 20 2014, pp. 49–57.
12 Jenny C. Aker and Isaac M. Mbiti, 'Mobile Phones and Economic Development in Africa', Journal of Economic Perspectives', Vol. 24, No. 3, 2020, pp. 207-32.
13 Amitabh Sinha, "COP28: What were the most important decisions, where they fell" short *Indian Express,* December 15, 2023 at https://indianexpress.com/article/explained/explained-climate/cop28-what-were-the-most-important-decisions-where-they-fell-short-9067358/ (Accessed 16 December 2023)
14 'Making South-South Cooperation Partnerships Work for Africa: A situational analysis and policy recommendations Vitalice Meja Reality of Aid Africa', at https://www.realityofaid.org/wp-content/uploads/2014/12/4.Making-South-South-Cooperation-Partnerships.pdf (Accessed 09 March 2024).

7

Energising the India-Africa Partnership

Shebonti Ray Dadwal

Energy plays an important role as a scale of economic and social development and as a basic humanitarian need. In fact, the per capita consumption of energy of a country is regarded as an important indicator of economic development. Unlike a decade or two ago, when the developed countries were the largest consumers of energy, today, the emerging economies, particularly in Asia, are witnessing increases in their economic growth – as well as energy consumption. Today, some of the countries with the largest populations currently without electricity are in Asia and Africa, including Nepal, Nigeria, Ethiopia, Côte d'Ivoire, Democratic Republic of Congo, Bangladesh and Afghanistan. India, despite an impressive of installed power generation capacity at 4,11,650 MW as of February 2023, and claims to have provided electricity to 99 per cent of its people, faces power deficit in several areas because of the intermittency of power generation as well as growing demand due to fast-paced economic growth. Sub-Saharan Africa too has seen rapid economic growth over the last decade with a concomitant growth in the demand for energy which has risen by 45 per cent. But with the lack of adequate energy infrastructure holding back development and living standards, many African governments are intensifying their efforts to tackle the regulatory and political barriers that are holding back investment in domestic energy supply.[1] At the same time, the impact of global warming and climate change – due largely to the use of fossil fuels – is making its presence felt, as with increasing incidence of rising sea levels, floods, hurricanes and storms wreaking havoc in many parts of the world. Unsurprisingly, the impact of these weather-related disasters is felt most in the developing world.

While these countries face a definite disadvantage due to energy poverty, they also have the option to develop their energy sectors without traversing the traditional fossil fuel route taken by most developed countries. This is particularly pertinent in the case of Africa, which is yet to take the massive leap towards development. Despite having some of world's energy resources – both in terms of fossil fuels as well as renewable energy – With nearly a fifth of the global population and accounting for only 3 per cent of carbon emissions, Africa as a continent is facing a disproportionate and negative effects of climate change, an indication of its consumption of traditional energy resources, along with reduced food production and low economic growth.[2]

Like Africa, India too has, albeit belatedly, realised the pitfalls of being a fossil fuel dependent country, both in terms of global energy geopolitics as well as environmental pollution and the impact of climate change. While India has been pushing to increase the share of clean energy for several years now, the current government has made it a policy goal to accelerate the pace of increasing the share of energy derived from renewable and clean energy resources, and has achieved with substantial progress in the same. Within a short span of time, India has succeeded in ramping up the share of renewable energy in installed power generation capacity to more than 40 per cent. While the overall renewable energy capacity was around 6.4 MW per year in 2005,[3] it has now reached 168,400 GW in 2023.[4] Moreover, it has committed to not only reducing its carbon emissions by 30-35 per cent by 2030 from 2005 levels and achieve net zero emissions by 2070, but is also looking to increasing the renewable energy capacity to 500 GW by 2030, which is expected to meet 50 per cent of the energy requirements, besides reducing cumulative emissions by one billion tonnes by 2030.[5] Hence, India, with its experience, is in a favourable position to assist African nations in their goal to achieve energy security through non-traditional energy sources.

According to the International Energy Agency (IEA), at present, 600 million people, or 43 per cent of the total population of Africa, lack access to electricity, most of them in sub-Saharan Africa, compared to 75 per cent in developed countries.[6] Therefore, in order to achieve economic development, all these countries need robust energy policies as without energy, there can be no agricultural, industrial or technological development. Moreover, access to electricity is a prerequisite for overcoming poverty and enabling nations to improve their health and education infrastructure. According to World Bank estimates, if sub-Saharan Africa's economies had dependable electricity, the GDP growth across the region could be up to 2 per cent higher per annum than current rates. Moreover, Africa is seen as an excellent home for grid scale and mini-grid power projects to reach all 1.2 billion of its inhabitants.[7]

The spread of renewable energy has the potential to change the nature of global geopolitics. Not only has the overwhelming use of fossil fuels impact on the environment, and increase incidences of drought and famine, hydrocarbons, particularly oil, has been a major factor in conflicts since the end of World War II, but also international oil majors, backed by their sovereign governments, have vied to gain control of oil production, supply and markets. On the other hand, renewable energy, due to its abundant availability and potential for decentralisation, lends itself to cooperation among states by encouraging regional grid integration.[8] For example, renewable energy micro and mini-grids have a huge potential to expand reliable electrification in thousands of remote villages which are not connected to the national grids.

The African Energy Scenario

According to the World Bank, if sub-Saharan Africa's economies had dependable electricity, the GDP growth across the region could be up to 2 per cent higher per annum than current rates. Overall, Africa's economic growth is also increasing, and is estimated to be 3.2 per cent in 2018, albeit with considerable variations between countries. Sub-Saharan African economies are expected to grow at 3.3 per cent in 2018, and 3.5 per cent in 2019, up from 2.5 per cent in 2017. The continent also hosts six of the world's fastest growing economies. As a result, their demand for energy, which is essential for economic and social development, is set to increase. However, data from most countries in sub-Saharan Africa, with an average of less than 35 per cent electrification, against 86 per cent in South Africa and 99 per cent in North African countries, indicate that the level of electrification remains far below par, which in turn has a negative impact on their overall productivity. In the rural areas, the problem is even worse with the average electrification rate at 16 per cent, against 71 per cent in Southern Africa and 99 per cent in North African countries.[9] With an estimated 80 per cent of those without access to electricity living in rural areas, many of them with no nearby grid, electrification remains one of sub-Saharan Africa's biggest socio-economic challenges. Since it is clear that grid extensions cannot be seen as the sole, or even the primary, answer to providing electricity for all, distributed energy for smaller power generation and storage systems that are used to power homes, businesses and communities would be far more beneficial, sourcing generation from renewable energy sources such as solar, wind, and hydropower.

Ironically, while Africa as a whole has an abundance of natural resources – hydrocarbons and renewable energy, including hydropower, large parts of Africa's power sector remains under-developed. This is despite the fact that almost 30 per cent of global oil and natural gas discoveries made since 2009-2014 have been in sub-Saharan Africa, reflecting the growing global appetite for African resources. However, following the 2014 fall in oil and natural gas prices, and a similar drop in global energy demand following the COVID-19 pandemic, its impact on the energy value chain affected the profitability of the energy sector and consequently on the ability to repay debt requirements, given that several of the projects had been financed at a time when oil was ruling above $100 a barrel.[10] Moreover, regulatory uncertainty, militant conflict and oil theft in some of the more profitable production areas in Africa, such as the Niger Delta, have also contributed to production deterrence. Hence while a number of smaller African countries like South Sudan, Niger, Ghana, Uganda and Kenya have seen rising oil production, by the late 2020s, production in most countries – with the exception of Nigeria – is expected to decline, while demand for oil products is set to double over that time.[11]

Moreover, with the growing public awareness in global and regional climate change, African governments are increasingly focusing on environmental impact of energy use. For example, in May 2018, all 54 African countries signed the Paris Agreement, with 46 of them having ratified the Agreement and made nationally determined contributions (NDCs). A number of African countries have also been developing energy policies that seek to balance renewable energy resources with fossil fuels to achieve the lowest-cost source of reliable fuel. Over the past few years, a number of solar energy programmes have been developed across the continent, including Zambia,

Ethiopia, Senegal, Madagascar, South Africa and Morocco. Hydropower too represents around one-fifth of current electricity production in Africa, although that still accounts for a tenth of its potential.

Despite the huge opportunities and potential for developing clean, mainly renewable, including hydro, energy resources in Africa, a key challenge is capital costs. The required investment needs in the energy sector have been assessed at around $ 65-90 billion per annum, depending on the energy mix, according to a study by the African Development Bank, "Strategy for the new deal for Energy for Africa 2016-2025". Although the economics of renewable energy has improved significantly over the last few years, witnessing a massive fall in solar and wind generated power, they are still not competitive when compared with conventional energy, namely coal-based, power plants, particularly in countries with limited experience. Many also lack the appropriate investment and regulatory environment, as well as economically feasible tariff regimes, to attract private sector participation in renewable energy infrastructure.

Why India and Africa should Cooperate in Energy

India has had substantial cooperation in the energy sector with several African nations. However, these are largely with respect to hydrocarbons, with India either purchasing oil and gas, or investing in upstream hydrocarbon blocks in Africa. However, following the high discounted oil being purchased from Russia over the last year, Africa's share of India's oil import basket has dropped to its lowest since 2001 to 3.6 per cent[12] from around 16 per cent in 2017.[13] At the same time, bilateral trade, which was at its peak at $72 billion in 2014-15, has yet to reach the target of $100 billion.[14] But now with climate change concerns increasing the world over, and governments recognising the need to reduce dependence on fossil fuels, there is a need to go beyond trade in hydrocarbons to bolster and sustain relations between India and its African partners.

An important forum that can foster more cooperation between India and the African States is the International Solar Alliance (ISA). With the Indian government having adopted a leadership role in developing renewable energy, particularly solar energy, African countries are a major factor in India's renewable energy policy and the Ministry of New and Renewable Energy

(MNRE), has established bilateral cooperation with various African countries for the promotion of renewable energy, especially solar energy, wind, small hydro, biomass etc. At present, 34 African countries are members of the ISA, forming the largest contingent of the alliance. The exchanges in the solar sector between India and Africa are shaped by the fact that African states have the required resources but little of the technology, which provides the opportunity for a collaborative platform through the provision of technology, capacity building and employment generation. In 2020, India's National Thermal Power Corporation (NTPC) procured the Project Management Consultancy Contract to develop a 500 MW solar park in Mali and Togo, supporting the ISA through private investment, marking the first step for India towards acquiring a role in the solar sector in Africa. NTPC is also looking at similar opportunities in other African ISA member countries like Sudan, Mozambique, Gambia, Malawi, etc.[15]

In its Global Energy and CO_2 Status Report 2017, the International Energy Agency (IEA) states that the overall share of fossil fuels in global energy demand continued to remain at 81 per cent as it has for more than three decades, despite the strong growth in renewable energy. Renewable energy resources have grown as well, but make up around a quarter of global energy demand growth, while nuclear use accounted for 2 per cent of the growth. This has led to global CO_2 emissions reaching a historic high of 32.5 gigatonnes in 2017, after three years of flat emissions.[16]

According to the IEA's Renewables 2017 report, three countries have contributed the most to the growth in generation from renewable energy resources, namely, China, the US and India. The IEA has also stated that India's economic growth has contributed to its rising energy demand and this has in turn continued to drive up emissions, albeit at half the rate seen during the past decade. Hence the pressure to cut emissions is growing.

Not too long ago, India's power scenario was quite similar to many of those in Africa and other developing economies, with an overwhelming dependence on fossil fuels and poor access to grid generated electricity. However, over the years, India has succeeded in having the third largest installed generation capacity of a little under 412 GW. Nevertheless, several Indian households either still do not have access to electricity with low last mile connectivity, or have to undergo several hours of load shedding. Therefore, in order to achieve the goal of delivering 24x7 electricity to all, India will require huge amounts of energy.

Hence India requires to look for alternative and indigenous resources of energy. Since it did not have sufficient fossil fuels to satisfy its increasing demand without increasing dependence on hydrocarbon imports, renewables and other cleaner sources of energy was seen as the way to go. Moreover, there are the pressures to reduce carbon emissions under the commitments under the Paris Agreement.

According to estimates, India's solar potential is greater than 750 GW, while its wind potential is 302 GW,[17] with some estimates pegging the actual potential at more than 1000 GW. The potential of power generation from biomass and small hydro is also significant. Therefore renewable energy therefore has the potential to anchor the development of India's electricity sector, besides preventive huge revenue outflows for expensive imported fuels.

Over the past four years, India has seen a massive increase in its renewable energy-powered generation, which stands at around 168,400 GW, as on February 2023, or around 41 per cent of overall installed generation capacity. Moreover, renewable capacity in India is expected to more than double by 2030 with solar and wind representing 90 per cent of India's capacity growth, which is the result of auctions for contracts to develop power-generation capacity that have yielded some of the world's lowest prices for both technologies. Currently, India holds the fourth and sixth positions, respectively, in global wind and solar energy installed capacity. More importantly, it has one of the lowest per unit tariffs for both solar and wind power.

To resolve the issue of last mile connectivity to remote areas that cannot be connected to the grids, India is pushing to increase the share of off-grid power generation from renewable energy as well. Around 63 solar micro grids totalling 1.89 MW have been installed under the country's Solar Off-Grid and Decentralised Applications Programme, which targets those villages and areas which are unable to access grid-based power. The rooftop solar scheme under the Jawaharlal Nehru National Solar Mission (JNNSM) is another scheme for off-grid solutions. Moreover, under the off-grid renewable system, as of November 2022, solar projects of the capacity of 61.97 GW have been commissioned, of which the capacity of 61.97 GW includes 52 GW from ground-mounted solar projects, 7.82 GW from rooftop solar projects, and 2.09 GW from off-grid solar projects.[18]

In the case of wind energy, a total capacity addition of 1761.28 MW has been achieved from January to October 2022. Moreover, the government has brought out a roadmap for achieving 30 GW of offshore wind energy target by 2030.[19]

India's Africa Focus

In many ways, the challenges that face many of the African countries today, are similar to that of India – a growing population, low per capita consumption of energy, and rapid urbanisation, which leaves many people starved of access to modern forms of energy.

While Eastern Africa has been a traditional partner, India is now looking at other regions of Africa, including countries of Francophone Western Africa, as a significant development partner. Specifically with regard to cooperation in renewable energy, "India has announced solar energy projects in parts of Africa, in consultation with local governments, and is seeking to ensure effective implementation of its Line of Credit (LoC) of $1 billion." At the International Solar Alliance meet in Delhi on March 11, 2018, India extended the LoC specifically for 23 solar energy projects in 13 African countries, including Benin, Burkina Faso, Chad, Mali, Niger, Togo, Guinea, and Democratic Republic Congo in Central Africa, as well as its traditional partners, Ghana and Nigeria. Some of these countries will house more than one solar project. Other countries where specific solar projects are being executed include Seychelles, Tanzania and Rwanda. The goal is to also produce solar panels in India for these projects at rates which are cheaper than those made in other countries.

Ironically, Africa's importance in the world of hydrocarbon market has grown, as it is seen as an alternative source of supply from the politically turbulent Persian Gulf region, prompting many countries to turn towards African oil and gas. Furthermore, technological advances have made it easier to extract Africa's offshore oil reserves, which are lighter, sweeter, and lower in sulphur content, and hence cheaper to refine than the Middle East's sour crudes. Yet, this has not benefited most African countries, as its own energy resources are not used for internal consumption, but for generating revenues for individual regimes. Moreover, fossil fuel-based power generation is the most expensive form of energy, and has deep negative consequences for the environment.

In a 2015 survey of leading executives and companies in the sector throughout the continent, 70 per cent of the survey respondents said that there was a medium to high probability that advances and cost reductions in renewable off-grid technology will deliver an exponential increase in rural electrification levels by 2025, particularly where grid connectivity was difficult to access due to a variety of factors.

However, several challenges remain such as the shortage of proven business models, adequate and appropriate forms of financing, established supply chains and implementation capacity.

The irony is that Africa is very rich in energy resources but most of the energy potential on the continent is unexploited. Research by McKinsey found that Africa's potential energy generation capacity is up to 1.2 terawatts, excluding solar and more than 10 terawatts, including solar energy, which Africa has in abundance. The good news is that many parts of Africa have the opportunity of accessing renewable energy, without going through the fossil fuel powered history that other developed countries did, which can have a positive effect on its environment. According to the IEA, renewable energy will play an important role in Africa's energy mix in the coming years, with more than 25 per cent of Africa's total energy coming from renewable energy – geothermal, hydro, solar and wind – by 2040.

Hence, a partnership between India and the African countries would benefit both sides. Taking a leaf out of the development policy for Africa in other areas, India could provide the relevant experience and technical and financial resources to assist African countries in exploiting their untapped potential for renewable energy – be it solar, wind, non-storage hydropower, biomass, etc. Moreover, under the aegis of the International Solar Alliance, India, together with other members of the alliance and its African partners can expand the scope of solar energy in Africa, particularly for off-grid generation in rural areas.

Conclusion

Renewable energy, and solar PV in particular, has become a game changer especially in developing countries, particularly for areas which are not or cannot be connected to national grids. No doubt, the infrastructure will have to be put in place to incentivise development of the sector and this is where national governments have a large role to play in ensuring that this development occurs. Government policies will need to prepare the market for private investors and promote regional integration to enhance savings on capital spending.

Just as there has been increasing global recognition of the need to shift to a low-carbon economy, and a concurrent interest in clean technology, such as solar power and zero-emission vehicles, there is also a growing awareness that the manufacturing of renewable energy technologies, particularly for wind turbines and solar PV cells, will require metals such as aluminium, chromium copper, iron, lead, manganese, neodymium, nickel, steel, zinc, indium and silver. Africa has large reserves in several of these mineral resources, such as platinum, manganese, bauxite, and chromium. However, given that Africa has a history of being exploited as a source for minerals, both for non-renewable (including hydrocarbons) as well as renewable (in the future), countries with mineral potential should position themselves to use these judiciously for their own development.

India is a leader in renewable energy technology; more importantly, it shares a legacy with African nations with regard to the exploitative practices of colonialism. Hence, while India has emerged as a key market for Africa's abundant natural resources, it is also a source of investment, technology and capital goods, making India Africa's fourth largest trade partner. No doubt, its development assistance is less than other actors in Africa, such as China and the USoward Africa is based on the concept of development cooperation and partnership based on mutual benefit, which would make it less exploitative in nature. On the one hand, through its concessional credit lines, India offers alternative project financing options for African countries and on the other hand, it aims to create opportunities for Indian public and private sector companies to enter new markets.

Africa is quickly becoming one of the most significant regions in the global expansion of the solar PV industry. With several African countries joining the India-driven International Solar Alliance, the role of renewable energy, particularly solar energy, can be a major area of cooperation for both. While the African Development Bank has entered into a partnership with the ISA to provide power to 250 million Africans through its Desert to Power Solar Initiative, India has also decided to use about $2 billion of the $10 billion line of credit it has committed to Africa for renewable energy projects in these countries, which include Tanzania, Togo, Benin, Congo, Chad and the Seychelles. The idea is to marry Indian tech and finance capabilities with specific projects around the world, and teams of experts are being sent to these countries to prepare the projects and work out the details.

Hence, while the push for moving the world towards cleaner energy resources is on, the India-Africa partnership in energy cooperation can bring multiple dividends to both sides. Given India's achievements in renewable energy, it is in a favourable position to share its experience with partner countries. However, New Delhi should take care to ensure that its engagement with African nations is different from other external actors in Africa. Therefore, while trade and investments are important components of bilateral interaction, the emphasis should be on enhancing the peoples' productive capacities, enhancing knowledge and developing local skills. Moreover, the focus should be on decentralised energy development. And finally, India should commit to a long-term engagement with Africa. It is only then will a truly India-Africa partnership be successful.

NOTES

1 "Africa Energy Outlook: A Focus on Energy Prospects in Sub-Saharan Africa", World Energy Outlook Special Report, International Energy Agency, 2014, at https://www.iea.org/publications/freepublications/publication/WEO2014_AfricaEnergyOutlook.pdf.
2 Africa in an evolving global context: Challenges and Prospects, Africa Energy Outlook 2022, world energy Oulook Special Report, International Energy Agency, June 2022, https://www.iea.org/reports/africa-energy-outlook-2022
3 Vikas Khare, Savita Nema, Prashant Baredar, "Status of Solar Wind Renewable Energy in India", Science Direct, Vol. 27, November 2013, pp 1-10.
4 Power Sector at a Glance, Ministry of Power, Government of India, https://powermin.gov.in/en/content/power-sector-glance-all-india
5 Renewable Energy in India, Press Information Bureau, Govt of India, September 9, 2022, https://pib.gov.in/FeaturesDeatils.aspx?NoteId=151141&ModuleId%20=%202#:~:text=Meeting% 2050%25%20of% 20energy%20requirements,)%20by%2045%25%20by%20 2030.

6 Africa Energy Outlook, World Energy Outlook Special Report 2022, International Energy Agency, pp.15, https://iea.blob.core.windows.net/assets/6fa5a6c0-ca73-4a7f-a243-fb5e83ecfb94/AfricaEnergyOutlook2022.pdf

7 Felicia Jackson, "Solar Investment Powers Ahead And Africa Opens Up", *Forbes*, April 11, 2018, available at https://www.forbes.com/sites/feliciajackson/2018/04/11/solar-investment-powers-ahead-and-africa-opens-up/#70095db67f74

8 How Renewable Energy Will Change Global Geopolitics", *Stratfor*, available at https://worldview.stratfor.com/article/how-renewable-energy-will-change-geopolitics

9 Laurence Harris, Financing System Challenges for Energy Transformation in Africa, The Oxford Institute for Energy Studies, September 2018: Issue 115, pp6, https://www.oxfordenergy.org/wpcms/wp-content/uploads/2018/09/OEF-115.pdf

10 Ade Adela et al, "Bridging The Gap: Can Africa Attract New Liquidity Sources To Its Energy Projects?" Africa Oil & Gas Report, *Petroleum Economist*, 2018.

11 See note 1, IEA 2014.

12 Russia tightens grip on India's oil mkt in Feb; Africa's share lowest", ET EnergyWorld, March 13, 2023, https://energy.economictimes.indiatimes.com/news/oil-and-gas/russia-tightens-grip-on-indias-oil-mkt-in-feb-africas-share-lowest/98605341

13 "India's Oil Imports in 2017 Surged to a Record 4.4 Million Barrel Per Day", *ET Energy World*, January 17, 2018, https://energy.economictimes.indiatimes.com/news/oil-and-gas/indias-oil-imports-in-2017-surged-to-a-record-4-4-million-barrel-per-day/62532977

14 Rajiv Bhatia, "Is Narendra Modi's India-Africa Partnership Working?", *Quartz*, September 10, 2018, available at https://qz.com/india/1384301/is-narendra-modis-africa-policy-working/

15 Latika Adlakha, "Future Prospects of India-Africa Energy Ties", Centre for Public Policy Research, 5 September 2022, https://www.cppr.in/articles/future-prospects-of-india-africa-energy-ties

16 Global Energy & CO_2 Status Report 2017, International Energy Agency, March 2018, at https://www.iea.org/publications/freepublications/publication/GECO2017.pdf

17 175 GW Renewable Energy by 2022 - Policy Options and Financial Support Mechanism, Lok Sabha Secretariat Larrdis, Research Paper, September 2020, https://loksabhadocs.nic.in/Refinput/Research_notes/English/11092020_174832_102120462.pdf

18 Solar Energy, MNRE, https://mnre.gov.in/solar/solar-ongrid#:~:text=The%20 capacity%20of %2061.97%20GW,from%20off%2Dgrid%20solar%20projects.

19 Year - End Review 2022 - Ministry of New and Renewable Energy, MNRE, GoI, December 20, 2022, https://pib.gov.in/PressReleasePage.aspx?PRID=1885147#:~:text=as%20on% 2031.10.-,2022.,Renewables%202022%20Global%20Status%20Report).

8

Food Security in Africa and India

Nitya Nanda

Introduction

Food security, in general, means everybody should have affordable access to nutritious food in sufficient quantity. In the basic definition, whether a country as a whole is producing enough to feed the people or not, is not an issue at a theoretical level. Certainly, a country can import food. But, there are several reasons why it cannot work in practice, at least in the context of India and Africa. Ironically, most of the people who face food insecurity, in both Africa and India, depend on agriculture for their livelihood. In such a situation, we need to ensure that the food growers grow enough for their own requirements and sell the surplus in the market.

Also, we have seen that the global market is not good enough when countries get into food crisis. In 2007-08, for example, several countries had trouble accessing food from the global market. Similarly in 2022-23, several countries including those from Africa, faced problems accessing food grains due to the Ukraine conflict. The global market is not deep enough. Most countries try to import food at the same time for whatever reason, the global market cannot supply. For most food items, global trade is a small fraction of total global production or consumption. It is smaller than the total production or consumption of some countries. For example, if India decides to import its entire rice requirement, it is not possible, as India's requirement is much higher than the whole world can supply.

Hence, self-sufficiency in food production is an important component of food security in a country like India or African countries. Food self-sufficiency does not mean that a country will not engage in trade of food items. A country will both export and import food. So, food self-sufficiency is defined in the following way: SSR=[Production/(Production+Imports-Exports)]x100. Empirical evidence suggests that it is difficult for a developing country to achieve food security with being self-sufficient in food production. Those who are food deficit and yet do not have the problem of food insecurity of the people are all developed or rich countries.[1]

Changing Food Security Situation in India and Africa

Now the question is how Africa is different from India? Historically, Africa and India had a lot of differences. Even today, Africa is very different from India. Today, Africa is the only continent which is a net food importer, while India is net exporter of food. India is of course also of continent size, and its population is actually higher than the combined population of Africa. Many would be surprised to note that in 1960s Africa was actually food self-sufficient. India, on the other hand, was a food deficit country and it depended on food aid at that time. Although many countries helped India, India thought it was a humiliating situation that it was running from country to country asking for food aid. So, India adopted a slew of measures to improve the food self-sufficiency. Today, India is one of the major food exporters in the world. The fact that India produces enough food to feed its own people is a big achievement considering where it was.

Africa went in the reverse. Africa was self-sufficient in food continent-wise. In the sixties Africa produced enough to feed its people. Some African countries were in deficit, but others were in surplus, way above their requirements. At the macro level the African continent produced enough food. However, it had problem of food security in terms of people's ability to access the food. Today, Africa faces huge trade deficit in agricultural goods, which went up to $46 billion in 2011. In case of food the deficit was about $30 billion on average during 2012-16. But now, Africa produces only 85 per cent of its requirement, and most countries are in deficit.

The reasons are not the same across all countries. Zimbabwe might have very different reason from South Africa which is very different from Malawi, which is different for Botswana. Thus, most countries in Africa went into higher deficit in food over the years. In the case of India as well, while the country as a whole ensures food self-sufficiency, the states have attained different levels of food security. Nevertheless, most states have become better in terms of food self-sufficiency.

Table 1: Food Security Situation in Africa and India

Regions/ Countries	*Prevalence of Undernourishment in the total Population*		*Prevalence of Severe Food Insecurity in the Total Population*		*Prevalence of Wasting Weight for Height (% of Children under 5)*		*Prevalence of Stunting Height for Age (% of Children under 5)*		*Prevalence of Overweight Weight for Height (% of Children under 5) 15-49)*		*Prevalence of Anaemia among Women of Reproductive Age (% of Women Ages*	
	2004-06	*2021*	*2014-16*	*2019*	*2016*	*2022*	*2005*	*2020*	*2005*	*2020*	*2005*	*2019*
World	14.1	9	9.1	10.5	7.7	6.8	29.5	-	5.3	-	30.6	30
Africa	20.8	-	25.9	-	7.4	-	36.2	-	5.0	-	41.6	-
Sub-Saharan Africa	23.7	22	29.4	24.6	7.3	5.9	38.6	-	4.4	-	43.9	41
India	20.5	17	-	-	21.0	18.7 (2020)	47.9	35.5	1.9	3.5	53.2	53

Source: World Bank: World Development Indicators.

When it comes to food security at micro level, India is not very different from Africa. If one looks at the different measures of food security, India is actually worse than Africa on an average. But if one compares India with Sub-Saharan Africa, then India appears to be slightly better (Table 1). So, at micro level in terms of outcome oriented measures, India is not yet far away from Sub-Saharan Africa. Both have similar problems in terms of making food accessible and that is because in some of the states in India, situation is bad and some states are quite comfortable and comparable to lower rung developed countries. While, this provides sufficient scope for cooperation and experience sharing within India, similar scope for cooperation exists between India and Africa as well.

If a country is food sufficient it does not mean that all of its people are food secure. Interestingly, if one looks at countries that are not food sufficient and yet food secure, they are all rich countries. They are either developed countries or oil-exporting countries. If one leaves aside these countries, then there is no country which is food insufficient, and yet food secure. So, food sufficiency is important. So, a country or a region has to fight the war on food insecurity in two stages. First, it has to have food sufficiency. At the second stage, it has to ensure that the food reaches everybody. So, the first part of the war has been won in India. The second stage is yet to be won. But, Africa has to win the first stage as well. Africa has to go back to where it was in 1960s. In some countries, of course, efforts are being made. Nigeria, for example, has a serious programme on reviving agriculture and some other countries are also trying. Once a country gets used to certain things it would develop all kinds of vested interests. Then changing that is very difficult.

Indian Experience: Lessons for Africa

Now, the question is what did India do to achieve food sufficiency or food security? It all started in the 1960s. Among other things, it provided minimum support prices for procurement, which is now a globally debatable issue. India believed that this was the best way it could support its farmers as it could not provide subsidies like other countries, which was a more expensive option. So, the government declared certain support prices to ensure that the growers were not dis-incentivised. It also provided subsidized inputs to some extent – it provided quality seeds, spent money on agriculture and research and development, extension services, etc.

Much of the technologies that India developed were in the government sector, so farmers could get those technologies free of cost. The state governments also spent substantial money on extension services. So, farmers were getting at a negative price in some sense. India also followed a different kind of Intellectual Property Rights (IPR) regime so that farmers could access agricultural technologies at relatively cheaper costs. While the world knows that India's pharmaceutical industry is dependent on the basis of a relaxed IPR regime, it sometimes ignores the fact that India has a different kind of IPR for agro-chemicals. So the companies could not patent agro-chemical products just like the pharmaceutical products. While India had to bring its IPR law at par with standards of WTO TRIPS, it has retained flexibility to some extent, as farmers rights have been protected in its law on plant varieties by adopting a sui generis law.

As noted earlier, food security is not the same as food sufficiency, and hence, additional efforts are needed to graduate from food sufficiency to food security. In fact, supporting farmers through minimum support prices can push up the prices of food stuff. Hence, government established a public distribution system through which poor are provided with subsidised food. This also works as a channel through which food procured by the government is disposed of. However, the public distribution system is not equally efficient or effective in all states. Within India, food insecure people are concentrated in states that are not only relatively underdeveloped in agriculture, but also have weak public distribution system. However, even public distribution system was not enough to ensure food security for poor people as they are very often subject to seasonal unemployment in particular, the people engaged in agriculture as wage labourer. Hence, the government also adopted public works programme to provide employment to poor people. Now rural poor have been given legal right to get 100 days of wage employment in a year through the Mahatma Gandhi National Rural Employment Guarantee Act, 2005.

African countries can draw lessons from Indian experiences that would be appropriate for them. While Africa has different countries with different situations, Indian experience is also quite varied as it varies from state-to-state. Hence, different African countries can pick up success stories and practices that will suit them well. There will be some scope for experience sharing whatever be the local context in an African country.

However, it is also important to note that the Indian agriculture has been stuck by the vices of unsustainability. A large number of farmers are in debt trap and they often commit suicide under debt burden. One more issue of sustainability, which is also linked to the problem of debt burden, is the issue of environmental degradation due to excessive use of water as well as of chemicals. While India needs to find solutions for these challenges, Africa also needs to be mindful when it draws lessons from Indian experience so that it can avoid creating similar problems.

Global Trade Regime: Scope for Africa-India Cooperation

As noted before, agriculture sector is very different. It is not like industrial sector because here production decisions are taken only twice or three times in a year. A farmer cannot cut back production or increase production on a daily basis. Related to the, market dynamics for agricultural goods is also very different. Given this, leaving the agricultural sector completely at the mercy of market can have its associated risks. Even in developed countries, agricultural sector has a long history of receiving substantial government support. Hence, liberalizing domestic market for agricultural goods to international competition creates further complications.

Goal 2 of the 2030 Sustainable Development Agenda seeks to end hunger and all forms of malnutrition, and double agricultural productivity by 2030. The UN members have also emphasised on global partnership for achieving the Sustainable Developmental Goals (SDGs) as articulated in SDG17. SDG 2b urges the UN member states to correct and prevent trade restrictions and distortions in world agricultural markets, including the parallel elimination of all forms of agricultural export subsidies and all export measures with equivalent effect, in accordance with the mandate of the Doha Development Round. Global agricultural market is still highly distorted not only by huge subsidies, but also by high tariffs. Developed country markets like the US, EU, Republic of Korea and Japan are the most-protected market in this regard. While the average tariff rate could be quite misleading as often tariffs are very high on products that matter, the Republic of Korea and Norway have quite high average tariff rates as well (Table 2).

Table 2: Tariff Structure for Agricultural Goods 2015

Country/Territory	*Simple average*		*Maximum duty*		*Coefficient of variation*		*Number of tariff lines*
	Bound	*MFN applied*	*Bound*	*MFN applied*	*Bound*	*MFN applied*	*MFN applied*
Australia	3.2	1.2	29	2.	149	169	883
Brazil	35.4	8.0	55	55	31	64	1083
China	15.7	13.9	65	65	75	85	1199
European Union	12.2	11.4	375	144	135	123	2126
United States	4.8	5.1	350	350	342	319	1752
India	113.1	39.6	300	150	46	73	1543
Japan	16.2	13.4	482	482	206	217	1917
Korea, Republic of	61.4	57.0	887	887	210	238	1708
Norway	139.0	35.5	>1000	>1000	121	200	1449
Russian Federation	10.7	9.7	100	100	116	116	2706
Indonesia	47.1	8.6	210	150	50	211	1457

Source: WTO ITC UNCTAD, World Tariff Profiles 2023.

Most developed countries (barring exceptions like Norway) committed for lower tariffs on agricultural goods as they supported their farmers through subsidies rather than import tariffs. Nevertheless, even though they had to reduce their tariffs, they still maintain high tariffs in some goods. However, they continued to provide higher real subsidies in absolute sense as their real subsidies remained almost at the same level as a percentage of total consumption. But, inclusion of market price support that is measured through price differential helped them obfuscate the issue and now they claim to have reduced subsidies. In reality, they have reduced the tariff barriers a bit while increasing the real subsidies. As can be seen from Figure 1, the total subsidy (OECD TSE) has increased over time in OECD countries as well as major countries/region like the United States and the European Union. It has also increased substantially in China, but remains low in India. Total support also includes market price support which is measured as the difference between domestic price and international price which is not estimated on accrual basis but it is a notional value. The fact that international price is also distorted; use of such a measure is problematic.[2]

Figure 1: Agricultural Support (Total Support – TSE) in Select Countries/Regions (US$ million)

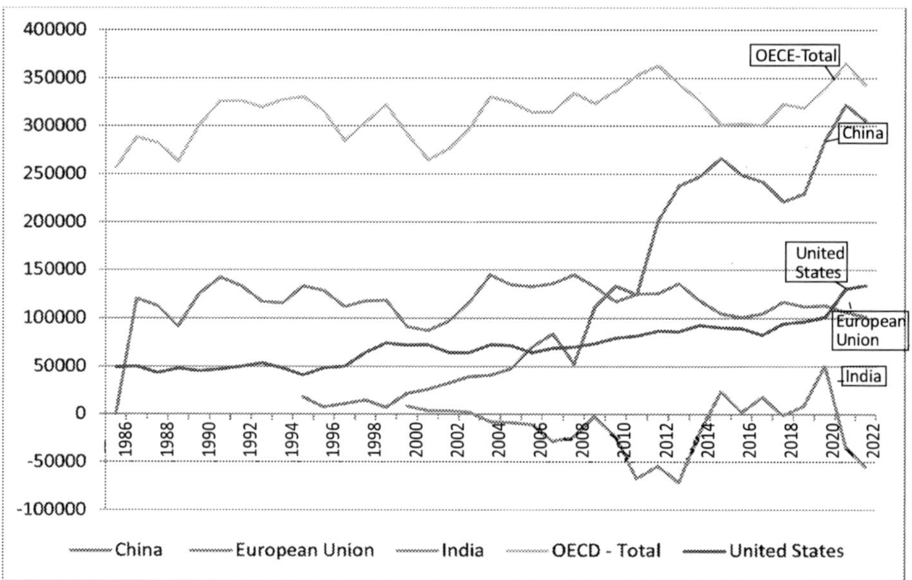

Source: OECD Statistics.

For developing countries, inclusion of market price support in the aggregate measure of support was risky from the beginning as the international price was at a lower level and far below the competitive level due to huge subsidies offered by the developed countries. However, they could not appreciate this as their domestic price at that time was even lower than that of "international price" even though the latter was subsidised due to the fact that they had very low wages for agricultural labour. About two decades of economic growth in some countries like India and Indonesia has ensured that both demand for agricultural goods as well as wages for agricultural labour have increased substantially. Prices for other agricultural inputs have also increased in tandem. What is more problematic is the fact that the international reference price against which the market price support is estimated is that of 1986-88 level. During this period, the international prices of wheat and rice were at their lowest levels and hence market price support would always be overestimated (Figure 2). Moreover, this measure would also capture the impacts of import protection through tariffs that countries are allowed to maintain otherwise. Such subsidy measure also favours the countries that provide huge subsidies as that will make domestic prices lower compared to countries like India who support farmers through minimum support price (MSP), making farm prices higher.

Figure 2: World Prices (US$ per metric ton) and Price Indices (1986-88=100) of Wheat and Rice

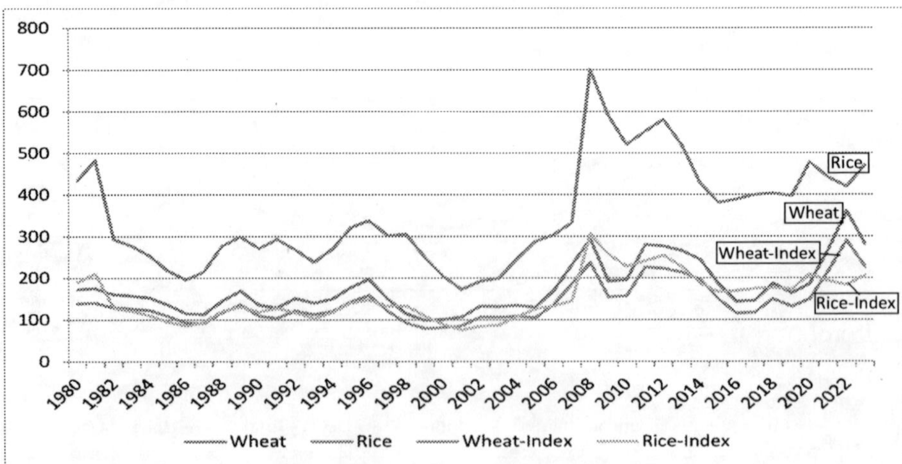

Source: WEO Statistics.

It is important to note that during the Uruguay Round of negotiations, all countries including the developing countries accepted commitment to reduce subsidies as well as tariff barriers. Accordingly, developing countries have also accepted bound rates of tariffs on agricultural goods. In fact, India's applied rates for agricultural goods are much lower than the bound rates. Nevertheless, developing countries have the right to impose import tariffs as long as they do not cross the bound rates. However, when aggregate measure of support is measured in such a way that it also captures the impact of tariffs then their right to maintain the tariffs is taken away. It is another matter that the international reference price that is used as the basis for measuring AMS is much lower than what should it be.

Developed countries are not showing much interest to conclude the Doha Round after what they wanted was agreed in the form of the trade facilitation agreement, while several issues that are of concern to developing countries remain unresolved. One such important issue is trade in agricultural goods; distortion of global market due to subsides, in particular. This is also against what countries committed at the time of adopting SDGs. What the global community needs to address is the real subsidies, rather than a theoretical construct on measure of support that also includes impacts of tariffs. While tariffs on agricultural goods are high in developing countries as well, it is legitimate to maintain such high tariffs as long as huge direct subsidies are there in developed countries.

Tools that were used by India to turn itself from a food-deficit country in 1960s to a food surplus country will not be available now if the subsidy commitments of developing countries are strictly implemented. While India is still able to maintain them thanks to the so-called "peace clause", countries in Africa might not be able to adopt them if they want. It is important to note that Africa was actually a food surplus continent in the 1960s, but today, they are similar to what India was then. Obviously, now they are looking towards India to improve their situation in this regard. Unfortunately, the tools adopted by India will remain prohibited for them, if the food security agenda of the WTO is not addressed in an appropriate manner. For India too maintaining food security will remain a challenge.

Conclusion

The fact that India has been able to achieve food sufficiency holds several important lessons for Africa. While it may not be possible to pick up Indian policies and programmes unaltered, several elements can be adopted in Africa as well depending on the local needs and situations. What is also of concern is that several of the policy tools that India used might be difficult to use now anywhere, including Africa due to restrictions imposed by the WTO regime. Moreover, the hopes raised by the WTO regime for developing countries did not come true as the WTO regime seems to be soft on subsidies provided by developed countries, at the same time extremely hard on "accounting subsidy" that might not exist at all. Mostly developing countries are affected by the restrictions imposed by the WTO regime. The fact that developed countries are reluctant to complete the Doha Round, would also mean that it will be difficult to have the necessary reforms at the WTO.

While, developed countries continue to provide huge subsides, in developing countries, especially in Africa, there is push from developed countries to open their markets, and Africa is now slated to be a one-trillion agriculture market. So, the agro companies of the world look towards Africa as the place for potential business, rather than making it self-sufficient and food secure. Africa needs to ensure that it can adopt the kind of policies it requires to ensure food security and the global regime should not be a barrier. It is important to note and understand how unfair the global regime is and how India is fighting a battle. While India received some support from Africa on this, in some African countries, the issue is not adequately appreciated because they have not yet started the mission of getting into self-sufficiency and food security. If they get into that mission they would realise what India is fighting for in the global regime is important for them as well. So, Africa and India needs to come together and work towards ensuring food self-sufficiency and food security on different fronts.

NOTES

1 Jennifer Clapp, "Food Self-sufficiency: Making Sense of it, and When it Makes Sense", *Food Policy*, 66 (2017), pp. 88-96.

2 Nitya Nanda, "WTO and Food Security: Challenges Ahead", *Economic and Political Weekly*, Vol. 52, No. 49, pp. 21-24.

9

The Imperative of Adopting a Security Response Approach and Cooperation for Cyber Security in Africa

Essien D Essien

Introduction

Emerging manifestations in contemporary studies surrounding the emergence of the digital society and cyber security in Africa have revealed two dramatic findings for scholarship. Firstly, the advent of new technology which started with the introduction of computers in the 1950s to the development of the internet in the 1980s has altered the notion of security in contemporary societies.[1] New types of crime perpetrated by means of sophisticated technology have replaced traditional crimes such as fraud, stealing by tricks, and obtaining under false pretence. Secondly, traditional boundaries have fallen away and a virtual borderless world has become a platform for crime. In recent years, cyber security related incidents have continued to increase in frequency and impact. In spite of the huge successes and positive attributes that the digital environment has introduced as an integral part of the modern information society, the resultant growth trajectory for cybercrime and related incidence heightens the extent to which cyberspace vulnerabilities and limited capacities prevent Africa from maximising the benefits of the digital economy.[2]

Given this scenario, the use of Internet and Information and Communications Technology (ICTs) has become a matter of strategic importance. With the increase in cybercrime activities, people are facing a growing number of uncertainties related to the use of the digital environment. Digital security threats and incidents have increased the financial and reputational consequences, reduced privacy and in some cases, produced physical damage. Although stakeholders are increasingly aware of these challenges raised by digital security risk, they often approach the problem only from the technical perspective, and in a manner that tends to play down on the ethical implications of the social cleavages in digital use and applications that accompany information poverty and insecurity challenges.[3] In the light of this turn of events, cyber security landscape and processes are redefining security in the 21st century everywhere in the world.[4] The Internet and the ICTs constitute vital infrastructure for growth and development. They are the new drivers for innovation and social well-being.

In fact, the role of the Internet in supporting the economy, delivering information and education, and in enabling creativity is well implicit and acknowledged.[5] The Internet economy is a dynamic environment where technologies, applications, uses and markets constantly evolve, often in a volatile manner. While the Internet benefits economic growth and innovation, attacks against Internet infrastructure represent a major risk to economic growth and innovation in any society. Apparently, the world's growing dependence on the Internet has revealed that cyber space is now as important as physical space. Its vulnerability to disruption and attack has highlighted the importance for a coordinated response for security in all spheres, be it national, regional or global levels.[6] This lends credence to the fact that as the society continues to be operated largely on technology and almost everything we do is dependent on it; the imperatives of cyber security cease to be an optional project. It follows therefore that as technology brings ever greater benefits, it also bring with it ever greater threats which by the very nature of the opportunities it presents it becomes a focal point for cybercrime, industrial espionage, and cyber attacks. Therefore, protecting it is of paramount priority. This explains why some scholars, analysts and theorists of the network society have argued that the global information revolution underpinning online transaction and movement as well as networked society is generating increasing threats, vulnerabilities and exploitable weaknesses which require responsibility for cyber security, especially with regards to essential infrastructure and governance.[7]

Theoretical Framework

The theoretical framework that underpins this study is the "protection motivation theory" which was propounded by Ronald Rogers in 1975. The theory measures the survival behaviour of a person, country and/or region when informed or aware of a threatening event such as cyber criminal activities.[8] According to the theory, such survival actions are directly subjective to a commensurate management response which indicates the idea of making provision for collaborative decision-making on cyber security. The management response in this regard is the net result of the country's evaluation of the threat appraisal and management appraisal. Cyber-crime threat appraisal in this perspective refers to a country's assessment of the level of danger posed by the threat.[9] The protection motivation theory, therefore, plays a significant role in determining one's ability to acquire skill, information and knowledge through collaborative policies and governance in cyber security. The tenability of the theory of "protection motivation" rests, therefore, upon the maintenance of cooperative strategy with strong guarantees for security and protection.

However, this is clearly exemplified in the perceived vulnerability, perceived severity, and perceived frequency of cyber criminal activities in Africa. The penchant for this behaviour involves the psychological pleasure as well as peer approval experienced today.[10] The second idea however, revolves around the security response consideration which has something to do with an individual, nation or regional assessment of the capacity to cope with and/or avert the accompanied loss and damage resulting from threats and/or danger of cyber-criminal activities. Another dimension of the theory is the self-efficacy, response efficacy, and response cost of adopting countervailing measures toward cyber-criminal activities. In cyber-crime for example, self-efficacy refers to criminal's confidence being involved in the act, response efficacy to the consequence of the act, and the response cost to pull out or stoppage of cyber criminality. For a people or continent plagued by growing level of insecurity such as food insecurity, conflict and poverty, vulnerability and dependency in technology and scientific advancement, averting cyber-crime activities, as well as developing effective security response strategy towards cyber threats in telecommunications and the Internet deserves critical thinking and cooperation of a very high precedence.[11]

Cyber Security Landscape in Africa

The landscape of cyber security in Africa is changing rapidly with the evolving technology and expanding digitization which are providing new opportunities and challenges. Accomplishing the culture of cyber security responsiveness is of utmost importance in today's technological landscape. The cyber-crime landscape in Africa is rapidly changing with vulnerability and threat actors growing in size, scope, complexity and capability. Latest scholarship on the subject show that the number of Internet users has grown from less than a million in 2003 to over 80 million in 2016 and 160 million in 2022.[12] In recognition of the increased importance of Internet, cyberspace has become an essential component of modern society. Cyber security is considered an emerging challenge in Africa in contemporary time. Africa's exponential growth, and the associated expansion of IT connectivity and business, has led to the continent becoming a high value target for cyber attack. Cybercrime in the African continent has moved far beyond the notorious 419 Nigerian email scams, coined after the code of legislation aimed to suppress such scams.

The sophistication of some attacks and tactics used by cyber criminals clearly demonstrates how vulnerable individuals are online and how they have disfigured public confidence in online security and commerce.[13] The infection rates for infrastructures in African countries runs between 57 per cent and 98 per cent. The cybercrime space in Africa is advancing so rapidly, such that it can be a challenge to deal with it. Regrettably, about 62 per cent of users of cyber space do not have any cyber crisis management plan in place to help them respond to a breach and vulnerabilities. This portrait can be compared with 40 per cent in Europe and Middle East and 31per cent in Asia. It would be useful to note that with the prevalent threats and vulnerability level, broadband services are opening in different parts of the continent, which means more users would be able to access the web, translating into more viruses and spam from online sources.[14] Unfortunately, those who use Internet in Africa do not have a clue as to how to protect themselves and their personal information against cyber attacks directed at their gadgets.

To make matters worse, cybercrime has started to exploit mobile devices in the African continent. The reason being mobile devices such as smart phones are reasonably cheaper and affordable in the rapidly evolving mobile landscape in Africa. The growth, however, has been fuelled in large part by the liberalisation effort resulting in the formation of independent regulatory bodies and increased competition in the market.[15] Currently, the total African mobile subscriber base is approximately put at 280.7 million people, about 30 per cent of the total population. Approximately, 15 mobile operators in countries like Nigeria, Kenya and Tanzania are already planning to introduce 3G and data service.[16] Already, in Nigeria, Glo Mobile is currently operating with 3G and about to introduce 4G data services. This magnitude of increase in mobile use (mobile phones with web connectivity) presents a veritable open door for all cyber criminals to exploit mobile users in Africa with little or no cyber safety knowledge. It has to be noted, that more individuals worldwide gain Internet access through mobile phones. Critically speaking, it is pertinent to note that cyber criminals in Africa are comfortable with millions of inexperienced users whom they deceive with unsophisticated scamming techniques than with more knowledgeable and experienced users who have grown wise over the years.[17]

Table 1: African Cyber Security Threat Landscape

Target sectors of cybercrime in Africa	1. Government Agencies, African Think Tanks 2. African Media, Communication service providers 3. Various Sectors of the African economy (Financial, Petroleum/ Oil and gas, Retail, Power and energy, ICT, etc.) 4. Critical Infrastructures-Health, Education, Power, Transport, Industry etc.4. High Profile Government Websites 5. Industries, parastatals and private establishments etc
Tactics adopted by cybercrime fraudsters in Africa	1. Spear Phishing 2. Software Hijacking 3. Specific Nigerian Firewall and AV Targeting 4. Malware, Spyware and Adware 5. DDOS 6. Colluding with insiders to defraud

It is therefore, obvious that in Africa, most people are not aware of the cyber danger surrounding them. They are just happy that they can operate their gadgets and can connect to the internet. It is important to train and educate this group of users in the art of using these gadgets and the cyber space safely. This definitely is the area that needs to be explored and action taken effectively to properly understand the cyber landscape.[18] The borderless nature of cybercrime makes African countries vulnerable to all threats already present elsewhere. In this context, African policy-makers find themselves in the compelling need to develop and implement effective policies, legislation as well as awareness and education initiatives to address the risk of cybercrime and cyber threats, in general. But any set of measures to be effective require a thorough understanding of the threat landscape. To this end, cyber intelligence is a crucial tool in the effort to increase cyber security and consequently confidence in the use of technology.[19]

Expectedly, Symantec, the world's leading cyber security company, with the largest set of sensors on the Web, organised what is called Global Intelligence Network (GIN). Every year, hundreds of skilled analysts, analyse trillions of bytes of telemetry gathered through these sensors, and distil the data into an annual report known as the "Internet Security Threat Report (ISTR)". Also, in order to overcome the information gap, the African Union (AU) and Symantec, through the Global Forum for Cyber Expertise (GFCE) and with the support of the US Department of State (DoS), engaged in a Public-Private Partnership to develop a report that collected and presented detailed technical data on the cyber security threats in Africa.[20] The report tagged "Cyber Crime and Cyber Security Trends in Africa" analyses the key technological trends in the continent and the cybercrime proliferation and its techniques. However, the unique feature of this report is that it incorporates online threat data from Symantec's comprehensive cyber threat monitoring network, as well as the perspectives of African Union Member State governments. It is pertinent to note that some key findings point to the proliferation of ransomware, social media scams and the explosion of mobile malware in the African continent.[21]

The Challenges of the Cyber Security Phenomenon in Africa

Despite the strong starting position of the digital society, the gains and benefits from the digital systems remains risky and complex. This is so because vulnerabilities remain widespread, attacks are also increasing, and breaches are incurred which cause substantial harm to individuals and businesses. Taking cognizance of this projection, the digital systems if not well-secured, would face more threats as they become more complex, and especially as the pay-offs to attackers increase. This, therefore, poses a serious challenge to cyber security, policy and management in protecting the cyber space, individuals and businesses against these threats. Cyber security no doubt is a multidisciplinary concept which needs to take into account the social and behavioural sciences. The understanding of the real-world behaviour of digital and human systems depends on a wide range of disciplines involved in the digital activities. It follows that effective cyber security measures would need to integrate insights from all the disciplines.[22]

Indeed, cyber security challenges are comprehensive in nature, with networks, services and attacks rarely confined to a single jurisdiction and/or discipline. This also explains why data transmitted around the world can be rapidly replicated. Moreover, the sensitive nature of the material protected by cyber security can affect how much information is shared about protective measures, vulnerabilities and breaches. This knowledge is an important collective resource for improving cyber security defences, even though its use is often limited by lack of transparency.[23] This lack of transparency is often based on justified concerns about the risks of releasing information. On the whole, cyber threats are hard and/or pretty difficult to predict simply because they are constantly evolving. This makes the attackers to exploit the vulnerabilities created by the complexity of the system and increased reliance on the digital systems.[24] A good example is the malware virus which has been noted to have extended its tentacles into highly targeted exploits. Also, we have cases such as ransomware and silent malware that remain undetectable until they are activated. It presupposes the fact that to deal effectively with these evolving threats, the digital sector must itself be diverse and responsive.

The Nature of Cyber Security Threats in Africa

Today, there are about 400 million internet users in the continent of Africa. But, the sorry story is that about 80 per cent of all personal computers on the continent are infected with different kinds of viruses and other malicious software. This however, costs Africa about $2 billion.[25] Africa is considered to have a permissive environment for cyber criminals due to lack of security capabilities, absence of relevant legislation and general lack of awareness of cyber security measures. Throughout the five regions of Africa, namely, Northern, Central, West, East, and Southern Africa, with their different levels of connectivity and penetration to the internet, cyber criminals in their nefarious activities are more businesslike, bold and professional.

The impact of the cyber criminals is not only felt by the targets they exploit, but also concerns the sums of money they seek.[26] These criminals' projects are for all intents and purposes fully-functioning business enterprise, covering a multitude of disciplines and individuals, each with their own area of expertise. The situation looks so real because of the weak infrastructure status of Africa in tackling cyber security vulnerability; also pertinent are issues of poor legal framework, inadequate security facilities, derisory manpower, and deficient resource base.[27] Nonetheless, the fight against cybercrime requires coordinated effort among all stakeholders such as government bodies, educational institutions, business organisations and law enforcement authorities.[28]

Cybercrime is on a dramatic rise on a worldwide basis, and Africa is not immune from it. In order to carry out their activities, cyber criminals look for fertile environments, both in terms of technological vulnerability and user behaviour. As an example, Africa is the leading force for mobile money transfers: 14 per cent of all Africans receive money through this medium. Further, the e-commerce business is estimated to reach a market value of $75 billion by 2025.[29] This immediately becomes an enticing proposition for increasingly sophisticated cyber criminals, who, like everywhere else in the world, exploit both vulnerable technology and users' carelessness. Moreover, outdated operating systems further compound the situation. Indicatively, about 25 per cent of personal computer users in Africa are still on Windows XP that were first released in 2001 and today unsupported and unpatched, or even pirated software. Meanwhile, in the mobile sphere, nine out of ten devices use the Android operating system which is by a long way the most vulnerable in the marketplace. It is worth mentioning that digital developments in Africa are already moving at a faster pace and the society is changing profoundly.[30]

However, new challenges arise alongside this growth tempo just as the increasing technological exposure poses its own vulnerabilities and risks. For instance, it is argued that the volume of threat in Africa is extremely massive and disturbing, with 286 million different virus samples counted (783, 562 samples per day; 32, 648 samples per hour; 544 samples per minute and about nine samples per second) on a yearly basis.[31] This development presents a very dangerous portrait as hackers could invade critical infrastructures such as the airport control tower and release information that could compromise weather and traffic signals to pilots in-flight. In this situation, the dire consequences are that planes may disappear just as it was popularly suspected when the Malaysian flight MH370 that departed from Kuala Lumpur International Airport on March 8, 2014 got missing en route to Beijing. This may have been a victim of cyber terror attack.[32]

The consequences could also be disastrous if hackers invade the defence, oil and gas installations, banking and telecommunication sectors. Considering the borderless nature of cybercrime and emerging cyber security threats in contemporary time, the only viable way forward in fighting cybercrime is through multi-stakeholder, inter-agency, bilateral and multilateral collaboration and cooperation. Today, the challenges of information communication technologies (ICTs) in Africa toward achieving a level of technological security in order to prevent and control risks; contribute to the economy and guarantee access to information to individuals while at the same time creating a climate of confidence and trust in ICTs and protecting rights and freedoms is quite enormous.[33] On the appendage of this development, the global tracking of cyber attacks in Africa indicate that many countries are struggling with high cases of software piracy, intellectual property theft and malware attacks.

Figure 1: Cyber Security Life Cycle and Measures

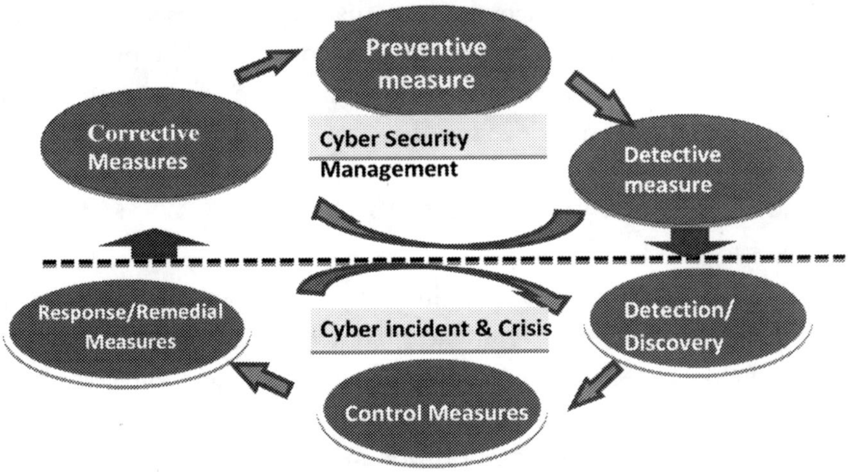

Source: Essien.[34]

This situation presents a serious challenge to the continent's resolve to take advantage of the enormous opportunities that the digital system offers, while balancing and managing its associated risks. However, what is particularly intriguing about cyber security and its challenges is the way and manner in which the cyber attacks are carried out and/or sponsored by the cyber fraudsters. Perhaps, this is due to the fact that cyberspace does not have defined jurisdiction by air, sea or by land, and hence, the perpetrators of cybercrimes not only remain ubiquitous but also dangerous. A good example of cyber security and its challenges in Africa is the incident in August 2012, when Boko Haram, the insurgent group responsible for several thousands of deaths, kidnaps and bombings in Nigeria reportedly hacked the personnel records and databases of the Directorate of Secret Service (DSS) or State Security Service (SSS). Nigeria's secret police is popularly known with the acronym DSS or SSS. Boko Haram group was able to successfully compromise the covert personnel data system of the DSS.[35] This however, culminated into database breach and revealed the names, addresses, bank information and family members of current and former personnel assigned to the country's undercover policy agency. Rationalizing the show of aggression on the security outfit, the Boko Haram group held that the security breach was carried out in order to get back at the government and protest the Nigerian Government handling of issues involving the insurgents, especially the non-release of their members detained in various prisons across the country. Interestingly, this case scenario obviously depicts the facts that no nation is strictly speaking immune from cyberspace attacks irrespective of status. The preponderance however, tends to swings heavier in developing economies such as Africa because of inability to prioritize security.[36]

Common Types of Cybercrimes in Africa

Though cybercrime encompasses a broad range of illegal activities perpetrated electronically, it can be generally divided into five broad categories with detachments such as intrusive offences, content-related offences, copyright and trademark-related offences, computer-related offences, and combination offences. However, the complexity in types and forms of cybercrime increases the difficulty to fight back and/or provide commensurate security. According to Symantec Corporation, there are several contributing factors that attract cyber criminals to operate in specific countries and regions of the world, such as access to broadband connections and/or uninterrupted internet connectivity. Nonetheless, the cybercrimes landscape in Africa can be categorised into two segments for easy comprehension as indicated in Table 2.

Table 2

Conventional Cybercrime through the Use of Computer	*Common Frequently Used Cyber Crimes and their Techniques in Africa*
(1) Identity Theft/Social Engineering	**Types**
(2) Financial Crimes	(1) Yahoo Boys
(3) Cyber Pornography	(2) The Next Level Criminals
(4) Online gambling	**Techniques**
(5) Intellectual property crime	(1) Phishing
(6) E-mail spoofing	(2) Unauthorised access to computer system and networks
(7) Forgery	(3) Theft of information contained in electronic form
(8) Cyber defamation	(4) E-mail bombing
(9) Cyber Stalking	(5) Data diddling and mobile pharming
	(6) Denial of service attacks
	(7) Virus/adware worm attacks
	(8) Trojan and malware attacks
	(9) Card/Data interception

Categories of Cybercrimes Prevalent in Africa

There is an endless list of possible crimes that can occur through the use of the Internet and computer. Worldwide, the predominance of electronic pathways in most payment system has made them ready targets for fraudsters. This study attempts a description of a good number of the widespread forms of electronic fraud technique common in many countries in Africa.

Basically, there are two common types of cyber criminals in Africa. Prominent among these emerging groups are known as the "Yahoo Boys" and "Next-Level Cyber Criminals." These two groups portray distinct characteristics and operate different types of scams based on their levels of experience.

Yahoo Boys

Studies have shown that the "Yahoo Boys", are so named as a result of their use of Yahoo apps to communicate. They are often part of groups operating in the same physical location and supervised by a more experienced ringleader.

These cyber criminals see a scam from beginning to end and often carry out multiple attacks at one time. They specialise in advance-fee, romance and stranded-traveller scams, such as the "Nigerian Prince" phishing emails that brought West Africa on the theoretical map of cybercrime in the early 2000s. Their goal is to convince unsuspecting victims to transfer large sums of money for a variety of illegitimate reasons. "Yahoo Boys" typically lack maturity and actively use social media to show off their ill-gotten wealth.[37]

Next-Level Cyber Criminals

The second most popular group is called the "Next-Level Cyber Criminals". This group is the opposite of "Yahoo Boys". The group consists of well-off and highly respected family men who are mature in terms of personal behaviour. Although new to the scene, "Next-Level Cyber Criminals" engage in more complex attacks, such as Business Email Compromise (BEC) and tax scams, by using malware and other crime-enabling software from Russia and other English speaking underground markets. They also maintain connections and accounts overseas as a way to feign legitimacy with their victims and keep law enforcement at arm's length. Due to the sophisticated social engineering tactics required to pull off these scams, significantly more research and effort goes into the crimes committed by "Next-Level Cyber Criminals."[38]

Identity Theft/Social Engineering

Identity theft is a form of fraud where a person uses another person's personal information to engage in fraudulent activities. It can take many forms, from fraudulent credit card use, to your entire identity being used to open accounts, obtain loans, and conduct other illegal activities. Be suspicious if anyone asks you for your personal information. Scammers use convincing stories to explain why you need to give them money or personal details.

Card (especially ATM) and/or Skimming

Card skimming involves the illegal use of a skimming device to copy, capture and collect data from magnetic stripe and PIN on credit and debit cards. The captured card and PIN details are encoded onto a counterfeit card and used by an identity thief to make fraudulent account withdrawals and transactions in the name of the actual account holder. Skimming can occur at any bank ATM or via a compromised POS machine. Usually, fraudsters would attach false casing and PIN pad overlay devices on genuine existing ATMs, or they can attach a disguised skimming device onto a card reader entry used in tandem with a concealed camera to capture and record PIN entry. This tactic has resulted into numerous fraudulent activities across many countries in Africa. The Central Bank of Nigeria reported recently that the Nigerian banking sector lost over ¦ 20billion through Internet fraud and the impact on the nation's cashless policy is significant.[39] Table 2 above simply give an unambiguous impression of the types of cybercrimes that exist in Africa. Although the volume of fraud cases reported in 2015 and 2014 had increased by 78 per cent and 70 per cent respectively, this is however, relative to cases reported in 2013. Similarly, the value of attempted fraud cases reported in 2014 and 2015 decreased by 60 per cent and by 50 per cent, respectively. The actual loss associated with fraud cases reported in 2015 and 2014 increased by over 1000 per cent relative to 2013 loss. Similarly, actual fraud loss as a percentage of attempted fraud increased to 80 per cent and 85 per cent in 2014 and 2015 respectively, from 3 per cent in 2013. Table 3 below shows the distribution of actual loss through cyber fraud.[40]

Table 3: Estimated Loss through Cyber Fraud in Africa Annually

Direct cost	*Type of crime*	*Amount*	*%*	*Indirect cost*	*Type of crime*	*Amount*	*%*
	Insider Threat	$179m	50		Insider Threat	$107m	20
	Attacks on Computer Systems	$79m	22		Attacks on Computer Systems	$155m	29
	Social Engineering and Identity Theft	$36m	10		Social Engineering and Identity Theft	$102m	19
	Email Spam & Phishing	$25m	7		Email Spam & Phishing	$64m	12
	Data Exfiltration	$25m	7		Data Exfiltration	$54m	7
	Online Fraud Scams	$14m	4		Online Fraud Scams	$54m	10
Total $358m				Total $537m	Overall total	$895m	100
Sectoral Loss to Cyber Fraud in Africa							
Banking & Financial Services	(a) Banking malware, (b) ATM Skimming (c) Insider threat, (d) Investments in technologies to detect, and prevent cybercrimes such as Antivirus etc., and (e) Audit and compliance with regulators					$206m	23

Government	Cyber Crime to African Governments activities and services such as: (a) Tax fraud, (b) Benefits fraud, (c) Local-government fraud, (d) Website defacements, and (e) Ransom demands	$170m	19
E-Commerce	(a) Online fraud, (b) Credit card fraud, (c) Social Engineering	$143m	16
Mobile based transactions/ e-commerce/e-payment	(a) Malware, (b) Social Engineering, (c) Insider fraud	$116m	13
Telecommunications		$98m	11
Hospitality		$90	10
Other Sectors		$72m	8
Total		$895m	100

Adopting Security Response Approach for Cyber Security in Africa

The African continent has become a nest for cyber criminals. For instance, those who specialise in the "419" scam, named after Article 419 in the Nigerian criminal law that penalises fraud and specifies the fines and other penalties for this sort of crime have now rebranded, re-strategized and operate on a bigger scale using sophisticated crime network.[41] Through the lens of critical thinking and analysis, there is a renewed attention, spirit and focus on the subject matter of cyber security in contemporary societies and Africa is not an exception. This lends credence to the fact that promoting a culture of cyber security and its interconnected disquiet is imperative for the African continent. This is because the African continent is collectively vulnerable and no country can tackle the question of cyber security alone.[42]

Practically speaking, the main objective for cyber security initiative in Africa is to make safe the online security of the African cyberspace. This, on a more practical note is to enable African countries enjoy the full benefits of the cyberspace as a springboard toward investing on human capacity development of all citizen. It is apparent that the continent of Africa which consists mostly of underdeveloped and developing countries is characterised by a limited awareness, knowledge, expertise and understanding of cyber security phenomenon.[43] There is no gain saying the fact that the rest of the world needs Africa to be aware and ready for cyber security. We are all connected in cyber space and our collective security is linked through either being hosts or targets of crime and attacks. This being the case, Africa can only be aware and ready for cyber security if and when it is internally organised and collaborated effectively with the rest of the world.

Currently, the African continent is particularly vulnerable to cyber security threats largely because of vast increased bandwidth that is attempting to bridge the "digital divide" for economic and social developments.[44] There is no mincing of words that lack of security awareness which includes shortage of local cyber security experts, and most importantly lack of funds, clearly justifies the need for cooperation for cyber security.

Ethical Implications of Cyber Security in the 21st Century

The question of ethics as the moral principles that govern human behaviour is a critical element of any sound cyber security defence strategy. Ethics have an important role to play in the promotion of collaborative effort toward social wellbeing and sustainable development in every society. This is because, security habits need to be formed which can hold people personally accountable and responsible for every actions or inactions performed in the society even when the leaders are impervious and/or circumstance changes.[45] For instance, in order to achieve a cyber secure society for all, certain policies, actions and inactions required to be exposed to some ethical scrutiny and critical thinking by asking the following questions: In the society, is living an ethical life all about doing one's duty (Deontological Ethics), or is it about bringing as much utility and happiness to one's family relations and friends or as possible for all concerned (Utilitarian ethics), or is it about following the natural law (Natural law ethics), or is living an ethical life about living up to the social contract that we have signed on to (social contract ethics), or is it about flourishing; that is maintaining and achieving well-being by developing excellent traits and characteristics (virtue ethics)? Certainly, the association between cyber security and matters such as knowledge sharing, responsibility, transparency, justice, and cooperation are all ethically based, and relates to the need for all stakeholders to make informed choices in the process toward securing the cyberspace for sustainable development.[46] Although the ethical element promoting information technology and cybersecurity is one of many other variables that should underlie a sustainable development policy, it is however considered as fundamental, in the context of digital economy. This is simply because it is associated with a set of values that should be upheld to promote the happiness of the current and future generations. In this regard, the issue of responsibility, protection, cooperation, accountability, truthfulness, and care towards the present and future generations deserves to take a centre stage.[47]

Cyber security is not only a matter of technology alone but also one of morality. It is particularly important for those in the cyber security business to act ethically given the understanding that cyber security is a process of making safe, secure, and reliable, the cyber space for its social and economic wellbeing advantages. As a process, cyber security requires some ethical obligations which define a moral course of action. This presupposes that considering the importance of modern technology, many organisations are supposed to commence imposing ethical cyber security obligations to their members. In ethics of cyber security, the IT security professionals have a very challenging job to handle especially when it comes to cybercrime.[48] Not only must the professionals guard against attacks, but they also must contend with other ethical issues such as privacy, reading of people private emails, monitoring the social media activity of others, capturing the keystrokes of everything an employee will type, as well as the reading of files stored on employees' machines. Within the corporate sphere, some of the methods used in helping to ensure the safety of data will certainly provoke ethical questions. This includes everything ranging from customer and employee information to financial records and product specifications. This is essential as personnel working in the IT industry are expected at best to be every bit as ethical just as the hackers are very unscrupulous in their nefarious activities.[49]

Conclusions

This study mirrored expressly on the imperatives for deepening the security engagement and cooperation for cyber security in Africa. It noted that cyber security is today recognised as global phenomenon, and there is currently no continental coordination and cooperation on cyber security. The study tried to establish a different argument that to stay on track and become one of the major drivers of the global economy in order that the continent and her people can reach its full potentials, Africa needs to urgently address efforts to combat cybercrime and improve its cyber security posture. This however, raises some critical ethical challenges bothering on responsibility on the part of the various stakeholders to tackle cyber security in Africa. The current cyber threat landscape in Africa shows that users (Africans) are being enormously impacted upon both by threats that are trending globally as well as some that are more specific to the region. This study demonstrates that with the existing trend of cyber security, it will certainly take a concerted effort from international governments, civil society organisations, and institutions to fight cybercrime and improve cyber security in Africa.

Recommendations

Given the complex nature as well as the magnitude of cyber security challenges in African continent in contemporary time, tackling the phenomenon requires a coordinated and well-focused policy. However, the composite character of the issues demands a multidisciplinary dimension in tackling the menace. The interaction between these dimensions nonetheless, reinforces the delicate and complex nature of cyber security which is apparent in our societies nowadays. The following recommendations will suffice for the problem:

(1) There is a need for governments at the continental level to create institutional capacity to respond to cybercrime and threats. This will involve setting up a minimum standards and procedures in tackling cyber security issues to enable the continent to obtain the full benefits of the cyberspace. The establishment of the necessary cyber security organisational structures with regional responsibility to curb cyber vulnerabilities is pertinent.

(2) The role of governments in putting in place the policy, legal and regulatory framework is of paramount importance. This is because the success of any cyber security initiative requires the full involvement and support of the political leadership and goodwill at the very highest level. Having regional frameworks, policies and strategies relating to cyber security are imperative for African countries. This is because they will allow stakeholders to use the technical, legal and regulatory tools available to promote a culture of cyber security concerns.

(3) Cyber security awareness and training ought to be a top priority for all African. Security awareness is the most important requirement for cyber security. It should be made to reach all levels and inform all users of the internet, from vulnerable sector or people in the society, school-going children to families, industry captains, critical national infrastructures handlers, government officials, and the entire African

continent with its unique needs.

(4) Employment and empowerment opportunities should be given a top consideration in order to cater for the large population of the youths who have finish school but remain jobless. Job security must be seen as a sine-qua-non for a functional cyber security in Africa. Effective cyber security involvement also has the capacity of creating job opportunities.

(5) The coordination of local as well as international partnerships on cyber security is apt. This will foster cooperation and coordination between governments, stakeholders, private sector and citizens in engaging cyber security in order to promote and strengthen international cooperation.

(6) The governments in Africa should engage in rigorous dialogue with others, especially among the academic community, and major stakeholders aimed at establishing a common understanding of the problem of cyber risk and vulnerability.

(7) Cyber security issues in the continent should constitute a broader range of the African bilateral relations programme.

(8) The Governments in Africa should make a concerted effort to establish one or more dedicated support funds under specialised and professional management to support the financing of cyber security innovation, targeting cases where innovation would have spill over benefits but might not otherwise be funded.

(9) The global nature of cyber security means that cyber security practice must take account of human, social, legal, regulatory and technological factors. The complexity of digital systems also means that the connections between the social, human and technological elements of a system themselves create opportunities for exploitation. Research challenges are therefore multidisciplinary, including the social sciences and humanities as well as

NOTES

1 Essien Essien, "Ethical Implications of the Techno-Social Dilemma in Contemporary Cyber-Security Phenomenon in Africa: Experience from Nigeria", *International Journal of Information Communication Technologies and Human Development,* Vol. 10, Issue 1, 2018, 17-30.

2 Fawzia Cassim, "Addressing the growing spectre of cybercrime in Africa: evaluating measures adopted by South Africa and other regional role players", *Comparative and International Law*

and Justice South Africa, 44, 2011, 123-138.

3 Ibid.

4 Ibid.

5 Essien 2018, note 1, p. 21.

6 Naresh Kumar, "Africa Could Become the Cybercrime Capital of the World, 2010" at http://www.psfk.com/2010/04/africacould-become-the-cybercrime-capital-ofthe-world.html (Accessed 17 March, 2018).

7 Essien 2018, note 5, p. 24.

8 Patricia Rippetoe and Ronald Rogers, "Effects of Components of Protection-Motivation Theory on Adaptive and Maladaptive Coping with a Health Threat," *Journal of Personality and Social Psychology*, Vol. 52, No. 3, 1987, pp. 596-604.

9 Steven Prentice-Dunn and Brain McClendon, "Reducing Skin Cancer Risk: An Intervention Based on Protection Motivation Theory," *Journal of Health Psychology*, Vol. 6, No. 3, 2001, pp. 321-328.

10 Ibid.

11 Ronald Rogers, "A Protection Motivation Theory of Fear Appeals and Attitude Change", *The Journal of Psychology*, 91(3), 1975, pp. 93–114. doi:10.1080/00223980.1975.9915803 PMID:28136248

12 Eric Akuta, Isaac Ong'oa and Chanika Jones, "Combating Cyber Crime in Sub-Sahara Africa; A Discourse on Law, Policy and Practice", *Journal of Peace, Gender and Development Studies, 1*(4), 2011, pp. 129–137; World Bank, *Digital transformation drives development in Africa*, 18 January 2024 at https://www.worldbank.org/en/results/2024/01/18/digital-transformation-drives-development-in-afe-afw-africa#:~:text=Over%20160%20million%20Africans%20 gained,payment%20 between%202014%20and%202021 (Accessed 20 January 2024).

13 Essien 2018, note 7, p. 26.

14 Brent Rowe, Douglas Reeves, Dallas Wood and Fern Braun, "The Role of Internet Service Providers in Cyber Security," Institute for Homeland Security Solutions, 2011, at https://www.ihssnc.org/portals/0/PubDocuments/ISP-Provided_Security_Rowe.pdf (Accessed 13 February 2018).

15 Alex de Joode, "Effective corporate security and cybercrime", *Network Security*, (3), 2011, pp. 16-28.

16 Ibid.

17 Ibid.

18 Mike Jensen, ICT in Africa, 2001, Retrieved 22/02/2018 from http://goo.gl/mYhTR

19 Namusa Kaiko, "Tackling the challenges of cyber security in Africa", *Times of Zambia*, 2014, at http://www.times.co.zm/?p=18423Cyber-crime-costs-Zambian-banks--4millio/- /979180/1883006/-/128vr2iz/-/index.html (Accessed 20 February 2018).

20 Hawes John, "An Epic Year for Data Breaches with Over 800 Million Records Lost", *Naked Security*, 2013, at http://nakedsecurity.sophos.com/2014/02/19/2013-an-epic-year-for-data-breaches-withover-800-million-records-lost. (Accessed 07 March 2018)

21 Ibid.

22 Alexander Klimburg, *National Cyber Security Framework Manual,* NATO CCD COE Publications, 2012.

23 Rayne Reid and Johan van Niekerk, *Towards an Education Campaign for Fostering a Societal, Cyber Security Culture,* Plymouth: Centre for Security, Communications & Network Research Plymouth University, 2014.

24 James Lewis, *Economic Impact of Cybercrime—No Slowing Down*, CSIS McAfee Report, 2018.

25 Elmarie Kritzinger and Basie von Solms, "A framework for cyber security in Africa", *Journal*

of Information Assurance and Cyber Security, 12(2), 2012, pp. 37-51. doi:10.1109/AFRCON.2013.6757708.

26 Frans Leeuw and Bastian Leeuw, "Cyber Society and Digital Policies: Challenges to Evaluation?" *Evaluation, 18*(1), 2012, 111–127. doi:10.1177/1356389011431777

27 Audrey Kumar, "Africa Could Become the Cybercrime Capital of the World", 2010. Retrieved 17 March, 2018 from http://www.psfk.com/2010/04/africacould-become-the-cybercrime-capital-ofthe-world.html

28 Friday Wada and Godwin Odulaja, "Assessing Cyber Crime and its Impact on E-Banking in Nigeria Using Social Theories", *African Journal of Computing and ICT*, *5*(1), 2012, pp. 69-82.

29 Ibid.

30 Fawzia Cassim, 2011, note 2, p. 131.

31 Olumide Longe and Stella Chiemeke, "Cybercrime and Criminality in Nigeria - What Roles are Internet Access Points in Playing", *European Journal of Social Sciences, 6*(4), 2008.

32 Adesopo Agboola, "Electronic Payment Systems and Tele-banking Services in Nigeria", *Journal of Internet Banking and Commerce,* 11(3), 2006, at http://www.arraydev.com/commerce/jibc (Accessed 13 February 2018).

33 Rashid Ahmed, "Nigeria: N10 Billion Lost to Bank Fraud in 2007", NDIC, *Daily Trust,* 2008.

34 Essien 2018, note 13.

35 Essien Essien, "The Challenges of Public Administration, Good Governance and Service delivery in the 21st Century", *International Journal of Civic Engagement and Social Change, 2*(2), 2015, pp. 55–66. doi:10.4018/IJCESC.2015040104.

36 Olumide Longe, Victor Mbarika, Mousto Kourouma, Friday Wada and Robert Isabalija, "Seeing Beyond the Surface: Understanding and Tracking Fraudulent Cyber Activities", *International Journal of Computer Science and Information Security, 6*(3), 2009, pp.124-135.

37 Omoneye Olasanmi, "Computer Crimes and Counter Measures in the Nigerian Banking Sector", *Journal of Internet Banking & Commerce, 15*(1), 2010, at http://www.arraydev.com/commerce/jibc/ (Accessed 12 March 2018).

38 Ibid.

39 Ibid.

40 Wada and Odulaja, note 28, p. 70.

41 Andrews Atta-Asamoah, "Understanding the West African Cyber-crime Process", *African Security Review, 18*(4), 2010, pp. 105-114.

42 Ibid.

43 United Nations Office on Drugs and Crime (UNDOC), "Comprehensive Study on Cybercrime", February 2013, at http://www.unodc.org/documents/ organized-crime/UNODC_CCPCJ_EG.4_2013/ CYBERCRIME_ STUDY_210213.pdf (Accessed 27 February 2018).

44 Agboola, note 32, p. 22.

45 Martins Hoffman, *Empathy and Moral Development: Implications for Caring and Justice,* Cambridge: Cambridge University Press, 2000.

46 Ibid.

47 Helen Nissenbaum, "Where Computer Security Meets National Security", *Ethics and Information Technology, 7*(2), 2005, pp. 61-73.

48 Ibid.

49 Ibid.

10

India and Africa in Cyberspace: An Agenda for Co-operation

Cherian Samuel

India and Africa have many similarities and face common challenges in cyberspace. In terms of similarities, while there are differing capabilities and capacities amongst the many states of India, the same could be said of countries in Africa with states like Kenya and South Africa faring very well on digital indexes, while other countries are lagging behind. These disparities have consequences not only for economic growth, but also provide opportunities for bad actors to take advantage of this borderless space. The relative absence of borders means that any cybersecurity issue, more often than not, has international ramifications. The unceasing waves of attacks around the world that affect individuals, individuals, companies, and entire countries bear testimony to the ravaging impact of cyber attacks.

India was one of the first countries to have an Information Technology Act, as far back as 1998; it was also one of the first to set up Computer Emergency Response Team (CERT) in 2004. The potential for Information and Communications Technologies to drive growth and development was seen as early as the 1970s when the National Informatics Centre (NIC) was established to provide IT support to the government. The 1980s saw the establishment of country-wide networks, including the National Informatics Centre Network (NICNET) which connected Ministries of the Central Government, State Governments, and down to the individual districts via satellite and cable. A similar network, the Education and Research Network

(ERNET) served the academic and research communities. Internet service for the public was made available from 14 August 1995 and today, India has over 850 million users.[1]

Successive Indian governments have utilised information and communication technologies (ICT) in their efforts to take governance to the masses. The present government has made internet connectivity and digitalisation a cornerstone of many of its activities. Campaigns like the Digital India Campaign have been designed with a number of ambitious goals, from creating broadband highways, improving delivery of government services, and reducing electronics imports. Others like *Start-up India* tie in with other larger campaigns like *Make in India* and endeavour to have digital products created in India rather than just consuming those created elsewhere. The Aadhaar unique identification card initiative, with over a billion numbers generated, functions on a digital backbone, with the biometric data stored in a central database.[2]

Some aspects unique to developing countries are the low level of cyber literacy, especially at the level of individuals which makes them easy targets for all manner of social engineering based crimes. Another aspect to be considered is the need to focus on mobile security as much as computer security given that most interactions and transactions in developing countries take place through mobile phones. Mobile vulnerabilities increased by 215 per cent in 2015 over 2014 according to a report commissioned by the Global Forum on Cyber Expertise.[3] Low income levels also are a cause of computer piracy, in turn leading to compromised systems which are then used for bot network activities. While botnet infections in India have come down after government-led initiatives such as the Cyber Swachh project to clean computers, it is still ranked second in the list of botnet infected countries.[4] The number of botnet victim detections in Africa was around 50,000, with a monthly average detection of 3,900.[5] The global percentage of bots originating from Africa stood at 13%.[6] Compromised systems and cybercrime activities originating from Africa have also led to reputational damage and even geo-fencing to prevent online transactions originating out of Africa.[7]

Other factors have included vulnerable systems and lax business practices, and the traditional tussle between viewing cyber security as a cost center by companies where governments have tried to encourage companies to enhance their cyber security practices through a combination of incentives and regulation. Cyber security budgets in many organizations are reported to be less than 1 per cent.

The global losses due to cybercrime have fluctuated widely since there is no verifiable method for measuring cybercrime. The latest report by McAfee in association with the Center for Strategic and International Studies gives a figure of $ 600 billion. Of this the loss to sub-Saharan Africa is estimated at $2 billion (.13% of GDP) and the loss to South Asia is estimated at $11 billion (.385 of GDP).[8] In addition to monetary loss, there are other losses including reputational loss to businesses, loss due to theft of intellectual property, loss of productivity and legal costs.[9]

A number of recent indices bear testimony to the efforts of governments in Africa and India to utilise cyberspace to resolve governance issues as well as the long way they have to traverse. The 2018 edition of the United Nations Annual E-government survey has four countries from Africa in the top-100. The countries from Africa are Mauritius, South Africa, Tunisia and Seychelles, ranked, respectively at 66, 68, 80 and 83.[10] India also broke into the top 100 for the first time in 2018, with a ranking of 96,[11] reaching a ranking of 10 in 2020.[12] From Africa, Mauritius and Egypt rank at 6 and 14 respectively.[13] In general, smaller countries rank higher on the indices by virtue of the smaller size of the population which facilitates better governance.

However, the root causes are not just the vulnerabilities in the software, but the use of those by cyber-criminals, as well as state-sponsored actors for purposes ranging from espionage, to attacks on critical information infrastructure. Attacks have ranged from ransomware attacks, to Dedicated Denial of Service (DDOS) attacks. Malicious ransomware attacks like Wannacry, Petya and Notpetya were rebuffed through a combination of luck and active response by governments and tech companies. Whilst Notpetya brought the operations of the shipping giant Maersk in India to a halt, a number of countries in Africa were impacted by the Wannacry ransomware.[14] India was affected the most by NotPetya in the Asia-Pacific region and was the seventh most affected globally. Wannacry was formally attributed to North Korea by the US supported by allies in December 2017 through North Korea rejected these allegations. While Petya's origins were murkier, like Wannacry, it was based on an exploit developed by the US National Security Agency

(NSA) which was leaked in March 2017 by the Shadow Brokers, a hacking group believed to be affiliated to Russian intelligence. According to reports, North Korea is even using the proceeds of cyber-criminal activities carried out by its agents as a source of funding. That much of this cannot be conclusively and independently verified speaks to the instabilities in cyberspace. As the above examples show, cyber attacks need not be targeted to be destructive, more often than not, countries find themselves affected as collateral damage. However, the absence of borders in cyberspace means that attackers can spoof their identities and even basic forensics to arrive at the source of the attacks is difficult.

Cybersecurity is much more than cybercrime, and discussion on the more fundamental issues is lacking as seen when examining even basic definitions which are largely borrowed from elsewhere. Cybersecurity, for instance, is a dynamic concept that has evolved over the years from the techno-centric definition put out by the International Telecommunications Union to broader all-encompassing definitions. The ITU definition was as follows: "Cybersecurity is the collection of tools, policies, security concepts, security safeguards, guidelines, risk management approaches, actions, training, best practices, assurance and technologies that can be used to protect the cyber environment and organization and user's assets.[15] Organization and user's assets include connected computing devices, personnel, infrastructure, applications, services, telecommunications systems, and the totality of transmitted and/or stored information in the cyber environment."[16] The US Department of Homeland Security in its glossary of Cybersecurity Terminology defines cybersecurity as follows: "Strategy, policy, and standards regarding the security of and operations in cyberspace, and encompass[ing] the full range of threat reduction, vulnerability reduction, deterrence, international engagement, incident response, resiliency, and recovery policies and activities, including computer network operations, information assurance, law enforcement, diplomacy, military, and intelligence missions as they relate to the security and stability of the global information and communications infrastructure"[17] Cybersecurity strives to ensure the attainment and maintenance of the security properties of the organization and user's assets against relevant security risks in the cyber environment. The general security objectives comprise the following: Availability, Integrity, which may include authenticity and non-repudiation, and Confidentiality.[18]

The Indian Cybersecurity Policy of 2013 does not create a definition but uses the definition found in the International Standards Organisation Guidelines for Cybersecurity released in 2012. This states that cyberspace is "a complex environment consisting of interactions between people, software services supported by worldwide distribution of information and communication technology."[19] The International Standards Organisation gave a caveat to this definition noting that "there are security issues that are not covered by current information security, Internet security, network security and ICT security best practices as there are gaps between these domains, as well as a lack of communication between organizations and providers in the Cyberspace.[20]

The fact remains that developing countries have very limited opportunities to provide inputs on fundamental issues such as defining the building blocks of cyberspace. In its June 2010 Report, the United Nations Group of Governmental Experts on Developments in the field of Information and Telecommunications in the context of International Security, had recommended "(v) Finding possibilities to elaborate common terms and definitions relevant to General Assembly resolution 64/25."[21]

The establishment of the UNGGE was pursuant to a resolution moved by Russia in 1998 calling on the UN General Assembly to examine the issue of information security. The first Group of Governmental Experts (UNGGE) set up in 2004 by the First Committee, one of the UN General Assembly's six committees, on Disarmament and International Security, couldn't even arrive at a consensus on recommendations to be submitted to the 1st Committee, with vastly divergent positions taken by Russia and China on the one hand, and the US and its European allies on the other, on even the issues to be discussed by the GGE.

In subsequent iterations, the basic pillars for securing cyberspace were conceptualised and sought to be fleshed out. The 2010 GGE Report recommended dialogue among States on the norms to address collective risks and for protecting the critical national and international infrastructure. It also called for measures to promote confidence, stability and risk reduction. The main achievement of the next GGE was to have an outcome document that recognised that existing international law was applicable to cyberspace.

This, to an extent, settled the longstanding debate whether cyberspace required new laws taking cognisance of its unique attributes or whether existing laws were enough.

The subsequent GGE tried to push ahead on all these tracks; it examined how international law applies in cyberspace. It recommended voluntary, non-binding norms, rules or principles of responsible behaviour of States aimed at promoting an open, secure, stable, accessible and peaceful cyberspace. It further elaborated on confidence building measures and capacity building in less developed countries. The GGE process seemed to be on track with the recommendations of the 2015 GGE containing clauses that reflected concerns and priorities of various countries. Some clauses emphasised that state security must go hand-in-hand with respect for human rights and fundamental freedoms, others that States must not use proxies to mask their activities, and that they must ensure that their territories are not used by non-State actors for unlawful activities. It was agreed that state sovereignty in cyberspace applied to conduct of ICT-related activities, and states had jurisdiction over ICT infrastructure within their territory. However, despite the veneer of agreement, there were fault lines connected not just to cybersecurity but geopolitical changes, and the 2015 GGE could not agree on a consensus report by the conclusion of its mandate in 2017, dealing a body blow to the UNGGE process which had coalesced around rights and duties of states in cyberspace. While earlier GGEs had seen agreement that both were to be derived from existing international law, the 2015 GGE had the crucial mandate of taking the process forward and spelling out how the laws applied as well as fleshing out norms that would fill in the gaps. Further progress was stymied for several reasons including mutual suspicion on the parts of opposing blocs about the motivations and interests of the other. Even though the UN processes were revived in 2019 with a fresh UNGGE being instituted along with an Open Ended Working Group (OEWG), despite a promising start with consensus reports released by both fora, a review of these reports show that very little progress has been made on constituting rules of the road with the existing entrenched positions further exacerbated by the Ukraine conflict.[22]

Though, by virtue of being an instrument of the UN, the GGEs have had broad representation from the various continents, the skew has still been largely in favour of the developed world. India has been a member of the

UNGGE in the very first iteration that ran from 2004-05. It was also a member of the 2009-10, 2012-13, and 2016-17 Groups. As far as African representation in this important apex for cybersecurity and global internet governance is concerned, the representation has been limited, to say the least. The 2004-05 grouping had 2 countries (Mali and South Africa), 2009-10 had only South Africa, 2012-13 again had single country representation in the form of Egypt, 2014-15 had Ghana, Egypt and Kenya, and the last iteration which had increased membership to 25 had 4 countries from Africa, Kenya, Egypt, Senegal and Botswana. It goes without saying that even as new fora within the ambit of the United Nations are being considered, there should be increased representation from regions that were evidently under-represented in the previous fora.

Scope for India-Africa Co-operation in Cyberspace

The Indian subcontinent and the African countries have had a symbiotic relationship over the centuries, marked by seamless flow of people, resources and knowledge. This has continued into the present age, especially with regard to the sharing of technology. For instance, in 2009, India used its expertise in satellite technology to set in place the Pan-African Network at a cost of $116 million.[23] This network was used for tele-medicine and educational purposes and was hailed as a shining example of South-South co-operation. In the reverse direction, a private sector initiative for money transfer in low income communities, M-Pesa, started by telecommunications company Vodafone in Kenya in 2007, revolutionised this sector and was expanded to India in 2014.[24]

Even as the avenues for multilateral co-operation between the developing countries are lacking, the record of bilateral co-operation also offers much scope for improvement. India has signed memoranda of understanding (MoU) with just three countries in Africa; Egypt (2013), Tunisia (2014), and South Africa (2016).[25]

A summary of the MoUs for Tunisia and South Africa available on the Ministry site are virtually identical with the addition of a few extra areas of interest for Tunisia:

> "The MoU intends to foster active cooperation and exchange of knowledge and best practices between private entities, institutions

> involved in enhancing Capacity building, Governments and other public and private organisations of the two countries in the field of ICT. The main areas of cooperation are e-Governance, e-commerce, HRD and Capacity building in ICT sector, electronics hardware manufacturing, Information Security etc."[26]

The ICT projects that have been undertaken in Africa include the Indo-Ghana Kofi Annan Centre of Excellence for Communications and Information Technology (CoEICT) at Accra, a Centre of Excellence for Communications and Information Technology (CoEICT) at Dar-es-Salam, Tanzania and the India-Lesotho Centre of Excellence in ICT (ISCEICT) at Maseru, Lesotho.[27] One other aspect that needs to be looked at is whether the respective division in the Ministry of Electronics and Information Technology has adequate human resources and bandwidth to nurture and sustain the bilateral and multilateral efforts that are usually initiated at a government to government level.

On cybercrime, while India has signed Mutual Legal Assistance Treaties with 40 countries, just two of them are in Africa, South Africa and Egypt.[28] The Indian Technical and Economic Cooperation Programme (ITEC) the flagship bilateral assistance program has only recently started to offer short-duration technical programs in cyber technologies with the 2018 session offering courses at the Centre For Development Of Advanced Computing, Pune and the Indian Institute of Technology, Kanpur.[29] Earlier sessions in 2016 and 2015 had a few courses on cybercrime and cyber forensics conducted by Bureau of Police Research and Development.[30] Even though there has been a major expansion in the TEC programme with 5,000 odd participants from Africa every year, only a tiny fraction come for training on cybersecurity.[31] Indian digital initiatives like Aadhaar have been advocated by many as a solution to Africa's many problems, with some going to the extent of saying Africa would benefit more from Aadhaar than Chinese investments.[32] The Indian Government has made sporadic efforts to promote Aadhaar elsewhere, but the consensus is that considering the sensitivities involved with cyber technologies, it is better to have countries approach India rather than the other way around.[33]

The record is quite uneven when it comes to the Indian private sector investment in Africa, and in the ICT sector in particular. Barring the much-touted investments by Airtel in Africa, much of the $50 billion of investments monitored between 2006 and 2016 have gone into the energy sector.[34] While the countries of Africa would seem fertile ground for Indian entrepreneurs and start-ups, given similarity in economic wellbeing of citizens as well as economic problems in search of technology-based solutions, it would seem that the regulatory and other problems faced by such entrepreneurs are also similar. Whilst India has jumped many spots in the World Banks "Ease of Doing business" annual index, as at rank 100, African countries are also in the same range with Kenya at 80, and South Africa at 82.[35] An additional constraint for digital entrepreneurs is enactment of data protection laws across the continent which, even though for a good cause, increases costs for businesses. Starting with the African Union Convention on Cyber Security and Personal Data Protection, 2014, many African countries have enacted data protection and privacy laws.[36]

Another area for co-operation would be military arena. India has had a long standing military relationship with the countries of Africa, beginning with the deployment of military training teams in a number of act in countries as well as providing seats for African officers in Indian military training academies. Over the years, this cooperation has also extended to helping with the establishment of defence colleges in various countries of Africa. These include the establishment of the Military Academy in Ethiopia, defence and naval war colleges in Nigeria as well as setting up the Ghanian Air Force.[37] This topic has formed part of the discussions in both the 1st and 2nd editions of the India Africa Defence Minister's Dialogue (IADD) held on the sidelines of the Defence Expo in Lucknow in 2020 and in Gandhinagar in 2022. The Lucknow Declaration of 2020 called for co-operation *inter-alia* in "joint ventures in defence equipment software and digital defence".[38] The press release on the occasion of the IADD 2022 also noted that the IADD "seeks to build on the existing defence partnerships between African countries & India and to explore new areas of convergence for mutual engagements including areas such as capacity building, training, cyber security, maritime security and counter-terrorism."[39] The one constrain would be that the Indian military's engagement with cyber is, as yet, at a nasecent stage with the establishment of a Defence Cyber Agency in 2018.

To summarise, Indian engagement in Africa has mainly revolved around capacity building and institution building, trade and investment, technology transfer, as well as providing financial resources to facilitate these efforts. India has much to offer on these lines in the field of ICT and cybersecurity, particularly when it comes to capacity development, and incorporating computer technologies in the financial and governance sectors. In the cybersecurity arena, meaningful co-operation could take place on exchanging information on cyber threats and in responding to incidents, strengthening IT infrastructure, prevailing cyber security policies, capacity building, and protecting critical Infrastructure. Military co-operation could also be explored. Supply chain security is another area of pressing importance with electronic and communications equipment being susceptible to having backdoors and increasingly becoming a national security threat. On the economic front, the common areas of interest would be Electronic manufacturing as a means of import substitution, sharing expertise and know-how on start-ups and Software Technology Parks, and operationalising a Digital Economy. International cyber governance is another area which calls for a co-operative approach. The interests of India and the African nations align in the need for an open, secure and stable cyberspace. Bilateral dialogues should necessarily incorporate discussion on pressing cyber issues, such as developing an open, inclusive, transparent and multi-stakeholder system of internet governance, the application of international law in cyberspace and active participation in the UN processes.

It may be seen that there is a scope for a comprehensive agenda of co-operation, and the discussions should take place not just at the government-to-government level but also amongst all the very many stakeholders including the private sector, non-governmental organisations and academia for optimum results.

NOTES

1 Telecom Regulatory Authority of India, Information Note to the Press (Press Release No.8/2023), "Indian Telecom Services Performance Indicator Report" for the Quarter July-September, 2022, p. 1 3 February 2023 https://trai.gov.in/sites/default/files/PR_No.08of2023.pdf

2 Aadhaar Dashboard, https://uidai.gov.in/aadhaar_dashboard/

3 "Cyber Crime and Cyber Security Trends in Africa Report," Global Forum on Cyber Expertise, 16 March 2017, p. 20.

4 "The Top 10 Worst Botnet Countries," The Spamhaus Project, www.spamhaus.org/statistics/botnet-cc/

5 Interpol, *African Cyberthreat Assessment Report 2021*, p. 7, at https://www.interpol.int/en/News-and-Events/News/2021/INTERPOL-report-identifies-top-cyberthreats-in-Africa

6 "Cyber Crime and Cyber Security Trends in Africa Report," Global Forum on Cyber Expertise, 16 March 2017, p. 22.

7 Nir Kshetri, *Cybercrime and Cybersecurity in Africa*, Journal of Global Information Technology Management, 22:2, p. 5.

8 Signé, Landry, and Kevin Signé. "Global Cybercrimes and Weak Cybersecurity Threaten Businesses in Africa," Brookings, 4 June 2018, www.brookings.edu/blog/africa-in-focus/2018/05/30/global-cybercrimes-and-weak-cybersecurity-threaten-businesses-in-africa.

9 United Nations, "UNITED NATIONS E-GOVERNMENT SURVEY 2018," at https://publicadministration.un.org/egovkb/Portals/egovkb/Documents/un/2018-Survey/E-Government%20Survey%202018_FINAL%20for%20web.pdf.

10 Ibid.

11 The Financial Express, "India Breaks into Top 100 Again in Modi Era! After Ease of Doing Business, It is UN's E-Government Index," 30 July 2018, at www.financialexpress.com/economy/india-breaks-into-top-100-again-in-modi-era-after-ease-of-doing-business-it-is-uns-e-government-index/1263147/.

12 ITU, *Global Cybersecurity Index 2020*, https://www.itu.int/epublications/publication/D-STR-GCI.01-2021-HTM-E

13 International Telecommunications Union, "Global Cybersecurity Index 2017", p. 49. www.itu.int/dms_pub/itu-d/opb/str/D-STR-GCI.01-2017-PDF-E.pdf

14 "ICT CS Joe Mucheru Calls for Information Sharing and Reporting on Cyber-Security Breaches." CIO East Africa, 18 May 2017, www.cio.co.ke/news/ict-cs-joe-mucheru-calls-for-information-sharing-and-reporting-on-cyber-security-breaches-2/

15 "Cyber Security and Cyber Threats in the Construction Industry', https://www.windover.com/blog/cyber-security-cyber-threats-construction-industry/

16 Martin Euchner, Adviser, ITU-T,ITU-T *CYBEX standards for cybersecurity information dissemination and exchange*, ITU-ATU Workshop on Cybersecurity Strategy in African Countries, Khartoum, Sudan, 24-26 July 2016, https://www.itu.int/en/ITU-T/Workshops-and-Seminars/cybersecurity/Documents/PPT/S5P1_Martin_Euchner_V2.pdf.

17 USA, Department of Homeland Security, National Initiative for Cybersecurity Careers and Studies, "Explore Terms: A Glossary of Common Cybersecurity Terminology" ND. http://niccs.us-cert.gov/glossary 13 The White House, *The National Strategy to Secure Cyberspace*. Washington D.C., February 2003, p. vii.

18 ITU, Definition of Cybersecurity, https://www.itu.int/en/ITU-T/studygroups/com17/Pages/cybersecurity.aspx.

19 India, Department of Electronics and Information Technology, *National Cyber Security Policy-2013,* Delhi: 2013, https://www.meity.gov.in/writereaddata/files/National_cyber_security_policy-2013_0.pdf.

20 "Information Technology – Security Techniques – Guidelines for Cybersecurity, *"International Standards Organisation*, 2012, Web. 14 Nov. 2015. < https://www.iso.org/obp/ui/#iso:std:iso-iec:27032:ed-1:v1:en>.

21 "Group of Governmental Experts on Developments in the Field of Information and Telecommunications in the Context of International Security," United Nations, 30 July 2010.

22 Agnese Olmati, "Multi-Stakeholder Governance of Cyberspace – Merely a Myth?," *Directions Blog*, 21 November 2022, directionsblog.eu/multi-stakeholder-governance-of-cyberspace-merely-a-myth/.

23 India, Ministry of External Affairs, *Pan African e-Network Project (PAENP)*, https://mea.gov.in/Portal/ForeignRelation/Pan_African_e_docx_for_xp.pdf

24 Business Today, *Can mobile money transfer service M-Pesa succeed in India?*, 23 November 2014, https://www.businesstoday.in/magazine/case-study/story/case-study-vodafone-mpesa-mobile-cash-transfer-service-future-140393-2014-11-06

25 Government of India, Ministry of Electronics and Information Technology, "Active MoUs | Ministry of Electronics and Information Technology", meity.gov.in/content/active-mous

26 Government of India. Ministry of Electronics and Information Technology, "International ICT Projects", meity.gov.in/content/international-ict-projects

27 Ibid.

28 Ministry of Home Affairs, "MLATs," Central Bureau of Investigation, https://cbi.gov.in/MLATs-list.

29 Ministry of External Affairs, India, *ITEC Program*, at https://www.itecgoi.in/index.php

30 Ministry of External Affairs, "Civilian Training Programme, Indian Technical & Economic Cooperation (ITEC) 2016-2017." The Indian Technical and Economic Cooperation Programme (ITEC), at www.itecgoi.in/downloads/2016-2017.pdf

31 Economic Times, "Benefits for Africa as India Expands ITEC Programme," 30 November 2015, at economictimes.indiatimes.com/news/economy/foreign-trade/benefits-for-africa-as-india-expands-itec-programme/articleshow/49982822.cms

32 Adam Minter, How India Could Transform Africa. Bloomberg.com, 7 October 2018, www.bloomberg.com/view/articles/2018-10-07/india-s-aadhaar-could-unlock-economic-growth-in-africa.

33 Amrit Raj, and Upasana Jain, "Aadhaar Goes Global, Finds Takers in Russia and Africa," Livemint, 8 July 2016, at www.livemint.com/Politics/UEQ9o8Eo8RiaAaNNMyLbEK/Aadhaar-goes-global-finds-takers-in-Russia-and-Africa.html

34 Malancha Chakrabarty, "India's Feeble Stakes in Africa." DNA, 20 February 2018, at www.dnaindia.com/analysis/column-india-s-feeble-stakes-in-africa-2586516

35 "Africa's Best, Worst Countries for Doing Business," CNBC Africa, 31 October 2017, at www.cnbcafrica.com/news/east-africa/2017/10/31/africas-best-countries-for-doing-business/

36 "Personal Data Protection Guidelines for Africa," Internet Society, 8 May 2018, at www.internetsociety.org/wp-content/uploads/2018/05/AUCPrivacyGuidelines_2018508_EN.pdf

37 Arvind Dutta, "Indo-African Defence Cooperation: Need for Enhanced Thrust," *Journal of Defence Studies*, IDSA, 2008, at www.idsa.in/jds/2_2_2008_IndoAfricanDefenceCooperation_ADutta.

38 Ministry of Defence, "Lucknow Declaration Adopted at the 1st India-Africa Defence Ministers Conclave, 2020, 6 February 2020", at https://pib.gov.in/newsite/PrintRelease.aspx? relid = 199072

39 Ministry of Defence, India-Africa Defence Dialogue held on the sidelines of DefExpo 2022 in Gandhinagar, Gujarat; paves way for strengthening of India-Africa defence relations, 18 October 2022, at https://mod.gov.in/sites/default/files/sidelines-of-DefExpo-2022.pdf

11

India's Capacity Building Initiatives in Africa

Donald P. Chimanikire

Introduction

India and Africa have a long-standing relationship that dates back to ancient times. Their long history of interaction is embedded in their shared colonial history. There are many people of Indian descent who live in Africa, many of whom have participated in Africa's quest for independence. The India-Africa relationship is thus viewed through historical lenses. For decades India has played a crucial role in the development of Africa. It is an important driver of South-to-South cooperation. This relationship has developed into a partnership over time and it is predicted that in years to come India's relationship with Africa will surpass that of other Asian giants. The century-long economic linkage between India and Africa has evolved from an ancient people-led mercantile exchange to the current private sector-led industrial trade and production partnership, with the facilitating political support. While there is a steady increase in the volume of trade and equity cooperation between two sides, the issues concerning equilibrium and content of trade remain major challenges in the recent years.

India established trade relations with African countries as long back as the 16th century. According to Dubey, modern history lays testimony to the fact that Indian merchants came to Africa working for trade routes across the Indian Ocean in quest for lucrative markets for their goods.[1] In the process they played an influential role in the history of African culture. Trading links also necessitated the movement of people and currently an estimated 1.5 million Indians live in East Africa. The colonial period however brought an end to this trading system. The works of the Indian philosopher, Mahatma Gandhi, inspired Africa's colonial period. Gandhi's non-violent philosophy helped India attain its independence in 1947; the same philosophy inspired a generation of African leaders including Kwame Nkrumah of Ghana, Obafemi Awolowo of Nigeria, Julius Nyerere of Tanzania and Kenneth Kaunda of Zambia.[2]

Historically, India's relations with Africa were multi-dimensional, and could be analysed into five strands that is fight against racism, support to liberation struggles, Afro-Asian assertion culminating into Non-Alignment Movement (NAM), policy of active Association with Indian Diaspora and economic diplomacy along with security and peace building under South-to-South cooperation. As the first colonial country to become independent soon after the War, India was historically placed under fully committed leadership of Nehru to carry forward the movement of liberation and struggle against racial discrimination in Africa.[3] Under the reign of Nehru, India pursued a policy of supporting Africa's struggle for independence and against apartheid in South Africa. Indian support to liberation struggles in Africa during the Nehru period was influenced by Indian's own strategy and experience of freedom struggle.

Africa's development is a huge opportunity for India, just as Africa's resources play a key role in driving India's economic growth, while creating wealth and jobs in Africa. The continent's progress will add great stability and momentum to the global economy and benefit India as well. With a view to significantly enhance India's trade with Africa, the Government of India (GOI) launched an integrated programme 'Focus Africa' from the year 2002-2003. The main objective of the programme was to increase interactions between the two regions by identifying the areas of bilateral trade and investment. The 'Focus Africa' programme was extended to cover the entire African continent. These developments can be attributed to the growing prowess of African and Indian companies, with the GOI playing a pivotal role in creating an enabling environment for expansion through investment.

According to former Deputy Managing Director of Export Import Bank of Indian, Mr Debasish Mallick, Africa has emerged as one of India's major export, on account of GOI's Initiatives such as Focus Market Scheme, among others. Effectiveness of the bilateral initiatives that exists between India and Africa can be gauged from the recent robust trends in Indo-Africa trade relations, wherein bilateral trade has increased around five-fold in the last decade, which stood at US$ 98 billion in 2022-23.[4] Africa accounts for nearly 10 percent of India's global exports and supplies 8.3 per cent of India's global imports. The Indian private investment in Africa has surged with major investments having taken place in the telecommunications, IT, energy, and automobiles sectors and this has led to significant changes in Africa's transport and technology sector. According to the RBI, Africa accounted for nearly one-fifth of Indian overseas direct investments during April 1996 to March 2016, with Mauritius, Mozambique, Sudan, Egypt and South Africa being some of the major investment destinations.

Apart from the Focus Africa Programme, India also hosts the 'India Africa Forum Summit (IAFS)'. It was initiated in the year 2008, the IAFS process, in particular, has been the most defining policy initiative that has ushered in a qualitative transformation of India's relations with Africa. It has elevated the relationship to the summit level and has provided an institutional framework for cooperation at continental, regional and bilateral levels. As a consequence, political understanding, security cooperation, trade and investment collaboration, energy partnership, development partnership, and diaspora linkages between both regions have been enhanced According to Dash and Ray, while preparing for the IAFS-III in 2014, New Delhi recognised issues and concerns that were affecting the sustainability of its relationship with Africa, thus necessitating a calibrated, coherent and holistic policy approach.[5] The third IAFS hosted by the Indian Government in 2015 revealed the agenda that would help to empower Africans and bring Africa and India closer in the future. During the summit, India pledged US$ 10 billion in concessional lines of credit to African countries.

India's partnership with Africa has been driven by the aim of empowerment, capacity building, human resource development, access to Indian market, and support for Indian investments in Africa. The Pan Africa e-network Project, a joint initiative with India and the African Union is a good example that shows the partnership between Africa and India.

International Solar Alliance (ISA), one of the recent major initiatives of the Government of India, was conceived as a coalition of solar resource rich countries to address their special energy needs and to provide a platform to collaborate on addressing the identified gaps through a common, agreed approach. The proposed ISA members would include solar resource rich countries lying fully or partially between the Tropic of Cancer and the Tropic of Capricorn. The GOI would support the ISA by hosting its Secretariat for an initial period of five years and thereafter, it is expected to generate its own resources and become self-financing. Many African countries are part of the ISA and this would lead to significant changes in Africa. This is especially so, given the strong focus of the governments in the region on rural electrification and the inadequate grid connectivity which renders cooperation on decentralised solar power an attractive proposition. India pledged to add 100 GW of PV capacity by 2022 under its National Solar Mission.

India's Capacity Building

The United Nations Development Programme defines Capacity Building as the process by which individuals, organisations, institutions and societies develop abilities to perform functions, solve problems and set and achieve objectives. Capacity building encompasses a broad spectrum of projects. According to Yaruingam, it includes human resource development; the process of equipping individuals with the understanding, skills and access to information, knowledge and training that enables them to perform effectively.[6] It also encompasses organisational development, the elaboration of management structures, processes and procedures, not only within organisations, but also the management of relationships between the different organisations and sectors (public, private and community). Institutional and legal framework development, making legal and regulatory changes to enable organisations, institutions and agencies at all levels and in all sectors to enhance their capacities is also included in capacity building. The focus of India in Africa has for years been on capacity building and human resource development. With the use of Lines of Credits (LOCs) the government of India has managed to empower Africans with capacity building initiatives.

As a move to bolster India–Africa relations, the Government of India embarked on a journey of strengthening capacity building initiatives in Africa.

Indian investment in Africa has increased over the years and this has improved South-to-South cooperation. India's investment and capacity building mechanisms have created a long lasting relationship of cooperation between India and Africa. Capacity building has been an important factor in bolstering the India-Africa relations. India's former Minister of State for External Affairs VK Singh was quoted saying, "We feel that capacity building will always remain as a very important element of our cooperation. Our approach of development has always been because we believe that when you partner for development you must build capacities and capabilities in that country and it should not be extracted in your engagement."[7] While addressing a 400-member delegation at the CII-EXIM Bank conclave, Mr Singh said: "India will make sure to partner and share with knowledge, resources, technology and other support to the nations in the African continent."[8] Focusing on strengthening India-Africa cooperation, Mr Singh said that the transfer of technology is a strong foundation for India-Africa relations. Fields such as health-care, space, pan Africa e-network and its new avatar e-ArogyaBharti and e-VidyaBharti also play a crucial role in the cooperation between India and Africa. The latest initiative by India is launch of first off shore campus of Indian Institute of Technology, Madras in Zanzibar, Tanzania.[9] Such initiatives pave way for Africa's development and for reducing the differences that exist between Africa and the Global North.

Yaruingam further reiterates that several Africans have undergone training in India under the Indian Technical and Education Cooperation Programme (TECP). Capacity building is one key pillar in India's cooperation with Africa.[10] India emerged as a third largest skilled human resource in the world due to substantial public investment in establishing academic and professional institutions.[11] This makes India a vital entity in capacity building and human resource development in Africa. The growth of India's economy and resource base has led to broadening of cooperation initiatives and capacity building in Africa. In 2005 India became a full member of the African Capacity Building Foundation (ACBF). The ACBF is a development institution that supports capacity building efforts in sub-Saharan Africa. Countries and institutions that join the ACBF provide the resource base of the foundation from which it is able to provide financial and technical support to capacity building projects and programmes in Africa. Investment in capacity building is a necessity in Africa so as to achieve the Sustainable Development Goals.

At the India-Africa Forum Summit held in New Delhi in October 2015, India unveiled a consolidated fund of $10 billion for a host of development projects, training institutes and scholarships. At that summit, India had also pledged $10 billion in concessional credit to Africa. Apart from the concessional credit India also offered Africa an additional grant assistance of $600 million, an India-Africa Development Fund of $100 million and an India-Africa Health Fund of 10 million. India also announced 50,000 scholarships for African students in India over the next five years, and provided support to the expansion of the Pan Africa E-Network and institutions of skilling, training and learning across Africa. India's commitment to Africa has been of great importance for Africa's development especially in capacity building in the technology sector.

According to Mullen and Arora, "At the first India Africa Summit in 2008, India introduced financial support in the form of US$ 300 million credit line to the New Partnership for African Development (NEPAD) programme."[12] There was also an increase in the 'Aid for Africa' budget for projects in areas of capacity building and human resource development. Indian Technical and Economic Cooperation (ITEC) training slots offered annually to Africa were also increased. Long-term scholarships were doubled for graduate and postgraduate students. The Indian private sector working together with the government of India has been conducting training programmes aimed at providing African researchers with opportunities to conduct collaborative research with leading researchers and Research and Development institutions at Indian universities in the areas of science and technology. An example of such an initiative is the CV Raman International Fellowship.[13] There is no doubt that India's engagement is highly appreciated by Africans. Akinwumi Adesina, President of the African Development Bank, noted, "This cooperation is both a mutual privilege and priority" and that "it is a pleasure to partner with such an inveterate and committed investor in Africa.[14]

Indian Technical and Economic Cooperation (ITEC)

The ITEC was established by a decision of the Indian Cabinet on September 15, 1964 as a bilateral programme of assistance of the GOI. The decision regarding the setting up of ITEC was predicated on the underlying belief that it was necessary to establish relations of mutual concern and interdependence. The relationship was to be based not only on commonly held ideals and aspirations, but also on solid economic foundations. "Technical and economic cooperation was considered to be one of the essential functions of an integrated and imaginative foreign policy."[15] The ITEC was formulated with the intention of providing technical assistance to partner countries by focusing on manpower development. African countries have been the largest recipients under the ITEC Programme.

The Indian Technical and Economic Cooperation Programme (ITEC) is a demand-driven, response-oriented programme that focuses on addressing the needs of developing countries through innovative technological cooperation between India and the partnering nation. "Since its inception, the programme has spent over US$ 2 billion and benefited thousands of students and professionals from around the globe and annual expenditure on the programme has averaged US$ 100 million per annum in recent years."[16] The ITEC is an important part of India's attempt in contributing to South-to-South cooperation. The ITEC has also been an important component of India's assistance to African nations. In recent years, India has increased its assistance to various African nations and groupings. The focus is now on areas such as transfer of technology and the development of projects like the Pan African e-network that will link the African nations with Indian institutions and expertise. India also continues to provide extensive opportunities for human resource development and personnel training in these countries. There is also a special corollary to augment ITEC for African nations called the Special Commonwealth Assistance for Africa Programme (SCAAP).

The ITEC programme covers a wide range of areas including the training for civil and defence personnel, projects and project related activities such as consultancy services, study tours, donation of equipment, deputation of Indian experts in the partner nation and aid for disaster relief.[17] Personnel's training covers a wide and varied range of sectors such as banking, Information Technology and computers, personal management and administrative and scientific areas. India's Ministry of External Affairs coordinates the ITEC programme and all expenses including international airfare, boarding, lodging and tuition fees of selected personnel are borne by the Indian authorities. Although the ITEC is essentially a bilateral programme, its resources have also been used for financing trilateral and regional undertakings such as with the Economic Commission for Africa. The Afro-Asian Rural Reconstruction Organisation, COMESA, the African Union Commission and the G-15 receive training and project support under the ITEC.

The ITEC programme helps in capacity building through offering of technical training slots to personnel from developing countries in the very large network of vocational and human resource development institutions in India. Indian experts are transferred to developing countries to train local personnel, impart specialised skills and know-how in different fields. In addition, the ITEC programme facilitates study visits to India by senior political leaders and decision-makers from developing countries to acquaint them with the opportunities India offers in enhancing developing cooperation with these countries. Under the ITEC programme India also provides scholarships to students from African countries.

Capacity Building in Education and Skills Development

Economies in Africa have grown at unprecedented rates in the last several decades, but continued success will hinge on the ability to build local workforce capacity. Companies operating in Africa continue to cite difficulty in training, mobilising and retaining a competitive workforce as one of the biggest issues they face. India, with its booming economy, experience navigating workforce development in the developing world, and interest in increasing its influence in the continent, is uniquely situated to address these issues.

Since the Second Africa-India Forum Summit (2011), over 24,000 scholarships across 300 training courses conducted at 60 training institutions have been utilised by African nationals in areas such as IT, renewable energy, agriculture, marine & aeronautical engineering, marine hydrography, SME entrepreneurship, rural development, parliamentary affairs, logistics and management, climate change adaptation, disaster management, cyber security, forensic sciences, and defence and security, among others.[18] India has a long tradition of providing opportunities for higher education to students from developing countries. The opportunities have been for graduate and postgraduate courses in prestigious Indian universities, covering a wide range of disciplines in the humanities, science and technology and professional areas such as engineering and medicine. "Scholarships to African countries are administered through the Indian Council for Cultural Relations (ICCR) and through the African Union Commission although some scholarships may also be offered under the other institutions."[19] A number of Indian universities are offering self-financing placements to foreign students and this number is now several times that of placements under government scholarships. Central Ministries of the Government of India have their own International Cooperation Divisions, which promote bilateral exchanges with their counterpart in other developing countries. Such exchanges involve joint projects, capacity building programmes and visits of experts, which contribute significantly to South-South Cooperation.

The multiplicity of fellowships and training programmes in turn has led to the rejuvenation of India's civilian train-ing programmes through the Indian Technical & Economic Cooperation Programme (ITEC) and Special Commonwealth Assistance for Africa Programme (SCAAP) to offer help to de-veloping countries in Africa. The programme takes into account the regional groupings, such as the African Union (AU), for which additional slots have been made available. India offers various educational scholarships un-der 21 different schemes. The Indian Council for Cultural Research itself offers nearly 3365 scholarships annually under 24 scholarship schemes, of which 900 are for African coun-tries. There has been a considerable increase in the Indian government's allocation for SCAAP programme, which rose from $2.56 million in 2009-10 to $5.43 million in 2015-16.[20] India's support to African countries through ITEC training slots was also increased from 1704 in 2008-09 to nearly 4000 in 2014-15. In the last ten years, India has trained around 23,000 African experts under the ITEC programme.[21]

At the first India-Africa Forum Summit which was held in Delhi in 2008, India formally identified and prioritised the creation of educational and vocational training opportunities for Africa. More specifically, India pledged to establish ten in-country training institutes and provide scholarships for African students to study at Indian institutions of higher learning. Though India is a country still on the cusp of development itself, its government views investments in African education and vocational training as an opportunity to increase "soft influence" in the region, and strengthen relations with a trading partner that is rapidly growing in importance. Reflecting a unique approach to capacity building, many of India's contributions (both in the private and public sectors) have been products of collaborations between India and a local African institution, and have centred on helping Africans acquire skills in mathematics and the sciences.[22]

Sudan and Ethiopia have been important partners in training initiatives with the Government of India. Sudanese judicial officials were provided training by India in 1954. In addition, the Government of India also advised the Sudanese administration on a compensation scheme for expatriate officials.[23] In some mineral-rich countries, Indian engineers have played a key role in setting up the knowledge base for extractive industries. In 1961, the government of Ethiopia requested assistance in providing facilities for its officials to study programmes related to community development and three such officials went to India for training.

Capacity Building Institutions

India has committed to establishing about 100 capacity-building institutions to build and strengthen capacities at the pan-African, regional and bilateral levels. According to Yaruingam some of the key institutions are listed below:[24]

- India-Africa Institute of Information Technology, Ghana
- India-Africa Institute of Foreign Trade, Ghana, Uganda
- India-Africa Institute of Education Planning and Administration, Burundi
- India-Africa Diamond Institute, Botswana
- India-Africa Civil Aviation Academy
- India-Africa Institute of Agriculture and Rural Development
- India-Africa University for Life and Earth Sciences – Ibadan University, Nigeria

India-Africa Institute of Foreign Trade

A project of the African Union and India's National University of Education and Planning, this institute is run out of the University of Burundi and will offer full-time and part-time MBA programmes to African students.

India-Africa Institute of Information Technology

A Ghanaian vocational training centre that will offer computer software courses developed by the state-run Educational Consultants India.

India-Africa Diamond Institute

A training centre located in Botswana (near De Beers rough diamond sales operation centre) that will provide vocational skills in gemology, diamond grading, and gem polishing.

Tata Motors

Established a partnership with the Engineering Faculty at the University of Pretoria in South Africa, providing training in various vehicle manufacturing processes to African students.

CV Raman International Fellowship

In its sixty years, this grant funds African students to pursue doctoral research in mathematics and the sciences at Indian institutions of higher learning.

Pan Africa e-Network (PAEN)

A collaboration between the African Union and the Indian government, PAEN currently connects African students in 34 countries to Indian online tele-education and tele-medicine services. To date, over 2000 students have enrolled in top-ranking Indian universities in fields such as finance, business, and IT. India aims to provide online education to 10,000 African students by 2015.

Capacity Building in Science and Technology

Technology co-operation has been an essential ingredient in India's development co-operation with Africa since mid-1960s when the Indian Technical and Economic Co-operation (ITEC) Programme was launched. The ITEC was formulated with the intention of providing technical assistance to partner countries by focusing on manpower development. African countries have been the largest recipients under the ITEC Programme. India has a global reputation as a leader in the software industry, information technology enabled services, and business process outsourcing, and, over time, the sector has employed more than 10 million people. "The high demand for ICT services in India has also created demand for education, especially for engineering and computer science. This in turn has positioned India as a key ICT knowledge exporter."[25] The need for technology cooperation has been a major issue between the countries in the South. Indian technology was considered suitable for developing countries of Africa as compared to the more advanced tech from the West, which would provide challenges for the African countries.

Indian engineers have played a vital role in development projects in terms of implementation and training in areas such as irrigation, electrical power and railway management. In 1956, India helped establish a residential Royal Technical College in Nairobi. The college was meant to provide higher technical, commercial and arts education bearing a cost of $1.5 million. India and Ghana are also involved in institutional and capacity building partnerships aimed at knowledge sharing and transfer. According to Malyan and Jindal, the Ghana India Kofi Annan Centre for excellence was set up in Accra. Ghana's first Advanced Information Technology Institute works to stimulate growth of ICT Sector in ECOWAS.

India signed technology cooperation agreements with four African countries namely South Africa, Tunisia, Egypt, and Mauritius. India's cooperation with South Africa in the field of technology started in 1995 with a renewal in 2015. As of 2015, 74 joint research projects have been undertaken in areas such as biotechnology, information science, astronomy, food science technologies for rural applications, indigenous knowledge systems, nanotechnology, and renewable energy and more than 220 South African researchers have received funding from the Government of India.

During the India-Africa Forum Summit in 2008, India committed substantial support towards science and technology development in Africa. The Department of Science and Technology is implementing a number of programmes and activities under the India-Africa Science and Technology Initiative. The CV Raman Fellowship for African researchers was started in 2010 with the objective of providing opportunities to African researchers to engage in collaborative research in science and technology in Indian universities and institutions under eminent Indian scientists. So far about 164 candidates from African countries have been awarded fellowships under this programme.

The Department of Science and Technology is also providing technical assistance to African institutions engaged in research and development by training African researchers, sharing technological know-how and developing academic linkages with African institutions. In 2022, India launched the India Africa Security Fellowship programme to encourage policy oriented research on security issues by researchers from African countries. This programme is hosted by Manohar Parrikar Institute for Defence Studies and Analyses (MP-IDSA).

India is also playing a significant role in the deployment of renewable energy technologies in Africa. It has extended credit lines to facilitate the construction of power transmission lines in Kenya and Mali, hydro power plants in Burundi, the Central African Republic, and the Democratic Republic of Congo, and solar power plants in Niger. Promotion of decentralised solar energy options and improved cook stoves not only provides energy access to the energy poor rural households in Africa, but also improves their quality of life.[26]

India-Africa technology co-operation in the field of agriculture, renewable energy technology, and information technology bears a special mention. India and Africa share the same agro-climatic conditions which makes their partnering in agriculture an important component of South-to-South cooperation. India-Africa science and technology co-operation has opened up a wide array of unique opportunities for the growth of Africa's agricultural sector. African agriculture suffers from low productivity and limited use of technology, India possesses the technological capacity that Africa needs to harness growth in agriculture. According to Saran and Chakrabarty, India set up two institutions, that is International Crop Research Institute for the Semi-Arid Tropics (ICRISAT) and International Livestock Research Institute (ILRI).[27] These institutions have led increased cooperation for India-Africa co-operation in agriculture. The ICRISAT has established agri-business incubators and value-chain incubators in five African countries namely, Angola, Cameroon, Ghana, Mali and Uganda by partnering with local bodies. ILRI focuses on reducing poverty and improving food security in African countries through more sustainable use of livestock. Some of the ILRI's ongoing India-Africa programmes are: IM Goats (India-Mozambique), Milk IT (India-Tanzania), Value-Chain Development (India-Tanzania, Ethiopia, Mali) and

South-South Dairy Development (India-Kenya). Its India-Africa Knowledge Management mechanism emphasises on dissemination of technologies, tools and approaches.[28]

India is also playing a significant role in the deployment of renewable energy technologies in Africa. It has extended credit lines to facilitate the construction of power transmission lines in Kenya and Mali, hydro power plants in Burundi, the Central African Republic, and the Democratic Republic of Congo, and solar power plants in Niger. Indian institutions such as The Energy and Resources Institute (TERI) are promoting the use of solar lanterns and clean cooking options in many African countries. Promotion of decentralised solar energy options and improved cook stoves not only provides energy access to the energy poor rural households in Africa, but also improves their quality of life.[29] 80 candidates from various Africa countries have participated in training programmes in IT sector in CDAC Noida and CDAC Pune. India's lines of credit was used to construct the Technology Development and Innovation Centre in Science and Technology Park in Mozambique, Technology Park in Cape Verde and the Mahatma Gandhi IT and Biotechnology Park in Cote d'Ivoire. There are also some significant Africa-India initiatives undertaken at multilateral level, particularly in the domain of South-South cooperation. Sub-Saharan African countries and India have established collaboration in the health biotechnology.

Pan African e-Network/e-VBAB

Pan African e-Network, the first initiative of India in Africa at the continental level was launched in 2009 and fully funded by the Government of India for an amount of around Rs. 530 crores. The network has three components that is tele-education, tele-medicine and VVIP connectivity. 48 countries in Africa have acceded to the Network. The Network was handed over to the African Union in July 2014. The Pan-Africa e-Network is one of the best examples of the growing partnership between India and Africa. It began as a visionary initiative of the former President of India, Dr. Kalam. The Pan-Africa e-Network was launched with the aim of narrowing the digital divide in Africa and harnessing socio-economic benefits of ICT. Forty-eight African countries are part of the project and 169 centres have been commissioned and integrated with the network. The tele-education and tele-medicine projects bear testimony to India's commitment and transfer of skills and technology and aims to change peoples' lives through bridging the digital divide between them and their African counter parts within the framework of 'South-South co-operation'. The goodwill generated by the project through its use of soft diplomacy will certainly help India further its economic and strategic diplomacy as well.

The Pan African e-Network is the biggest project in South-South Cooperation. It is giving Africa-India relations a new substance and content. It is not only bridging the digital divide, it is bridging the hope divide between the have and the have nots. It is one of the most ambitious projects for distance education and tele-medicine undertaken in Africa. In addition, the network is also equipped to support e-governance, e-commerce, and infotainment, resource mapping metrological and other services in African countries. A total of 47 African countries have joined the project in two phases. The first phase was inaugurated in February 2009, with 11 African countries signing up. The second phase was launched in August 2010. The objective of tele-education is to impart quality education to 10,000 students in Africa over a 5-year period in various disciplines. Some of the best educational institutions are participating in this project. According to Malyan and Jindal, currently 2000 African students are already enrolled in several distance education programs. In tele-medicine, on-line medical consultation with Indian medical specialists is now available to African medical practitioners at the Patient End Location in Africa. The project cost is $125 million.[30]

Malyan and Jindal are of the view that "the project is aimed at providing under graduate and post graduate courses in sunrise sectors such as human resources, international marketing, business administration, tourism management and finance investment and analysis by the Indian counterparts".[31] In addition, diploma and certificate courses in subjects that have current relevance and demand in the market, such as database and information systems, networking and operating systems, electronic instrumentation, accounting, child care and HIV/Aids and language courses in Arabic, English, French and German, are being taught through e-connectivity.

The African Union short-listed three leading regional universities and two regional hospitals for participation in the e-network. These include, the Makerere University, Uganda (east Africa), Kwame Nkrumah University of Science and Technology, Ghana (west Africa), University of Yaounde, Cameroon (Central Africa), Ebadan Hospital, Nigeria (west Africa) and the Brazzaville Hospital, Democratic Republic of Congo (Central Africa). In Africa, 53 e-learning, tele-education centres, tele-medicine centres and VVIP communication nodes for hotline connection between Heads of States (i.e., one in each country) were set up by TCIL. The second phase of Pan Africa e-network called e-Vidyabharti and e-ArogyaBharti (EVBAB) was launched in 2019.[32]

Conclusion

India's initiatives have brought forth development within the African continent. The growing economic and financial potential of India and other emerging economies has strongly impacted and changed the existing status quo. Under the India-Africa partnership, several initiatives have been taken to promote capacity building, skill transfer and infrastructure development in Africa. This necessitated change within the African continent and has further enhanced South-South cooperation. For Africa to develop, it has to use its strength in natural resources to build up its weak industrial sector. Strategic starting point is to carry out processing of raw materials, agricultural and mineral, within African countries. Processed exports will always earn more money overseas and local industrial capacity will be increased and diversified. But, while Africa will have its natural resources as the basis for transformation, it is the development of human resources that will in the final analysis, determine the course and content of the transformation process. It is, therefore, critical that India continues to provide assistance to Africa in the area of human resources.

NOTES

1 Ajay K. Dubey, "India-Africa Relations: Historical Goodwill and a Vision for the Future," in Ajay K. Dubey and Aparajita Biswas (eds.), *India and Africa's Partnership: A Vision for a New Future*, Springer, New Delhi, 2016, pp. 11-30.

2 A. Mazrui, "Africa's International Relations: The Diplomacy of Dependency and Change," Boulder, Colorado, 1977.

3 Ajay K. Dubey, 2016, note 1.

4 "Remarks made by External Affairs Minister, Dr. S. Jaishankar at the Business Community Interaction," Ministry of External Affairs, Government of India, 8 July 2023 at https://www.mea.gov.in/Speeches-Statements.htm?dtl/36766 (Accessed 30 July 2023).

5 N. Ray and S. Dash, *India's Africa Policy: Continuity, Change and Challenges,* Indian Council of World Affairs Policy Brief, 2 July 2014.

6 A.S. Yaruingam, *India's Capacity Building Diplomacy in Africa,* 5th Conference on African Studies, ECAS 2013.

7 "India moves to boost bilateral ties with Africa," at www.indiawrites.org/diplomacy/ (Accessed 18 May 2018).

8 Ibid.

9 "IIT Madras opens offshore campus in Zanzibar, Tanzania" *The Hindu*, 6 November 2023 at https://www.thehindu.com/news/national/tamil-nadu/iit-madras-opens-offshore-campus-in-zanzibar-tanzania/article67503984.ece (Accessed 21 November 2023).

10 A.S. Yaruingam, "India's Capacity Building Diplomacy in Africa," 5th Conference on African Studies, ECAS 2013.

11 Ajay K. Dubey, 2016, note 1.

12 R Mullen and K Arora, *India's Reinvigorated relationship with Africa,* Policy Brief, Centre for Policy Research, 2016.

13 Ibid.

14 *Africa and India: A Shared Development Agenda,* African Development Bank Group, May 2017.

15 www.mea.gov.in, Ministry of External Affairs, Government of India, October 19 2015.

16 www.mea.gov.in, Ministry of External Affairs, Government of India.

17 Ibid.

18 India Africa Framework for Strategic Cooperation, *Partners in Progress: Towards a Dynamic and Transformative Development Agenda*, Third India Africa Summit, 29 October 2015.

19 R Malyan and L Jindal, *Capacity Building in Education Sector: An Exploratory Study on Indian and African Relations*, Procedia Social and Behavioural Sciences (157), 2014, pp. 296-306

20 *Enhancing India Africa Development Cooperation*, Brookings Report 2016 at www.brookings.edu/research (Accessed 13 May 2018).

21 Annual Report, Ministry of External Affairs, Government of India at https://www.mea.gov.in/Uploads/PublicationDocs/36286_MEA_Annual_Report_2022_English_web.pdf (Accessed 23 November 2023).

22 *India Leverages Capacity Building Experience in Africa to Train and Mobilise Workers* at www.covafrica.com (Accessed 18 May 2018).

23 *Enhancing India Africa Development Cooperation*, Brookings Report 2016 at www.brookings.edu/research (Accessed 13 May 2018).

24 A S Yaruingam, *India's Capacity Building Diplomacy in Africa,* 5th Conference on African Studies, ECAS 2013.

25 *Africa and India: A Shared Development Agenda*, African Development Bank Group, May 2017.

26 www.mea.gov.in Ministry of External Affairs, Government of India, 19 October 2015.

27 S Saran and M Chakrabarty, *India Africa Cooperation in Science and Technology*, In Focus, Ministry of External Affairs, 2015.

28 M Purvi, *Extending India-Africa Cooperation in Science & Technology,* Presentation made at the Conference on Africa-India Cooperation for Science, Technology and Innovation held in New Delhi on 22 October 2013.

29 *India Africa cooperation in Science Technology goes a gear up*, at www.herald.co.zw (Accessed 15 May 2018).

30 R. Malyan and L Jindal, L *Capacity Building in Education Sector: An Exploratory Study on Indian and African Relations*, Procedia Social and Behavioural Sciences (157), 2014, pp 296-306.

31 Ibid.

32 Official Launch of e-VidyaBharti and e-ArogyaBharti Project by External Affairs Minister (October 09, 2019) Ministry of External affairs, Government of India, 9 October, 2019, at https://www.mea.gov.in/press-releases.htm?dtl/31928/Official+Launch+of+eVidyaBharti+and+ eArogyaBharti+Project+by+External+Affairs+Minister+October+09+2019%20 (Accessed 20 October 2023).

12

Skill Development and Capacity Building in Africa: Opportunities for Development Cooperation

Pranav Kumar

Introduction

Africa and India have similar challenges on skilling millions of young people who are joining workforce every year. While in India roughly 12 million people enter workforce each year, in Africa for the next three decades, 15-20 million increasingly well-educated young people are expected to join the African workforce every year. Investors across the globe including India identify skills gaps as a major constraint to their ability to do business in Africa. According to World Economic Forum Report 41 per cent of all firms in Tanzania, 30 per cent in Kenya, 9 per cent in South Africa and 6 per cent in Nigeria identify inadequately skilled workforces as a major constraint to their businesses. This pattern may get worse in the future. This scenario is adversely impacting Foreign Direct Investment flow into majority of African nations.

Skill development was identified as one of the priority sectors in the "Framework of Strategic Cooperation" adopted by the leaders at the Third India-Africa Forum Summit held at New Delhi in 2015. The Public-Private Partnership (PPP) model was identified as the preferred mode to encourage Indian businesses to set up skills development units in African industrial zones with the aim to train African engineers, technicians, managers, and workers.

This would not only help achieve the commitments made by the Government of India but also help fulfil the needs of Indian businesses who have invested in Africa. In this context, it is important for the Indian Government to synergize its missions on skill development in Africa with the interests of private sector.

With the advent of the fourth Industrial Revolution, a reorientation towards skilling has become of the essence. It has brought a range of new technologies, making the need for cooperation in skill development all the more important. It is high time for both African and Indian governments to bring together different businesses' efforts for addressing future-oriented skills development and supports constructive public-private dialogue for urgent and fundamental reform of education systems and labour policies to prepare workforces for the future of jobs.

Employment Trends in Africa

According to the World Economic Forum Human Capital Index, "Sub-Saharan Africa only captures 55 percent of its human capital potential.... By 2030, the continent's working-age population is set to increase by two-thirds, from 370 million adults in 2010 to over 600 million in 2030."[1]

Data from the International Labour Organisation's World Employment and Social Outlook's data finder shows that the level employment in industry has gone from 22.2 million in 2001 for Sub-Saharan Africa to 42.9 million in 2018. For Northern Africa in the same time period, employment in industry went from 10.5 million to 18.6 million. Overall, employment in this sector in Africa went from 32.7 million in 2001 to 61.5 million in 2018 which is a mere 0.04 per cent increase in employment for a period of 18 years (Figure 1).[2]

There was a similar percentage increase for employment in services for the same time period. In people terms, Employment in Services for Northern and Sub – Saharan Africa increased from 78.2 million to 152.7 million people (Figure 2).

One notable trend is that, unlike other nations where the general trend has been to see a decrease in the number of people employed in the agriculture sector, with the world average falling from 38 per cent in 2001 to 26 per cent in 2018, in Africa, employment in the sector has increased. The sector employs

Figure 1: Employment in Industry Sector in Northern and Sub-Saharan Africa for the Period 2001-2018

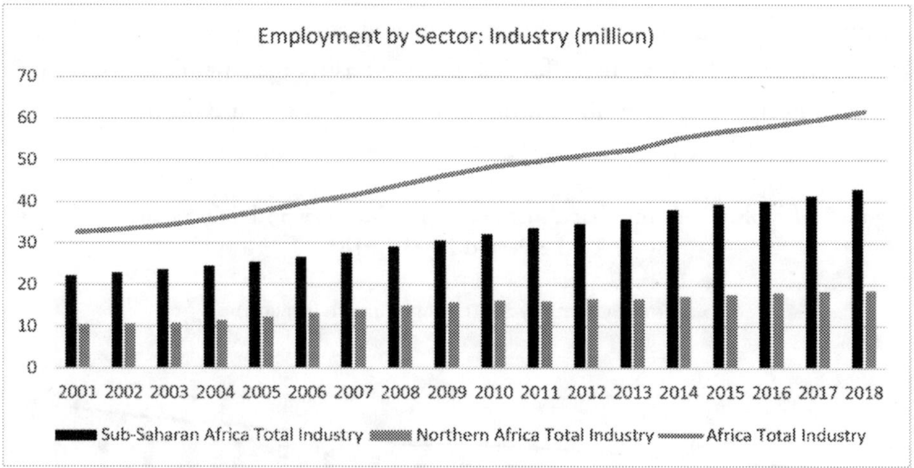

Source: Author generated based on International Labour Organisation data (International Labour Organisation, 2018)

Figure 2: Employment in Service Sector in Northern and Sub-Saharan Africa for the Period 2001 - 2018

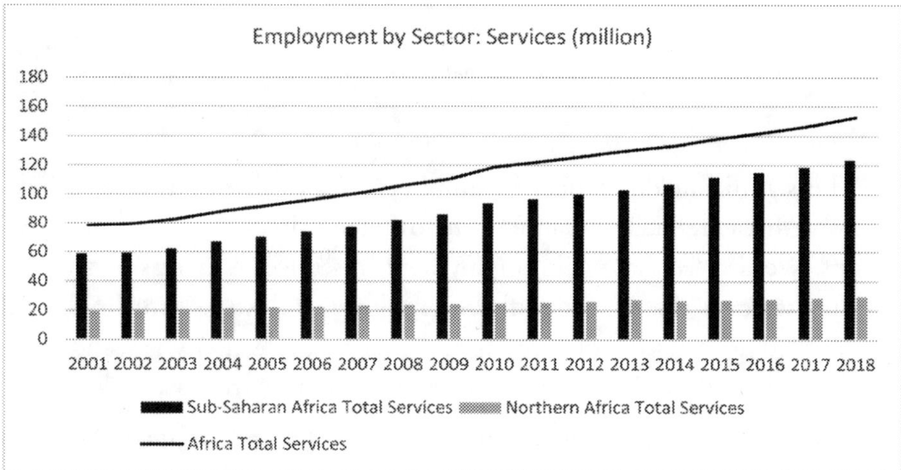

Source: Author generated based on *International Labour Organisation data* (International Labour Organisation, 2018).

239.9 million people in 2018 versus 166.9 million in 2001 (Figure 3). While this is significant, it should not be surprising to us given the amount of cultivable land on the continent. If harnessed correctly, Africa could be the key to ensuring food security for itself as well as its near neighbours. This is something that countries like India have already noted and accounted for in their pivot to Africa.

Figure 3: Employment in Agriculture Sector in Northern and Sub-Saharan Africa for the Period 2001-2018

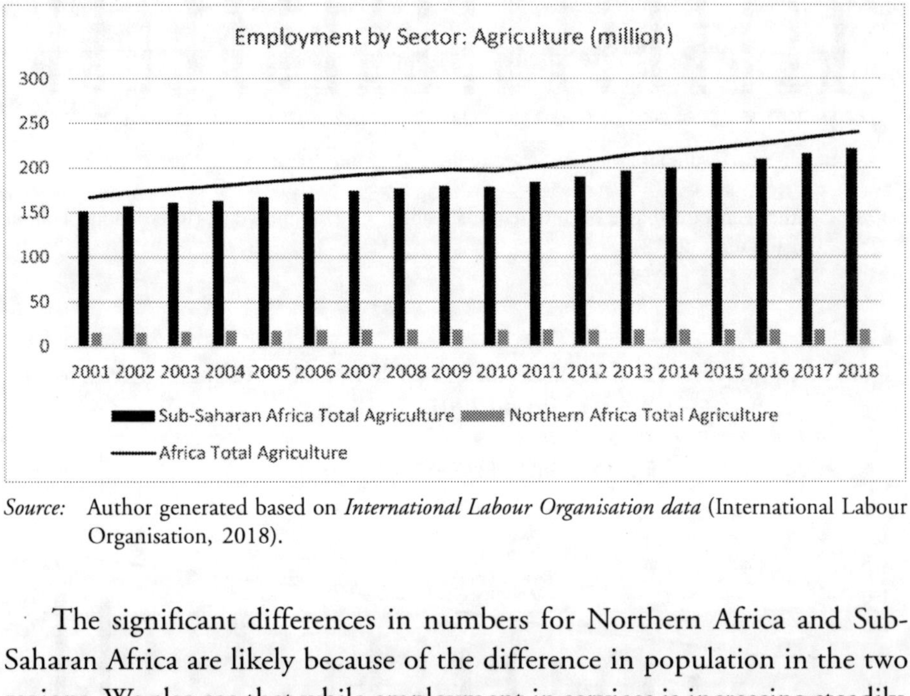

Source: Author generated based on *International Labour Organisation data* (International Labour Organisation, 2018).

The significant differences in numbers for Northern Africa and Sub-Saharan Africa are likely because of the difference in population in the two regions. We also see that while employment in services is increasing steadily, industry sector is the most significant employer. Industry sector implies all manufacturing, construction, mining and quarrying, electricity, gas, and water supply work. Services implies both market and non-market services.[3]

This sort of employment trend implies that any policy made for skills and education would not only have to be market oriented, it would also be dependent on the socio-political needs of these countries. Given the diversity of needs within Africa, it is hard to pinpoint any particular sector that needs more attention than others. The only constant through these sectors has now become, and will be for the foreseeable future, digital technology.

Tradability of Skills

Countries with a growing population of young people, what sociologists term as a "demographic dividend", are usually seen as having an advantage. This is because their level of human capital is increasing and therefore have a bigger workforce as a national resource. However, an obvious but sometimes neglected fact is that levels of education and skills need to grow in tandem with the population and according to the market's demand. If countries fail to maintain this balance, the demographic dividend soon becomes a "demographic burden".

There are very few countries now that see this demographic dividend, India and most countries in Africa are part of this small group. Given this, education and skilling are of the essence for them.

In the context of trade, skills are defined only in terms of their usefulness for employment. This includes knowledge which is job-relevant, personal attributes, as well as specific competencies relevant for the job.[4]

The pressure to ensure that education and skills levels meet market demands is further exacerbated by the fact that countries have to cater to global trends in addition to domestic demand due to the elevated level of proliferation of global value chains (GVCs). According to a WTO – ILO study, skills development is important for the export performance of a country and its ability to absorb Foreign Direct Investment (FDI). This is directly linked to the existence of GVCs.[5]

A further complication is that a country's position in GVCs can become fixed which counterproductive for a country trying to diversify its production and be further downstream in the GVC – a goal most African countries have. This has repercussions for a slew of policies from international trade policy, education policy, skills policy and even policies regarding environmental sustainability. Employment generation is also a key social concern for governments given the proven link between higher unemployment and higher crime rates.

Another challenge to employability is now posed by the Information Revolution. The fast pace at which technological change is occurring creates pressures on the economy which, while not new, have gained a greater urgency. This is true for all countries but especially significant for countries in Africa.

Technology, if harnessed correctly can be a great enabler for African growth. To make technology work for them, African countries will have to ensure that all aspects of technological innovation are accounted for when creating policies for skilling and education. This includes, TVET (technical and vocational education and training), human resource development, skills retraining, and Lifelong Learning.

In 2015, the World Bank prepared a report for the G20's Employment Working group. It found that the nature of employment was changing such that it had become more short term. Risks have shifted from the organisation to the individual. So, a new informal economy which was technology based was being created as a "virtual sweatshop".[6] This has created more uncertainty. The report also points to the importance of promoting transition from those jobs which have become automated and therefore redundant. It points to the example of the job of a typist and how it is no longer necessary. It notes that low-skilled workers at a greater risk of unemployment due to automation than those with higher skills.

This creates a Catch 22 for policy makers as if they promote higher skills, it will impact negatively on the mobility of workers in case of job loss and retraining also becomes difficult. The World Bank report suggests four strategic policy positions that governments could take to maximize the positive effects of technology – enabling the creation of digital jobs, empowering workforce to adapt to digital technology, find ways to increase access to digital tools, and assist workers in the transition period.[7]

African countries need to ensure that their skill development policies are future oriented in the sense that they are constructive and best utilise technology to meet their current needs. To close the skills gap they have and prepare for the "future of work" is essential for them. Technology now feeds most sectors which may be a key national concern for most African countries – from healthcare to sustainable development.

A brief study by the World Economic Forum, done in partnership with LinkedIn showed that for employers in the Sub-Saharan African region "inadequately skilled workforces" are a significant hurdle to their businesses.[8] The skills gap is created by the changing nature of work, which has become more and more technology oriented. It is evident, therefore, that more attention needs to be given to updating education and skills policies to meet the demands created by the job market. For this, it is important for African countries to go beyond the narrative of technology leading to job – loss. They must instead see it as an opportunity in other sectors and orient their policies to meet this demand.

It is important therefore that any efforts that governments make need to be keyed into the private sector demands of that country and context. The same is true for those countries involved in development cooperation arrangements with countries in Africa. While they can be motivated by an idea of mutual benefit, the benefits will not materialise unless the efforts are synchronised with the ground realities of the target country.

There are various models that can be used to ensure efficient cooperation. One model is entirely private sector led. Another is an entirely government to government system. A third is that of public private partnerships (PPPs). The latter model has been seen as the most significant one as it helps involve all the relevant stakeholders. Theoretically, it could be the most efficient way to disperse government resources while ensuring accountability and spreading and therefore reducing risks. Central to making this model more efficient now would be harnessing technology correctly.

> "Skills matter for efficiency.... Trade facilitates technology diffusion and helps firms increase their productivity through access to new technologies."[9]

There are two elements to consider here. Firstly, the relation between trade and technology should be seen as a virtuous circle. Just as greater trade helps increase access to new technologies, these technologies also promote greater trade. Secondly, enabling human capital digitally has become essential to increasing productivity and ensuring the sustenance of this virtuous cycle. This means ensuring that new market opportunities are taken due cognizance of and Research and Development is encouraged in innovative fields. To ensure this, education and skills policies would have to be pro-active, as would aid-for-trade and development cooperation arrangements.

Technology and Jobs

Skills development, increased literacy, and employment generation are co-dependent. The former is essential for the latter. Conversely, greater literacy rates without the corresponding job growth becomes a burden on the economy. Due to a trend of "routine biased technical change...", there is, what scholars call, '..."jobless recoveries" (periods following recessions in which rebounds in aggregate output are accompanied by much slower recoveries in aggregate employment).[10] This sort of trend makes it more difficult to assess whether the skills being created in the economy are meeting market demand. After a crisis, indicators for the stability of an economy, like growth rates, do not pay as much attention to levels and pace of employment generation as the mark of a healthy economy. This leaves them open to a relapse and larger socio-economic problems. Such a trend has implications for policies governing skills as it indicates the importance of an information loop between government and industry. While industry depends on government for efficient policy, governments can depend on industry for efficient implementation of said policies. This feedback loop is especially urgent in places like Africa and other developing regions of the world where the industrial revolution did not just come late, due to the unique experience of colonialism, but also came with the added disruptions of digital technology.

There are a few things to keep in mind when it comes to technology and the future of work. Firstly, technological innovation does not replace human capital as a workforce is still required to produce the technology and ensure its maintenance, Secondly, technology gives a boost to the competitiveness of firms by increasing productivity – for both goods and services. Thirdly, technology can also aid labour productivity by ensuring efficiency. Fourthly, technology may cause job loss in the short run but in the long run it is likely to help create new jobs just as with other revolutions. The reason why job disruptions are felt more keenly now are due to the fast pace of adoption of new technologies.[11]

Historically, there has always been resistance to new technology. The Luddite Movement against the industrial revolution in England in the 1800s is the most visible case in point. Today, technological innovation is more or less seen as inevitable. Also, while the pace of adoption of technology has increased, it varies across sectors. A concentrated effort, to make technological adoption central to policy making might yield more inclusive results.

Partnership for Skills Development

Given all of these realities, it is no surprise that technology transfer is also central to any form of development aid and cooperation, just as it has led to transformation in systems of production, employment, management, governance, and overall business.[12]

Africa and India are no exception. There are several ways in which skills development has already been incorporated into the aid and development relationship of the two partners. This has included the government-to-government model, the government to industry model, the industry to industry model, and the PPP model.

One unique way is when public sector enterprises (PSEs) in India take up government led development projects in Africa. This leads to what may be seen as a cross-sectional model where it is a government led industry entity which is leading the development work. Ostensibly, the PSE will have all the elements of a private sector industry body with its focus on efficiency and increasing productivity. However, it may not be working by the profit motive but a government's social motives of employment generation and large-scale production.

The following case studies will help highlight the same.

Pan Africa e-Network Project (PAeNP)

The Pan Africa e-Network (PAeN) is a Government of India (GoI) initiative started in 2009 post the first India Africa Forum Summit in 2008. It was first conceptualised by India's former President Dr. A.P.J. Abdul Kalam. Since inception, the project has had significant impact on cooperation in Tele-Education and Tele-Medicine between India and Africa. The project is a joint undertaking of the Government of India and the African Union (AU). The implementing agency of the project is Telecommunications Consultants India Limited (TCIL), which is a GoI owned engineering and consultancy company. PAeN aims

> "...to provide seamless and integrated satellite, fiber optics and wireless network to connect the African countries ... (and) at creating significant linkages for tele-education and tele-medicine, internet, video conferencing, and VoIP (Voice over Internet Protocol) services by

> linking them to premier educational and institutions and super-speciality hospitals in India. The project also supports e-governance, e-commerce, infotainment, resource mapping and meteorological services.... The project has two main components: Tele-Education Services and Tele-Medicine Services."[13]

TCIL played a central role in ensuring the success of the PAeN. As of July 2017, the project was handed over to the AU for implementation. It has been a positive contributor in terms of many of the challenges that African countries face and there has been wide demand to expand and sustain the project.

One of the unique features of the PAeN was that the beneficiary countries were not expected to contribute monetarily for the first ten years of the project. It was entirely housed and maintained by TCIL. There were 5 Indian Universities and 5 Regional University Centres in Africa chosen for the project. With 47 learning centres already set up, at least 22,000 African students have obtained degrees through the programme. This is a significant achievement considering the education infrastructure present in Africa and India. The project has gained enough momentum that now, with the AU leading the project, discussions are under way for a Pan African University. The AU and India are currently negotiating the extension of Indian technical and financial assistance for some more time.[14]

This model then, can be seen as a success given the widely positive reception it has had and the commitment the AU has to keeping the project alive. This is an example of the PSE model mentioned earlier. One of the reasons for its success may be the fact that it was modelled on the needs of the African nations as presented at the AU Congress meeting to then President Kalam in 2006. Secondly, given the project's success depended on the handling agency completely following government directions on demand, it is no surprise that the management of the project was left to a PSE. Thirdly, the model also allowed for a government and industry balance to occur because PSE's while controlled by government, are still industry members. The model therefore also allows for a reduction of political risk as there is full government commitment.

Such projects, if made sector focused, after in-depth market research, could have a greater positive impact on skills development in Africa. The

PAeN tries to focus on the entire continent. The model could also be effective if the focus was made more federalized and targeted at the needs of specific countries, increasing its relevance and ensuring its continued applicability. This model also holds significance for the PPP model which should be promoted further.

A Private Sector Model: TATA in Africa

TATA Africa Holdings was officially set up in 1994, although the company had been present on the continent even before that. The company, through its various subsidiaries, is present in various sectors in Africa, including the social sector.

In recent time, the TATA group has oriented itself towards the Sustainable Development Goals and has made Sustainability a main focus of most of its functioning given the business case for SDG's.[15] It has been argued that if employment levels are low or if there is too much of the workforce in at risk employment, the demand for social protection becomes higher.[16] It is in the interest of the private sector to have greater stability in employment as it acts as a motivator for productivity.

TATA Africa Holdings is active in both education and skills development. For education, it partners with universities in South Africa to support post-graduate students through scholarships. It has also been taking up specific efforts to promote women in Science and Technology by collaborating with the Department of Science and Technology in South Africa.

In the area of skills development, TATA group has put the goal of job creation at the centre and does capacity building for the local workforce as part of its Corporate Social efforts. It partners the South African government in the Priority Skills Acquisition Programme, by offering internships to internationally placed South African students at various TATA companies in India. It also does project basis skills development at the local and provincial levels. For instance, TATA Consultancy Services (TCS) has a local capacity building programme in South Africa called the Initial Learning Programme which enables local recruitment, skills development, and local capacity building for previously disadvantaged youth who later join TCS as interns. TATA Automobile Corporation South Africa (TACSA) provides skill development in its own areas of operation.[17]

This case has some specific learnings for us. Firstly, the private sector is evidently limited in its reach by presence in an economy. The fact that most of TATA's skill development work in Africa is focused on South Africa is a proof of this. Secondly, the private sector is also limited by its own areas of interest. It is less likely to invest in skill development in a field where there is no scope of obtaining human capital for its benefit. That is unless the project under discussion is specifically aimed to be a CSR project. A third learning which may be seen as an issue is that the skills needs of these particular companies may not reflect the needs of the country or continent as a whole.

On the other hand, private sector work is more focused, more reliable in terms of outputs, and specific in terms of targets. It can prove to be more efficient and overall have a more positive impact in terms of meeting market needs.

Given these realities, it is obvious that both the Government led and the Private led models have positive and negative repercussions. Government led has a greater reach and larger socio-economic focus. Private led has efficiency and productivity benefits. Both can complement each other if harnessed correctly.

In the area of digital skills development, the balance between public and private becomes even more important. Widespread development of digital skills has positive effects on inclusiveness and equality. It feeds into the larger development goals of these countries and needs to be at the centre of policy making. Finding the right compromise between public interest and market demand would be essential for a robust education and skills policy.

This brings us to the PPP model for skilling. The question arises, how the best elements of public and private led skills development can be used to meet the skills needs of specific economies. This model would not have to meet the market demand for new skills, but also fill the already existing skills gap.

Conclusion and Way Forward

A profound demographic transformation is sweeping across the African continent as the world's oldest inhabited continent is paradoxically the youngest today, with 40 per cent of its population under the age of 15. Further, as per the projection, by 2050, Africa will have a staggering 25 per cent share in planet's population. In other words, one in four people in the world will be from Africa, two-thirds of whom will be under 30. This demographic surge in Africa not only commands attention but presents unprecedented challenges for providing them meaningful skills and jobs.

Given the current and future emerging scenario in Africa, there exists an urgent need for comprehensive skilling initiatives. Government alone is not sufficient equipped with resources to accomplish this job. Private sector involvement is a must and therefore PPP model is the tried and tested method to realise this ambitious goal.

The PPP model is being increasingly used globally to get private sector involvement in infrastructure and social sectors projects such as health and education and skilling. Since African nations have huge requirement to skill the human resources, theoretically PPP model can make a big turnaround. However, one big challenge for majority of African nations is lack of a strong domestic private sector. In Africa since capital is scarce, they are largely dependent on foreign capital for their investment needs across sectors.

NOTES

1 World Economic Forum, 'The Future of Jobs and Skills in Africa - Preparing the Region for the Fourth Industrial Revolution', May 2017.

2 International Labour Organisation, World Employment and Social Outlook, 2018.

3 The ILO's descriptions of economic activity are based on the International Standard Industrial Classification of All Economic Activities (ISIC).

4 WTO - ILO, "Report on 'Investing in Skills for Inclusive Trade', 2017.

5 Ibid.

6 The World Bank Group, 'The Effects of Technology on Employment and Implications for Public Employment Services', 2015.

7 Ibid.

8 World Economic Forum, no. 1.

9 WTO – ILO, no. 4.

10 Ibid.

11 Ibid.

12 Ibid.

13 Abhishek Mishra, "Pan Africa e-network: India's Africa outreach", at https://www.orfonline.org/expert-speak/pan-africa-e-network-indias-africa-outreach (Accessed 10 February 2024).

14 Ibid.

15 'The TATA Group and the SDG's', TATA Sustainability Group, Mumbai 2017.

16 Torben Iversen & David Soskice, 'An Asset Theory of Social Policy Preferences', *American Political Science Review,* 2001, pp. 875-893.

17 "Tata: An African success story", at https://mg.co.za/article/2013-04-19-00-tata-an-african-success-story/ (Accessed 4 February 2024).

13

Skills Development in India and Africa: Interactive Agendas?[1]

Kenneth King

Introduction and Background

This chapter explores what are the inter-relations and possible synergies between the massive national ambitions to build capacity for skill development within India on the one hand, and the on-going needs within Africa to develop substantially its own technical and vocational capacities, on the other.

India shares with most African countries a situation in which the great majority of its skilled people are in the informal or unregulated economy. Formalising these informal skills is on the agenda of 'Skill India' as well as of the Africa Union's *Agenda 2063*.

The historical patterns of exchange between India and Africa have focused primarily on higher education rather than skills development. In other words, the movement of thousands of Africans to India has been driven by the desire for undergraduate and graduate qualifications, and not by the search for Technical and Vocational Education and Training (TVET). On the Indian side, in the last several decades, the migration of very large numbers of skilled and semi-skilled people has been to the Gulf and not to Africa. Historically, however, during the colonial period, substantial numbers of Indian workers settled in Anglophone Eastern and Southern Africa, bringing with them their skills in wood, metal, tin, glass, and in welding, food preparation and much else. Over time, these Indian communities were the source of what has been called Indo-African skill transfer, particularly in East Africa.[2] This process was far from being what might now be called a capacity-building project. Rather it was a case of African unskilled workers gradually acquiring, on-the-job, the skills of their Indian very small-scale employers in the 1930s, 1940s and 1950s.

On the other hand, and in the current period, especially in the last decade, there have been a series of India-supported TVET projects in Africa which derive from the pledges of the India-Africa Forum Summits of 2008, 2011 and 2015, as well as from bilateral agreements between India and particular African countries before and after this period. The chapter reviews their current status and the options for their substantial expansion. Beyond these, the activities of Indian non-state actors should be noted, since Indian enterprises today as well as Indian NGOs have been involved in skills development processes in Africa.

Finally, it should be noted that under the *Vision Document* of the Asia-Africa Growth Corridor, there are significant plans for India as well as Japan to be the source of large-scale skills capacity building in Africa.[3] Equally, there are World Bank plans for an India-Africa Knowledge Exchange in respect of skills development.[4]

India's Skill Development Ambitions, 2009-2018

The skill development missions of both the Singh and Modi governments have laid out targets of 500 million and 400 million people, respectively, to be upskilled within India by 2022. There has also been a huge range of initiatives in skills development in the last ten years.[5] The 'numbers game' of skilling almost one in two or one in three Indians by this deadline has had an international dimension, since it had been calculated that these 'skills missions' would also allow India to provide no less than 47 million skilled workers to meet the alleged global skills shortage.[6] Though there is therefore an international lens of the 'Skill India' campaign, so far this has meant the planning of what are called 'India International Skills Centres' (IISCs). These 50 planned centres, announced in 2016, are not concerned with providing training for other countries, but rather with India 'reaping the demographic dividend' of its youthful labour force by preparing them to work overseas.[7]

Beyond this, India's 'Skill India' campaign is also being linked internationally to a 'Make in India' ambition. There are clearly training dimensions within India in some of these 'Make in India' initiatives, including those associated with Japan's support for India's high-speed rail as well as its metro development and many other initiatives.[8] From a different angle, there are implications for both India and Africa in the World Bank's India-Africa Knowledge Exchange Mission which is being organised with India's Ministry of Skills Development and Entrepreneurship (MSDE), in partnership with six African countries.[9] But what will also need to be explored is what implications there are for India's international cooperation, as a so-called emerging donor, of these different national initiatives for skills development within India. What models of skills development, if any, is India drawing upon as it begins to offer institutions for vocational training in Africa? We return to this in later sections. But first we review the situation in Africa.

Africa's Skill Development Situation

Compared to East Asia where government policies towards technical and vocational education and training have been more positive than in Africa, and where it has been credited with contributing to the East Asian success story.[10] Africa has figured negatively in many of the key texts on vocationalisation.[11] However, with the rediscovery of a global role for TVET in a whole series of influential accounts (NN48), skill development has begun to take a more central role in national strategies including in Africa. The positioning of technical and vocational skills in several of the targets of the Sustainable Development Goals (SDGs) in 2015 has reinforced this new status.[12] It should not be surprising therefore that in the same year and month as the SDGs were agreed in New York, September 2015, the African Union's *Agenda 2063: The Africa we want* should underline the importance of TVET along with many other key ambitions:

> Strengthen technical and vocational education and training through scaled up investments, establishment of a pool of high-quality TVET centres across Africa, foster greater links with industry and alignment to labour markets, with a view to improve the skills profile, employability and entrepreneurship of especially youth and women, and closing the skills gap across the continent[13]

It is intriguing to note that the AU's pledge on TVET parallels the UN's SDG 4 in failing to distinguish between the proportions of young people going into TVET and into higher education: 'By 2030, ensure equal access for all women and men to affordable and quality technical, vocational and tertiary education, including university'[14]

> In the Africa of 2063, at least 70 per cent of all high school graduates will go on to have tertiary education at technical and vocational education and training (TVET) institutions, and Universities with 70 per cent of them graduating in the sciences, technology and innovation programmes....[15]

It is also important to underline the point that the African Union, like India, is aware that the great bulk of all the training of young people in skills actually takes place in the informal or unorganised sector. Hence, any really substantial programme for skills development has to take account of the massive training requirements of this unregulated sector of the economy:

> Improving the quality and relevance of technical and vocational skills development to address the needs of both cutting edge skills and training the majority who are involved in the informal economy[16]

Indeed, seasoned analysts of TVET in Africa have argued that it is not so simple as merely formalising the informal sector; rather the informal sector can be seen as a creative source of training for several key groups in society: "The skills needs of out-of-school youth, early school leavers, and adults are best addressed by informal sector training providers"[17] More generally, the AU has a vision for TVET and higher education that over the next decades will see the youth of Africa electing to stay in Africa rather than contributing to the massive flight of human capital from the continent:

> By 2063, the mass out-migration of talented, educated, innovative Africans that characterized the brain-drain of earlier years will change to a situation where Africa is the centre of convergence of the world's best and brightest; akin to the role and status, in ancient times, of the famed city of Timbuktu in the empire of Mali.[18]

In contrast to this very much too positive and promising account of the future of TVET in Africa, current analysis by the World Bank points to a continuing acute shortage of skilled workers in many countries, particularly in Eastern Africa[19] A similar account is available from the African Development Bank's *Human Capital Strategy 2014-2018.*[20] Skills is one of the red threads that runs through its 45 pages, and there is a powerful message about the need for Bank support to "foster transformation in technical and vocational education and training."[21] There are similar recommendations in the OECD Development Centre/African Union volume on *Africa's Development Dynamics 2018: Jobs, Growth and Inequalities.*[22]

A Role for Indian Cooperation in African Skill Development

Having very briefly sketched out some indication of the ambitions and challenges for TVET in these very different environments of India and Africa, we shall turn to examine some perspectives of cooperation in skills development and capacity building. There are several lenses on such cooperation – including at the state level, as well as through non-state actors.

However, it should be acknowledged, as mentioned at the beginning, that a good deal of India's human resources (HR) cooperation with Africa, like China's, is at the higher education level, and not related to TVET. This is the case for India's main scholarship schemes, as well as for the majority of its Indian Technical and Economic Cooperation (ITEC) courses. It was also the case with the Pan-African e-Network (PAEN) which provided e-health and e-education from 2009 till 2017 to over 40 countries in Africa. The India-Africa Forum Summits (IAFS) did make a large number of HR pledges to Africa in the area of institutional development in a whole variety of different sectors, including educational planning and administration.[23] Again, these are being delivered through partnerships with different Indian higher education institutions, such as the National Institute of Educational Planning and Administration (NIEPA). Thus, they will be more linked to higher education than to TVET.

In the specifically TVET sphere, one of the most clearly vocational pledges from the IAFS series was the provision of ten vocational training centres (VTCs). Interestingly, this was not delivered through India's Ministry of Skill Development and Entrepreneurship (MSDE) or its predecessor, but through the National Small Industry Corporation (NSIC) which is under the Ministry of Micro, Small & Medium Enterprises of India. These VTCs were first proposed at the 2008 Summit, and already by mid-2017 half of them were in place in Ethiopia, Rwanda, Burundi, Egypt, Burkina Faso, Zimbabwe and Gambia, and a further was under execution in Mozambique. It is important to note that they do not just provide technical and vocational courses, but strongly emphasise enterprise development. In the case of Rwanda, this initially single institution is being multiplied nationally through a new and much larger agreement with the Indian government.

There is a tendency in the study of India's HR cooperation with Africa to focus on some of the so-called flagship projects – such as those mentioned in the series of India-Africa celebratory volumes.[24] These are often the Pan-African items which have been sanctioned at the continental level like PAEN, or the many Pan-African institutes, supported by India but allocated to particular countries by the African Union.

What is less commonly noticed is the range of smaller HR bilateral items that appear under country-to-country agreements. Thus, in a 2017 account of India-Tanzania relations[25], there is a note of a new vocational training centre being set up in Zanzibar. Equally, there is information about the completion of two information and communication technology (ICT) projects: a Centre of Excellence in ICT in Dar-es-Salaam Institute of Science and Technology; and another ICT Centre at the Nelson Mandela African Institute for Science and Technology. Beyond this, there is the distribution of Science and Mathematics books for public secondary schools; the activities of the Indian Cultural Centre; and an Indian Council for Cultural Cooperation (ICCR) Chair at the University of Dar es Salaam, as well as the ICCR and ITEC scholarship allocations to Tanzania. These are just some of the items related to education and skill development in this much more detailed, multi-sectoral account of bilateral relations. Only a minority of the projects are TVET-related.

It would be possible to map other examples of such bilateral cooperation in TVET, such as the industrial training institute being promised to KwaZulu Natal in South Africa by the Indian High Commission in that country:

> The proposed skills training institute will be similar to Industrial Training Institutes (ITIs) in India and will cover training in key skills. It will support infrastructure traits and also give training in hardware, software, machinery, tools and provide teachers and trainers.[26]

There is a further South African illustration of bilateralism; one of the TVET outcomes of Narendra Modi's African trip in July 2018 was the agreement to set up a Gandhi-Mandela Centre of Specialisation for Artisan Skills in Tshwane South TVET College near Pretoria, South Africa.[27] This was formally launched in October 2018 with agreements to develop boiler-making, electrical engineering, mechanical fitting and turning, and millwright.

It is difficult, therefore, to generalise about India's bilateral and multilateral HR cooperation with Africa, precisely because of the variety and specificity of the bilateral relations with individual African countries as have just been illustrated for Tanzania and South Africa.

But it would appear that, despite these bilateral examples, there is still little explicit, overall connection between India's own massive efforts in national skills development discussed above and the challenges Africa is itself facing in skills development. The main contribution of state-level Indian cooperation with Africa in human resource development remains in the sphere of higher education, with an expanding programme of cultural cooperation and soft power.

Non-state Actors in India-African Skills Development

It is worth noting that there has been activity by Indian non-state actors in skills development in Africa. These cover both the non-profit and for-profit domains.

Non-governmental Organisations

Thus, in some five African countries, there has been exploration by the NGO, the Self-Employed Women's Organisation (SEWA), from Gujarat, of a range of skills development activities, including in microfinance, microenterprise, micro-insurance and leadership capacity-building. The Tanzanian government has asked SEWA to set up a SEWA in Tanzania, and there has been strong interest from a civil society organisation in Mozambique for SEWA to help in setting up their own informal workers' organisation. Indeed two-way relations are already underway to explore what learning from SEWA would mean in Mozambique. Similarly, the Barefoot College in Tilonia, Rajasthan, has promoted skills in the assembly and maintenance of solar panels mainly by rural women with basic levels of education. While this latter has not been exclusively targeted at Africa, there are now plans for five vocational training hubs to be located in Africa. The first of these is in Zanzibar, which already operates as a regional centre for skills development, and others are under execution in South Sudan, Burkina Faso, Liberia, and Senegal.[28]

Private Sector Skills Development in Africa

With the exception of the Indian large-scale, multi-national firms where formal industrial training either in Africa or in India has been the norm,[29]many smaller Indian firms have trained their African workers on the job, in preference to using the formal TVET institutions in country. The latter have tended to be supply- rather than demand-driven. There is, furthermore, a large disconnect between the great majority of African skilled workers who are trained, on the job, in the informal sector and the very small number of formally trained workers from TVET institutions. There is in fact much in common between the approaches to on-the-job training of small-scale Indian investors in Africa and those pursued by African entrepreneurs in what is termed the informal (*Jua Kali)* sector.[30]

We turn in a final section to examine the skill development side of the Asia-Africa Growth Corridor (AAGC), but it is worth noting that the next phase of the Pan-African e-Network (probably renamed from early 2019) may be able to provide for some of the skill needs of Indian companies operating in Africa without the expense of their bringing Africans for training in India.

Skill Development in Africa via the Asia-Africa Growth Corridor and World Bank's India-Africa Knowledge Exchange

Although the *Vision Document* of the AAGC was a year old in May 2018, there is still very little flesh attached to its skeleton. What is, however, clear in its preliminary *Vision*, developed by just three Asian think-tanks with little apparent African participation, is that 'Enhancing capacity and skills' and 'People-to-people partnership' are two of its four key pillars. Within the first of these, 'human resource training' and 'vocational/industrial training centres' are underlined as important.[31] Some indication of what this might involve in India-Japan cooperation for Africa is suggested in three AAGC discussion papers which focus on skills and human resource development, and which were produced by the New Delhi think-tank, Research and Information System for Developing Countries (RIS).[32]

While India and Japan's national skills systems can be individually described, along with the challenges to skills systems in Africa, there is no experience yet of India-Japan cooperation in skills development, except in India itself.[33] Japan's HR cooperation in Africa has focused on science and maths, along with community based education for all, and higher education, while India's cooperation with Africa, as we have seen, has also emphasised higher education, though there has been some support to vocational training.

We await, therefore, the translation of these many ideas from the Indian side of AAGC into the still-awaited *Vision Study* of the AAGC. It is assumed that there will be much more significant African agency in this next detailed round of putting flesh on the skeleton of the AAGC framework than in the development of the *Vision document*. It would also be important to emphasise that capacity building should not be a one-way street of building African capacity, but of Japan and India also learning from Africa. We have suggested elsewhere, however, that one of the biggest challenges for both Japan and India will be to rebrand their existing, separate, bilateral and continental engagements with Africa as something specifically collaborative under the umbrella of the AAGC.[34]

Equally, there has been one other significant marker of possible significance to India-Africa skill development. That was the five-day summit in Delhi in late October-early November 2017 entitled 'India-Africa Knowledge Exchange Mission' organised by the Ministry of Skills Development and Entrepreneurship, Government of India, and the World Bank.[35] Ministers and other senior figures in skills development were present from Rwanda, Nigeria, Ethiopia, Senegal, Tanzania and Ghana. According to the World Bank, these countries are keen to learn from India's experience as it strides to implement one of the world's largest skills development programmes.[36] Amongst the objectives of this meeting were the challenges of skills development in the informal sector, employer-led skilling strategies for enhancing industry competitiveness, and institutional reforms for the delivery of skills training, both long and short-term.[37]

In a path breaking development, India's National Skills Development

Corporation (NSDC) International, subsidiary of NSDC, signed a MoU with Sub-Saharan African Skills & Apprenticeship Stakeholders Network (SASASNET) in March 2024. The main objective is to develop a "skill ecosystem" in the region. This MoU will hopefully lead to greater collaboration between India and Africa on skill development. One of the aims of this agreement is to digitalise TVET systems across Sub-Saharan Africa.[38] It is still too early to say what may be the financing mechanisms for Indian skills development experience to be supported in Africa, but this, too, is clearly an area to watch.

Conclusion

We have noted that skills development has been identified both in Africa and in India as a crucial arena for urgent support. This will be essential if the currently high growth rates of India and of a significant number of African countries are to be maintained. However, skills development on its own, without accompanying industrial and agricultural development strategies, especially in Africa, will not be sufficient. Indeed, rapid increase in skilled graduates in Africa with no change in the job market for their skills will merely result in even greater pressures than at present to migrate out of Africa – to Europe and the Gulf. Or it will mean that these newly skilled young people will have to be resigned to joining those millions already working in Africa's large but technically underdeveloped informal economies. Neither outcome will necessarily lead to the fulfilment of the aspirations of the African Union's *Agenda 2063:*

> Youth employment will be eliminated, and Africa's youth guaranteed full access to education, training, skills and technology, health services, jobs and economic opportunities, recreational and cultural activities as well as financial means and all necessary resources to allow them to realise their full potential.... The creativity, energy and innovation of Africa's youth shall be the driving force behind the continent's political, social, cultural and economic transformation.[39]

NOTES

1 The term, technical and vocational education and training (TVET), has historically been used to refer to formal initiatives, whether in technical schools or streams within schools of the Ministry of Education, or in vocational training schemes of the Ministry of Labour, private employers or of non-governmental organisations (NGOs). By contrast, skills development is a wider term that is not only used to cover foundation skills such as literacy and numeracy, transferable, soft or interpersonal skills such as problem-solving, but is also used to identify technical and vocational skills, whether picked up in education and training schools and institutes or in work-based employer settings. For a discussion of these three dimensions of skills development, see *Education for All Global Monitoring Report 2012: Youth and skills: Putting education to work*, UNESCO, Paris, 2012.

2 K. King, "Indo-African skill transfer in an East African economy," *African Affairs*, 74 (1975), pp. 65-71; Kenneth King, *The African artisan: Education and the informal sector*, Heinemann Educational Books, London, 1977.

3 Asia-Africa Growth Corridor (AAGC), *Asia-Africa Growth Corridor: Partnership for sustainable and innovative development: A vision document*, African Development Bank meeting, Ahmedabad, India, 22-26 May 2017.

4 World Bank, *The World Bank India-Africa Knowledge Exchange Mission*. Brief report of proceedings and outcomes, 30 October–3 November 2017.

5 A. Sharma and K King, '"Skill India": The "modification" of skill development in India', in McGrath, S., Papier, J., Mulder, M. and Suart, R. (Eds.) *International handbook of vocational education and training for the changing world of work*, Springer, New York, 2019.

6 K. King, "The geopolitics and meanings of India's massive skills ambitions," *International Journal of Educational Development*, 32 (5), 2012, pp. 665-673.

7 *Economic Times* 17 July 2016, at https://economictimes.indiatimes.com/news/economy/policy/government-launches-15-india-international-skill-centers/articleshow/53252497.cms (Accessed 24 March 2018).

8 AAGC, 2017, note 3, p. 19.

9 World Bank, 2017, note 4.

10 S. McGrath, "Where to now for vocational education and training in Africa?", *International Journal of Training Research* 9, 1-2 (2011), pp. 35-48.

11 J. Lauglo and K Lillis (Eds.), *Vocationalising education: An international perspective*. Pergamon Press, Oxford, 1988. For several dimensions of skills in Africa, both historical and contemporary, See K. King, *Education, skills and international cooperation: Comparative and historical perspectives*, CERC Studies in Comparative Education, Comparative Education Research Centre (CERC), the University of Hong Kong, 2019.

12 United Nations, *Transforming our world: The 2030 agenda for sustainable development*, 2015; See also McGrath, VET Africa 4.0: Reducing inequality and enhancing sustainability through skills development, Global Challenge Research Fund, 2018.

13 African Union, *Agenda 2063: The Africa we want. Popular version*, African Union, Addis Ababa, 2015, pp. 14-15.

14 United Nations, 2015, note 12, p. 17

15 African Union, 2015, note 13, p. 31.

16 Ibid., p. 58.

17 Afeti, G. and Adubra, A.L. 2014. *Skilling Africa: The paradigm shift to technical and vocational skills development*. ADEA, Abidjan, at http://www.adeanet.org/en/blogs/skilling-africa-the-paradigm-shift-to-technical-and-vocational-skills-development (Accessed 23 March 2018)

18 African Union, 2015, note 16, p. 32.
19 World Bank, *East Africa skills for transformation and regional integration project.* Report No: PAD2715, World Bank, Washington, 2018.
20 African Development Bank, *Human capital strategy.* African Development Bank, Washington DC, 2014.
21 Ibid., p. 2; The word 'skills', in several different senses, occurs no less than 89 times in this Bank paper of 45 pages.
22 African Union Commission (AUC) and OECD Development Centre, *Africa's development dynamics 2018: Jobs, growth and inequalities,* AUC, Addis Ababa & OECD Publishing, Paris, 2018.
23 The precise number of these institutions promised to Africa fluctuates between 19 and 100, K. King, *India-Africa cooperation in human resource development: Education, training and skills.* IDSA Occasional paper, New Delhi, 2018.
24 K. King, *India-Africa cooperation in human resource development: Education, training and skills.* IDSA Occasional paper, New Delhi, 2018.
25 MEA (Ministry of External Affairs). 2017. *India-Tanzania Relations,* Available at http://www.mea.gov.in/Portal/ForeignRelation/Tanzania_August__2017.pdf (Accessed 24 March 2018).
26 M. Pandey, "Modi diplomacy at work: African nations looking up to India for entrepreneurship tips," *India Today*, Available at https://www.indiatoday.in/mail-today/story/modi-diplomacy-african-nations-looking-india-entrepreneurship-tips-1115223-2017-12-24 (Accessed 10 April 2023).
27 V. Gwangwa, TVET colleges key 'to building skills'. *Pretoria News,* October 9, 2018. Available at https://www.iol.co.za/pretoria-news/tvet-colleges-key-to-building-skills-17405860 (Accessed 12 October 2018).
28 Barefoot College. 2016. *The Barefoot model for global sustainability.* Barefoot College, Tilonia, Rajasthan.
29 P. Kumar, Skill development and capacity building of Africa: How to build synergy between government commitment and private sector interest, presentation to 4th India-Africa Strategic Dialogue on India and Africa: Parlaying the security engagement, March 27-28, 2018, IDSA, New Delhi.
30 K. King, *Jua kali Kenya: Change and development in an informal economy.* James Currey, London, 1996.
31 AAGC, 2017, note 3.
32 S. Mehrotra, Asia-*Africa cooperation in human resource development.* RIS/AAGC discussion paper 218, RIS, New Delhi, 2017; M. Agarwal, *Skill development in Africa: Scope for India-Japan cooperation in Asia-Africa Growth Corridor.* RIS/AAGC discussion paper 214, RIS, New Delhi, 2017; R. Beri, *India-Japan cooperation for promoting people-to-people partnership in the Asia-Africa Growth Corridor.* RIS/AAGC discussion paper, 213, RIS, New Delhi, 2017.
33 See for example: "The two Prime Ministers [of India and Japan] decided to cooperate on the human resource development in the manufacturing sector in India through 'Manufacturing skills transfer promotion programme'. This programme will enhance the manufacturing base of India and contribute to 'Make in India' and 'Skill India', through training 30,000 persons over the next 10 years with Japanese style manufacturing skills and practices through the establishment of the Japan-India Institutes for Manufacturing" AAGC,2017, p. 19.
34 K. King, Japan, India and China on Africa: Global ambitions and human resource development, in Panda, J. (Ed), *China-India-Japan in the Indo-Pacific: Ideas, Interests, and Infrastructure,* Pentagon Press, New Delhi, 2018.

35 World Bank, 2017, note 4.
36 'India and Africa exchange knowledge in a workshop organized by Skill India and World Bank', Available at http://www.nationalskillsnetwork.in/knowledge-sharing-workshop-for-african-delegates/ (Accessed 10 April 2018).
37 Ibid.
38 "NSDC International partners with SASASNET to develop skill ecosystem across Sub-Saharan at Africa"https://nsdcindia.org/sites/default/files/Press%20Release_NSDC%20 International % 20partners%20with%20SASASNET%20to%20develop%20skill%20ecosystem%20across %20Sub-Saharan%20Africa.pdf (Accessed 24 March 2024).
39 African Union, 2015, note 18, p. 9.

Index